U.S. NAVAL RADIO STATION— APARTMENT BUILDING (Bldg 1)

HISTORIC STRUCTURE REPORT

**Acadia National Park
Bar Harbor, Maine**

By

James J. Lee III
Architectural Conservator

Historic Architecture Program
Northeast Region, National Park Service
U.S. Department of Interior
Lowell, Massachusetts

2009

CONTENTS

LIST OF FIGURES AND CREDITS xi

ACKNOWLEDGMENTS xvii

INTRODUCTION 1

EXECUTIVE SUMMARY 3

PURPOSE AND SCOPE 3
BRIEF DESCRIPTION 3
RESEARCH CONDUCTED 4
RESEARCH FINDINGS 4
RECOMMENDED TREATMENT AND USE 5

ADMINISTRATIVE DATA 7

LOCATION OF SITE 7
NATIONAL REGISTER OF HISTORIC PLACES 7
LIST OF CLASSIFIED STRUCTURES INFORMATION 8
PROPOSED TREATMENT AND USE 9
RELATED STUDIES 10

DEVELOPMENTAL HISTORY 11

HISTORICAL BACKGROUND AND CONTEXT 13

INTRODUCTION 13
ACADIA NATIONAL PARK 14
John D. Rockefeller, Jr. 14
Grosvenor Atterbury 15
Schoodic Peninsula 18
U.S. NAVAL RADIO STATION 20
Otter Cliffs Radio Station 20
The Disposition of the Otter Cliffs Radio Station 21

    Schoodic Point 25
        The Road to Schoodic Point... 25
    U.S. Naval Radio Station, Winter Harbor, Maine 28

CHRONOLOGY OF DEVELOPMENT AND USE 33

INTRODUCTION 33
PLANNING 33
CONSTRUCTION 37
    Landscaping 44
ORIGINAL APPEARANCE 47
    Introduction 47
    Exterior Elements 48
        Design 48
        Foundation 50
        Walls 50
        Entrance Stoops and Terrace 52
        Doorways 54
        Window Openings 57
        Roofs and Related Elements 61
        Chimneys 63
        Utilities and Fixtures 64
    Structural Elements 64
    Interior Elements 68
        Basement Story 68
            Northeast Pavilion 68
            Main Block 69
            Southwest Pavilion 70
        First-Story Plan 71
            First-Story Northeast Pavilion 71
                Operations Rooms 71
                Bachelors'/Commanding Officer's Apartment 72
            First-Story Main Block 72
                Northeast (NE) Hallway 72
                Center Hallway 73
                Apartment No. 1 73
                Apartment No. 2 74

  Southwest (SW) Hallway 74
 First-Story Southwest Pavilion 74
  Apartment No. 3.. 74
  Apartment No. 4.. 75
Second-Story Plan 76
 Second-Story Northeast Pavilion 76
  Apartment No. 5.. 76
  Apartment No. 6.. 77
 Second-Story Main Block 78
  Northeast (NE) Hallway 78
  Center Hallway 78
  Apartment No. 7.. 79
  Apartment No. 8.. 79
  Southwest (SW) Hallway 80
 Second-Story Southwest Pavilion 80
  Apartment No. 9.. 80
  Apartment No. 10.. 81
 First-Story and Second-Story Elements 81
  Floors 81
  Walls.. 82
  Ceilings 83
  Doorways 83
  Window Openings 84
  Staircases 86
  Built-in Features 86
  Fireplaces 87
  Utilities and Appliances 87
 Attic Story 88
POWER HOUSE 93
ALTERATIONS.. 96
 Introduction 96
 U.S. Navy Occupancy 96
  Brief Chronology 1935 through 2002 97
 Landscape 102

CURRENT PHYSICAL DESCRIPTION...105
 INTRODUCTION 105

EXTERIOR ELEMENTS 106
Design 106
Foundation 106
Walls 106
Entrance Stoops and Terrace 107
Doorways 108
Window Openings 113
Window Schedule 113
Basement-Story Exterior Window Opening Elements 114
First-Story Exterior Window Opening Elements 115
Second-Story Exterior Window Opening Elements 117
Attic-Story Exterior Window Opening Elements 120
Roofs and Related Elements 121
Utilities and Fixtures 122
Landscape 123

INTERIOR ELEMENTS 135
Basement Story 135
Northeast Pavilion 135
Room 001 135
Room 002 135
Room 003 135
Room 004 135
Room 005 136
Main Block 136
Room 006 136
Room 007 136
Room 008 136
Room 009 137
Room 010 137
Room 011 137
Room 012 137
Southwest Pavilion 137
Room 013 137
Room 014 138

- Room 015 138
- Room 016 138
- Room 017 138

First-Story Elements 139
- First-Story Northeast Pavilion 139
  - Commanding Officer's Apartment 139
- First-Story Main Block 141
  - Northeast (NE) Hallway 141
  - Center Hallway 142
  - Apartment No. 1 142
  - Apartment No. 2 143
  - Southwest (SW) Hallway 143
- First-Story Southwest Pavilion 143
  - Apartment No. 3 143
  - Apartment No. 4 144

Second-Story Elements 144
- Second-Story Northeast Pavilion 145
  - Apartment No. 5 145
  - Apartment No. 6 145
- Second-Story Main Block 146
  - Northeast (NE) Hallway 146
  - Center Hallway 146
  - Apartment No. 7 146
  - Apartment No. 8 147
  - Southwest (SW) Hallway 147
- Second-Story Southwest Pavilion 148
  - Apartment No. 9 148
  - Apartment No. 10 148

Attic Story 149
Power House 155

CHARACTER-DEFINING FEATURES AND GENERAL RECOMMENDATIONS 157

INTRODUCTION 159
CHARACTER-DEFINING FEATURES 161
APARTMENT BUILDING EXTERIOR ELEMENTS 161
- Design and Context 161
- Walls 161
- Entrance Stoops and Terrace 162
- Doorways 162
- Window Openings 162
- Roof and Related Elements 163
- Utilities and Fixtures 163
- Landscape 163

POWER HOUSE EXTERIOR ELEMENTS 163
- Design and Context 163
- Walls 164
- Doorways 164
- Window Openings 164
- Roof and Related Elements 164

APARTMENT BUILDING STRUCTURAL ELEMENTS 165
APARTMENT BUILDING INTERIOR ELEMENTS 165
- Plan 165
- Floors 165
- Walls 166
- Ceilings 166
- Doorways 166
- Window Openings 167
- Staircases and Related Elements 167

GENERAL RECOMMENDATIONS
APARTMENT BUILDING AND POWER HOUSE 168
INTRODUCTION 168

EXTERIOR ELEMENTS	168
Design and Context	168
Walls	169
Entrance Stoops and Terrace	169
Doorways	170
Window Openings	170
Roof and Related Elements	171
Utilities and Fixtures	171
Landscape	171
STRUCTURAL ELEMENTS	172
INTERIOR ELEMENTS	172
Plan	172
Floors	174
Walls	174
Ceilings	174
Doorways	175
Window Openings	175
Staircases and Related Elements	175
ACCESSIBILITY	176

BIBLIOGRAPHY 179

PRIMARY SOURCES 181

SECONDARY SOURCES 182

APPENDICES 185

APPENDIX A

Apartment Building Architectural Drawings, 1933...187

Appendix B

Apartment Building Progress Reports Photographs,
1933 through 1935..227

LIST OF FIGURES AND CREDITS

Historic maps, drawings, and photographs were reproduced from the Archives at Acadia National Park (ACAD), Bar Harbor and Winter Harbor, Maine, unless otherwise noted. All photographs from 2008 are by the author, James Lee, unless otherwise noted.

Figures

1. Acadia National Park location map 6
2. Apartment Building, northwest (NW) elevation, 2008 8
3. Apartment Building, southeast (SE) elevation, 2008 8
4. Current USGS Map of Schoodic Peninsula, Winter Harbor, Maine 19
5. Lieutenant Alessandro Fabbri (front row, center) and his men at Otter Cliffs Radio Station, Bar Harbor, Maine, March 27, 1919 20
6. The remote transmitter site at Seawall Station, near Southwest Harbor, Maine, circa 1919 21
7. Detail of Naval Radio Station from Map of U.S. Naval Radio Station, Winter Harbor, Maine, June 30, 1935 32
8. Detail of Naval Radio Station from Map of U.S. Naval Radio Station, Winter Harbor, Maine, June 30, 1944 32
9. Preliminary Study, Apartment House, Schoodic Radio Station, Big Moose Island, Acadia National Park, February 25, 1933 34
10. Sheet 5 of 37, Apartment Building, Acadia National Park, Naval Radio Station, Schoodic Point, Hancock County, Maine 36
11. View of the SW elevation and roof framing from SW radio tower, December 9, 1933. 37
12. Apartment Building, SW elevation, March 8, 1934 38
13. Apartment Building, SE elevation, April 14, 1934 39
14. Apartment Building, SE elevation depicting completed exterior of building and debris removal, September 15, 1934 40

15.	Apartment Building, NW elevation and courtyard, looking NE, October 1934	43
16.	Apartment Building, SE elevation, looking SW. Power House in the right hand foreground, June 1935	43
17.	Apartment Building, NW elevation courtyard before grading and topsoil was deposited, November 1934	45
18.	Apartment Building, NW elevation courtyard, June 1935	45
19.	Apartment Building, Landscape Plan depicting planting completed in fall 1934 and proposed planting for spring 1935	46
20.	Panoramic view of Apartment Building, NW elevation, November 1934	47
21.	Apartment Building, SE elevation, center bay and cross-gable bay, September 1934	49
22.	Apartment Building, bracket detail, Grosvenor Atterbury, drawing number 8 of 37 sheet	51
23.	Apartment Building, NW elevation, entrance stoop and steps, August 1933.	52
24.	Apartment Building, NE elevation of Northeast Pavilion, steps to NE entrance and staircase to the back of the building. Sheet 21 of 37, Drawing No. 116387, Navy Dept. Bureau of Yards and Docks, June 1933 (ACAD Archives)	53
25.	Apartment Building, typical doorway hood, drawing number 12 of 37	54
26.	Apartment Building, SE elevation, September 1934	57
27.	Apartment Building roofs, looking north with Southwest Pavilion in foreground, photograph taken from south radio tower, June 2, 1934	61
28.	Steel framing details depicting steel Lally columns and beams, drawing number 21 of 37 sheets	65
29.	Apartment Building roof framing, view from SW tower	66
30.	Apartment Building drawings depicting typical window opening elements, drawing number 9 of 37 sheets	84
31.	Apartment Building, Grosvenor Atterbury Architect, John Tompkins, Basement Floor Plan, May 26, 1933; drawing number 1 of 37 sheets	90

32.	Apartment Building, Grosvenor Atterbury Architect, John Tompkins, First Floor Plan, May 26, 1933; drawing number 2 of 37 sheets	91
33.	Apartment Building, Grosvenor Atterbury Architect, John Tompkins, Second Floor Plan, May 26, 1933	92
34.	Power House, Naval Radio Station, Winter Harbor, Maine. drawing number 17 of 37 sheets	93
35.	Power House, SE elevation, window opening, 2008	95
36.	Power House, SE elevation, window opening interior elements, 2008	95
37.	Apartment Building, NW elevation, of June 1935	104
38.	Apartment Building, NW elevation, circa 1990	104
39.	Apartment Building, NW elevation, 2008	105
40.	Apartment Building, basement-story floor plan with window opening and doorway numbers assigned during the current project (not to scale)	110
41.	Apartment Building, first-story floor plan with exterior window opening and doorway numbers assigned during the current project (not to scale)	111
42.	Apartment Building, second-story floor plan with window opening numbers assigned during the current project (not to scale)	112
43.	Apartment Building, NW elevation of Main Block and Southwest Pavilion including NE courtyard elevation of pavilion, 2008	124
44.	Apartment Building, SE elevation, 2008	124
45.	Apartment Building, NE elevation with Power House on the left, 2008	125
46.	Apartment Building, SW elevation, 2008	125
47.	Apartment Building, SE elevation, cross gable and projecting center bay, 2008	126
47a.	Apartment Building, SE elevation, cross-gable bracket, 2008	126
48.	Apartment Building, SE elevation, cross-gable brackets supporting second-story window opening bay, 2008	126
49.	Apartment Building, NW elevation entry stoop to D102, 2008	127

50.	Apartment Building Northeast Pavilion, SE wall of NE entrance stoop to D108, 2008	127
51.	Apartment Building, SE Terrace, 2008	128
52.	Apartment Building, SE Terrace staircase, 2008	128
53.	Reproduction door hardware from 1940 P. & F. Corbin catalog	129
53a.	Extant Suffolk-style latch and escutcheon on interior door to NE Hallway vestibule	129
53b.	Extant reproduction strap hinge on Northeast Pavilion entrance door, D108	129
54.	Apartment Building, SW elevation, window openings depicting exterior elements of different window types, 2008	130
55.	Apartment Building, SW chimney, 2008	130
56.	Apartment Building, SE elevation, exterior light fixture on Northeast Pavilion, 2008	131
57.	Apartment Building, NE elevation, exterior light fixture above D108, 2008	131
58.	Apartment Building, basement-story floor plan with room numbers assigned during the current project (not to scale)	132
59.	Apartment Building, first-story floor plan with room numbers assigned by apartment number during the current project (not to scale)	133
60.	Apartment Building, second-story floor plan with room numbers assigned by apartment number during current project (not to scale)	134
61.	Apartment Building, Center Hallway NW vestibule interior doorway, 2008	150
62.	Apartment Building, NE Hallway utility closet, 2008	150
63.	Apartment Building, typical interior of window opening with four sashes (W237), 2008	151
64.	Apartment Building, typical interior of window openings with two sashes (W227) and three sashes (W226), 2008	151
65.	Apartment Building, SW Hallway looking NW at staircase and interior of D104, 2008	152

66. Apartment Building, SW Hallway looking SE at staircase,
    utility closet doorway, and doorway to Apartment No. 4, 2008 152

67. Apartment Building, typical apartment interior elements,
    Apartment No. 9 looking NE from Living Room to Dining Room, 2008 153

68. Apartment Building, typical apartment kitchen elements,
    Apartment No. 9, Room 902, 2008 153

69. Apartment Building, attic story, typical framing of roof and
    cross gable, 2008 154

70. Apartment Building, typical steel framing of hipped roof and
    "nailcrete" sheathing panels, 2008 154

71. Power House, adjacent to the Apartment Building,
    SW and SE elevations looking north, 2008 155

ACKNOWLEDGMENTS

The preparation of this report would not have been possible with out the assistance of the staff members of Acadia National Park (Acadia NP). Rebecca Cole-Will, Cultural Resources Program Manager, provided direction and coordinated the efforts of her staff. Rebecca also provided assistance with archival research at Acadia NP Headquarters, Bar Harbor. Phil Church, Schoodic Maintenance Foreman, gave a tour of the Apartment Building and provided access to the building during the site visits. Phil also provided access to the architectural drawings and maps stored in the Winter Harbor facility. John McDade, Museum Technician/Curator, provided access to historic documents and copies of historic photographs, plans, and documents in the Acadia NP Archives Collection, Bar Harbor. Jim Vekasi, Chief of Maintenance, reviewed the proposed projects for the Apartment Building and discussed the issues concerning the rehabilitation and reuse of the building. Clayton Gilley, Civil Engineer, also reviewed some of the issues concerning the proposed rehabilitation of the building.

The current report used information compiled by Deborah Thompson, Ph.D. for the National Register of Historic Places Nomination, 2001. The report also relied upon previous research preformed by Lee Terzis at the Rockefeller Archive Center, Sleepy Hollow, New York. Monica Blank, Rockefeller Archive Center, researched and photocopied documents that were requested from the Archive Center. Heather A. Miller, Architectural Historian (HAP), made further inquiries with the Rockefeller Archive Center and performed preliminary research on Grosvenor Atterbury. Richard Crisson, Historical Architect (HAP), and Maureen Phillips, Historic Preservation Conservator, participated in the discussion of the nomenclature for the Apartment Building and the Schoodic Peninsula site. Their assistance helped clarify the building name and create consistent nomenclature between the current report, the National Register of Historic Places Nomination, and the List of Classified Structures.

James J. Lee III

INTRODUCTION

EXECUTIVE SUMMARY

Purpose and Scope

The Apartment Building, also known as the Rockefeller Building, is one of three extant buildings that were constructed as part of the U.S. Naval Radio Station, Winter Harbor, Maine, in 1934. The current project is focused on the Apartment Building and immediate adjacent landscape as identified in Project Management Information System (PMIS) 134906. The *U.S. Naval Radio Station – Apartment Building (Bldg 1), Historic Structure Report* (HSR) identifies significant historic features of the building and provides guidance for the treatment of the building. The project included archival research at the local and regional level, along with building investigation and research. The project was phased over two fiscal years (FY 2008 and FY 2009) and culminated in the HSR. In accordance with National Park Service (NPS) standards and as outlined in *Director's Order – 28*, the HSR contains "Part 1. Developmental History" that includes sections on "Historical Background and Context," "Chronology of Development and Use," and "Current Physical Description." The HSR also includes an additional subsection to Part 1 in the form of "Character-Defining Features (CDFs) and General Recommendations" for the Apartment Building. Identification of the CDFs will assist in guiding appropriate repairs and improvements, including fire-detection and -suppression systems, universal access, and potential modifications to accommodate new uses. The report does not include a "Part 2. Treatment and Use" or "Part 3. Record of Treatment," the latter of which should be accomplished by the contractor after the treatment is completed.

Brief Description

The Apartment Building is located near Schoodic Point on Big Moose Island in the Schoodic Peninsula portion of Acadia National Park, Winter Harbor, Maine. It and the adjacent Power House are two of the three surviving structures from the original U.S. Naval Radio Station facility on Schoodic Point. Construction of the Apartment Building began in 1933 and was completed in December 1934. It was commissioned as part of the U.S. Naval Radio Station, Winter Harbor, Maine on February 28, 1935[1] and served as a residential facility for the radio station and later the U.S. Naval Security Group Complex through 2001.

The location and construction of the U.S. Naval Radio Station on Big Moose Island was made possible in part through the influence of John D. Rockefeller, Jr. In his efforts to expand the motor road system on Mount Desert Island, Mr. Rockefeller, Jr. lobbied for the removal of the then-existing Naval Radio Station at Otter Cliffs on Mount Desert Island and the relocation of the facility to Big Moose Island. John D. Rockefeller, Jr. was also influential in

---

[1] *A History of the U.S. Navy at Schoodic Peninsula* (publication funded by the U.S. Navy, 2001; copy ACAD Archives) p. 5.

the choice of New York architect Grosvenor Atterbury who would design the original five buildings at the Schoodic Point Naval complex, of which the Apartment Building and the Power House are extant. Based on the association of the site and building with John D. Rockefeller, Jr., the Apartment Building is alternately referred to as the Rockefeller Apartment Building or the Rockefeller Building.

The Apartment Building is a two-and-a-half story H-shaped châteauesque structure that faces northwest. The Main Block is flanked by two pavilions that enclose a courtyard at the façade of the building and an expansive terrace at the back of the building. The design of Atterbury's buildings incorporated French Eclectic and Renaissance style with half-timbered and masonry exterior walls and steeply pitched terra-cotta roofs. The interior of the Apartment Building has eleven apartments on the first and second stories and utility rooms, offices, storage, and garage bays on the basement story. The Apartment Building is in good condition and retains a high degree of historic integrity.

Research Conducted

The *U.S. Naval Radio Station—Apartment Building (Bldg 1), Historic Structure Report* documents the evolution of the Apartment Building relying on physical investigation of extant materials and documentary research using both primary and secondary sources. To a certain extent, research for the "Historical Background and Context" relied on primary documents compiled by Lee Terzis during previous research at the Rockefeller Archive Center, Sleepy Hollow, New York. Terzis's research was assembled in a binder of correspondence whose contents related to the transfer of the U.S. Naval Radio Station from Otter Cliffs to Schoodic Point. The binder is entitled "Rockefeller Family Archives, John D. Rockefeller, Jr. correspondence—Naval Radio Station, Schoodic Peninsula, Acadia National Park" and is housed at the Acadia NP Archives, Bar Harbor, Maine. Repositories consulted and utilized for materials pertaining to the subject are as follows:

Acadia National Park, Bar Harbor and Winter Harbor, ME;
Cary Memorial Library, Lexington, MA;
National Archives and Records Administration, Northeast Region, Waltham, MA;
NPS, Historic Architecture Program Library, Lowell, MA;
NPS, Northeast Museum Services Center, Boston, MA;
NPS, Technical Information Center, Denver Service Center, Denver, CO;
Rockefeller Archives Center, Sleepy Hollow, NY;
U.S. Navy Historical Center, Washington, DC.

Research Findings

Primary and secondary research provided valuable information about the history of the site and the Apartment Building. The history of the U.S. Naval Radio Station and relocating the station from Otter Cliffs on Mount Desert Island to Schoodic Point provided an important context for the development of the site. The primary documents from the Rockefeller Archives Center included correspondence and reports to and from John D. Rockefeller, Jr., which contributed greatly to better understanding his involvement in all aspects of the development of the site and the construction of the Apartment Building. Correspondence with architect Grosvenor Atterbury and his notes regarding the architecture of the national parks provided greater insight into his involvement in the design of the Apartment Building and his choice of architectural style for the building. Atterbury's specifications for the Lodge at the Brown Mountain Gatehouse were also helpful in determining the construction methods used at the Apartment Building.

A more thorough understanding of the building relied on original plans, original construction drawings, historic photographs, architectural plans for rehabilitation, and the current physical investigation. The original plans and drawings provided information regarding the materials used, method of construction, and the original appearance. Likewise the collection of historic photographs documented the construction of the building, the original appearance of the building, and the appearance of the immediate landscape. Various plans from past rehabilitation efforts documented the alterations to the building. That information, coupled with the current building investigation, helped determine the extent of the changes to the building. Consequently the research determined that the building has had minimal alterations and retains a high degree of historic integrity.

Additional research should focus on the U.S. Navy Historical Center, Washington, D.C. to determine whether a set of original specifications for the Apartment Building do exist. Additional research at the Rockefeller Archive Center, Sleepy Hollow, New York, should further review any plans and photographs in their collection that might refer to the site and the Apartment Building. The current research discovered a limited amount of information directly related to architect Grosvenor Atterbury. Further study should include ferreting out any primary source material pertaining directly to Atterbury and researching the types of construction materials Atterbury was experimenting with and using in his buildings, such as nailable concrete or "nailcrete."

Recommended Treatment and Use

It is recommended that the Apartment Building be preserved through Rehabilitation. The rehabilitation of the building should conform to *The Secretary of the Interior's Standards for Rehabilitation* and *Guidelines for Rehabilitating Historic Buildings*. It is important that the specified rehabilitation strive to preserve the character-defining features (CDFs) of the building, and any changes to the building should be undertaken with attention to the CDFs.

The rehabilitation of the building should be done in a manner that does not diminish the historic integrity of the structure. The reuse of the building may require the installation of fire-suppression systems, additional fire-protection equipment, and ADA-compliant access to part of the building. These changes should be made with minimal impact to the CDFs of the building. It is further recommended that any reuse of the building that would require the creation of larger meeting rooms be planned with awareness to the historic elements of the building. The feasibility of any alterations to the exterior or interior should be studied, and any alteration should be planned with minimal impact to the CDFs (see subsequent section "Character-Defining Features and General Recommendations").

Figure 1. Acadia National Park location map. Schoodic Peninsula is indicated by the red circles.

ADMINISTRATIVE DATA

Location of Site

Acadia National Park (Acadia NP) is located on the coast of Maine and includes approximately 35,500 acres and 13,000 acres in conservation easement (fig. 1). The majority of the park is located on Mount Desert Island and occupies nearly half of the island's mass. A smaller portion of Acadia NP is located on Schoodic Peninsula, which is situated across Frenchman Bay from Mount Desert Island in Winter Harbor, Maine, and currently includes 2,366 acres of park land (fig. 1, inset).[2] The former U.S. Naval Security Group Activity (NSGA) complex is located on Big Moose Island at the southwest tip of the peninsula near Schoodic Point. The former Navy facility occupies approximately 25 acres, and the Apartment Building is located near the southeast end of that complex.

National Register of Historic Places

The Maine State Historic Preservation Officer (SHPO) concurred that the Apartment Building and the Power House were eligible for the National Register of Historic Places on September 20, 2000.[3] The buildings were nominated to the National Register in 2002 and the nomination was fully endorsed by the Main SHPO.[4] However, the nomination has not been finalized by the Keeper of the National Register of Historic Places.

The National Register nomination proposed that the Apartment Building and the Power House are nationally significant under Criteria A and B for their association with philanthropist John D. Rockefeller, Jr. The nomination also suggested that the buildings qualify for the National Register under Criterion C "as an outstanding example of French Renaissance architecture."[5] The stated period of significance for both the Apartment Building and the Power House is from the date of construction in 1934 through 1943. Acadia NP has determined that they must be preserved and maintained through rehabilitation.

---

[2] *Schoodic General Management Plan Amendment, Acadia National Park, Maine* (Washington, DC: U.S. Department of the Interior, National Park Service, April 2006) p. 6.

[3] Earle G. Shettleworth, Jr., SHPO, to Tina A. Deininger, P.E., Command Historic Preservation Officer, Northern Division, Naval Facilities Engineering Command, September 20, 2000. LCS Records, NPS, NER, HAP, Lowell, MA.

[4] Shettleworth, Jr., SHPO, to Commanding Officer Williamson, Naval Facility at Winter Harbor, Maine, March 1, 2002. LCS Records, NPS, NER, HAP, Lowell, MA.

[5] Thompson. Continuation Sheet, Section 8, Page 2.

List of Classified Structures Information

Figure 2. Apartment Building, northwest (NW) elevation, 2008.

Figure 3. Apartment Building, southeast (SE) elevation, 2008.

The current views of the Apartment Building depict the physical appearance of the two primary elevations of the building (figs. 2 and 3). The following is selected from the current List of Classified Structures (LCS) information for the Apartment Building:[6]

Preferred Structure Name:	Schoodic Point Naval Complex—Apartment Building
Structure Number:	SPNC – 2 *(B-1001-SD)
Other Structure Names:	Rockefeller Building Building 1 Atterbury Building U.S. Naval Radio Station—Apartment Building Schoodic Point Naval Complex—Housing
LSC ID:	235169

UTM:

	Zone	Easting	Northing
1.	19	574960	4909410

National Register Status:	Determined Eligible—SHPO (State Historic Preservation Officer)
National Register Date:	09/20/2000
Significance Level: Short Significance Description:	Contributing Nationally significant under Criteria A and B for association with John D Rockefeller, Jr., and under Criterion C as excellent example of Tudor-revival architectural style.

---

[6] *List of Classified Structures-Acadia National Park* (NPS website http://www.hscl.cr.nps.gov).
 *Note: The Structure Number "B-1001-SD" is used in the Facilities Management Software System (FMSS) and corresponds to the building number used by NPS site staff.

LCS information for the Apartment Building continued:

Long Physical Description:	The Apartment Building and attached Power House are located in the central 25-acre portion of the 110 acres that comprised the former Schoodic Point Naval Security Group Complex. The Apartment Building is a two-and-a-half-story H-shaped structure in the French Norman Revival style that faces northwest. It is comprised of a rectangular central block and flanking projecting pavilions that are connected to the central block by hyphens. The central block, pavilions, and hyphens all have steep, terra-cotta-clad hip roofs of varying heights; a large brick and stone chimney is located on each hyphen. The walls are composed of irregular granite blocks and layers of schist set between horizontal bands of brick on the first story, and patterned brick set within hewn, pecky cypress half-timbering on the upper stories. The main entrance is centered on the northwest façade; additional doorways are located at the center of the rear (southeast) façade and in the angle between the hyphens and pavilions. The basement level, exposed on the southeast elevation, holds ten garage doorways on the central block and east pavilion, each holding original, vertical-plank, glazed paired doors w/ original hardware. A flat roof over the center garages forms a projecting terrace at the first-story level that is rimmed by a masonry parapet. Windows of varying sizes hold anodized aluminum casement sashes (replacements).
Management—Category:	Must Be Preserved and Maintained
Management—Treatment:	Rehabilitation

Proposed Treatment and Use

The *Schoodic General Management Plan Amendment* (GMPA) determined that the National Park Service (NPS) will implement the Collaborative Management alternative for the Schoodic District of Acadia NP. In doing so the NPS has partnered with a nonprofit organization, Acadia Partners for Science and Learning (APSL), to develop the former Navy base as the Schoodic Education and Research Center (SERC) that focuses on promoting the understanding, protection, and conservation of natural and cultural resources of the National Park System.[7]

The goals of the NPS at Schoodic Peninsula include the preservation of the character and quality of the area. The Apartment Building is currently used for some programs and as a laundry facility, but is otherwise unoccupied. The Schoodic GMPA proposes the rehabilitation and reuse of the Apartment Building in conjunction with the SERC activities at the site. The rehabilitation and reuse may require modifications for ADA accessibility; upgrading utilities; installing fire-protection systems; and reconfiguring interior spaces for offices, conference rooms, visitor contact, exhibit space, and/or housing.[8]

---

[7] *Schoodic GMPA*, p. 35.
[8] *Schoodic GMPA*, p. 40.

Related Studies

Some publications identified in the Cultural Resources Management Bibliography were consulted in the preparation of this report. Should the reader desire a broader discussion of the history of Acadia National Park, U.S. Navy Communications, or John D. Rockefeller, Jr., he or she should consult the publications listed below.

George B. Dorr. *Acadia National Park: Its Origin and Background, Book I* (Bangor, ME: Burr Printing Company, 1942).

George B. Dorr. *Acadia National Park: Its Growth and Development, Book II* (Bangor, ME: Burr Printing Company, 1948).

Raymond B. Fosdick. *John D. Rockefeller, Jr.: A Portrait* (New York: Harper and Brothers, Publishers, 1956).

William D. Rieley and Roxanne S. Brouse. *Historic Resource Study for the Carriage Road System, Acadia National Park, Mount Desert Island, Maine* (Charlottesville, VA: Rieley and Associates, Landscape Architects, May 1989).

A History of the U.S. Navy at Schoodic Peninsula (publication funded by the U.S. Navy, 2001; copy ACAD Archives).

General Management Plan, Acadia National Park, Maine (Bar Harbor, ME: U.S. Department of the Interior, National Park Service, October 1992).

Navy Cold War Communication Context: Resources Associated with the Navy's Communication Program, 1946 – 1989 (Frederick, MD: R. Christopher Goodwin and Associates, Inc., December 1997).

Schoodic General Management Plan Amendment, Acadia National Park, Maine (Washington, DC: U.S. Department of the Interior, National Park Service, April 2006).

Deborah Thompson, Ph.D. National Register of Historic Places Registration Form: Apartment Building; Building 1. Naval Security Group, Winter Harbor, Maine, September 2001.

Brandon Wentworth. *The Fabulous Radio NBD, Otter Cliffs, Acadia National Park* (Southwest Harbor, ME: Beech Hill Publishing Co., 1984; copy ACAD Archives)

DEVELOPMENTAL HISTORY

HISTORICAL BACKGROUND AND CONTEXT

Introduction

The history of Mount Desert Island and Acadia National Park is well documented on the National Park Service website (http://www.nps.gov/acad/historyculture/stories.htm) and by previous publications including two volumes by George B. Dorr, *Acadia National Park: Its Origin and Background, Book I*, and *Acadia National Park: Its Growth and Development, Book II*, and by William D. Rieley and Roxanne S. Brouse, *Historic Resource Study for the Carriage Road System, Acadia National Park, Mount Desert Island, Maine*, as well as the *General Management Plan, Acadia National Park, Maine* and the *Schoodic General Management Plan Amendment*. The park was first established on Mount Desert Island as a National Monument and was later designated as a national park. The park was eventually named Acadia National Park (Acadia NP), which will be the park designation for the purposes of this report. Land on Schoodic Peninsula, Winter Harbor, Maine, which is across Frenchman Bay from Mount Desert Island, was later added to Acadia NP. Park land on Schoodic Peninsula originally included two islands as well as the picturesque Schoodic Point on Big Moose Island at the southernmost tip of Schoodic Peninsula. Acadia NP currently occupies much of Mount Desert Island and over 2,000 acres on Schoodic Peninsula, as well as four islands.

During World War I a U.S. Naval Radio Station was established at Otter Cliffs on Mount Desert Island. The subsequent transfer of that radio station to Big Moose Island at the tip of Schoodic Peninsula, Winter Harbor, and the establishment of the U.S. Naval Radio Station, Winter Harbor, would include the construction of the Apartment Building for Navy housing and radio operations, as well as radio towers and several support structures for the Navy facility.

The development and expansion of Acadia NP is inextricably linked to the influence and generosity of John D. Rockefeller, Jr. His desire to develop scenic motor roads on Mount Desert Island would directly affect the transfer of the U.S. Naval Radio Station to Big Moose Island. In addition, John D. Rockefeller, Jr.'s association with New York architect Grosvenor Atterbury would lead to Atterbury's commission to design the Apartment Building and four other buildings at the U.S. Naval Radio Station, Winter Harbor.

The following sections will briefly describe the founding of Acadia NP and the contributions of John D. Rockefeller, Jr. and Grosvenor Atterbury to the park. They will also describe the addition of Schoodic Peninsula to the park, the establishment of the U.S. Naval Radio Station at Otter Cliffs, and the transfer of the radio station to Winter Harbor as they pertain to the construction of the Apartment Building.

Acadia National Park

The establishment of park lands on Mount Desert Island, Hancock County, Maine, began through the efforts of conservation-minded summer residents. The increased development of the island during the 1880s and 1890s led to the creation of the Hancock County Trustees of Public Reservations (HCTPR) in 1901 by some of the areas more prominent residents. The organization was founded by Charles W. Eliot, President Emeritus of Harvard University, and modeled after a similar organization founded by his son, Charles Eliot, Jr., in Massachusetts, The Trustees of Reservations.[9] The primary purpose of the HCTPR was the conservation of land that it acquired through private donations and purchase.

The land managed by the HCTPR was to be set aside for public use and enjoyment. However, increasing pressure to exploit the resources of the area led trustee George B. Dorr to seek the support of the federal government to accept a donation of a portion of the HCTPR property. Dorr was successful in his efforts, and in 1916 Sieur de Monts National Monument was established and George Dorr was named the superintendent. The park was granted national park status as Lafayette National Park in 1919 and was the first national park east of the Mississippi River. The park was renamed Acadia National Park in 1929, and George Dorr remained as superintendent of the park until he died in 1944.[10]

John D. Rockefeller, Jr.

Acadia NP was the first national park created solely from donations of private organizations and individuals. Though he was not involved in founding the park, philanthropist John D. Rockefeller, Jr. (JDR Jr.), the most prominent heir to the John D. Rockefeller, Sr. Standard Oil fortune, was quite important to the expansion of Acadia NP. Mr. Rockefeller, Jr. purchased a summer residence, "The Eyrie," on Mount Desert Island in 1910 and became instrumental in the future of the park.[11] His friend and biographer Raymond B. Fosdick articulated John D. Rockefeller, Jr.'s interests and contributions to Acadia NP in the following passage:

> After the park had been officially created, he began to purchase additional land in order to enlarge its boundaries and join the mountain summits to one another so that ultimately a park road might extend from ocean on one side to Frenchman's Bay on the other. ... Land acquisition was but one phase of Mr. Rockefeller's participation. There was, in fact, no aspect of the park's development which did not

---

[9] William D. Rieley and Roxanne S. Brouse. *Historic Resource Study for the Carriage Road System, Acadia National Park, Mount Desert Island, Maine* (Charlottesville, VA: Rieley & Associates, Landscape Architects, May 1989) p. 20.

[10] *General Management Plan, Acadia National Park, Maine* (Washington, DC: U.S. Department of the Interior, National Park Service, Oct. 1992) pp. 1–2, & Appendix A: Legislation.

H.E. Foulds and Lauren G. Meier. *Cultural Landscape Report for Blackwoods and Seawall Campgrounds, Acadia National Park* (Boston, MA: U.S. Department of the Interior, National Park Service, Olmsted Center for Landscape Preservation, Sept. 1996) pp. 3–4.

[11] Rieley and Brouse, p. 28.

interest him – from the architecture of park buildings to landscaping, forestry, roads, or the destruction caused by beavers and deer. Through his long years of association with Acadia he would come to know and love the island almost inch by inch, and his total expenditures for land acquisition, buildings, roads, bridges, forestry, and planning would reach large sums.[12]

JDR Jr. took an active part in the development of Acadia NP. His involvement in developing the park roadway system was well documented by William D. Rieley and Roxanne S. Brouse in the *Historic Resource Study for the Carriage Road System, Acadia National Park, Mount Desert Island, Maine*. Soon after purchasing "The Eyrie" near Seal Harbor, Rockefeller started planning the development of the grounds and expansion of the roads. Between 1913 and 1919 he created plans for roads on his own property and a more extensive road system for public enjoyment of the park.[13]

Some of the roads were to be built on land of the HCTPR that would eventually become Acadia NP. JDR Jr.'s impetus in creating the road system was to establish carriage roads and bridle paths that were "motor free" and would allow the public to experience the natural beauty of Mount Desert Island from horseback and carriages. His contributions would eventually extend to motor roads as well.[14] Rieley and Brouse documented Rockefeller's extensive involvement in the development and construction of carriage roads, bridle paths, auto roads, bridges, gate lodges, and other structures at Acadia NP. His desire to expand the park roads in the 1920s would lead to an ambitious road construction project on Mount Desert Island. The road that was "to be constructed at private expense at an estimated cost of $4,000,000 and to be donated to the Government as the principal highway in Acadia National Park"[15] was apparently constructed at least in part, if not completely, at the expense of JDR Jr. That particular project included the reconstruction of Ocean Drive through Otter Creek and would lead to the expansion of the park property on Schoodic Peninsula, Winter Harbor, Maine, and the development of the U.S. Navy facility on Big Moose Island at the tip of Schoodic Peninsula.

Grosvenor Atterbury

In his efforts to create structures at Acadia NP that would harmonize with the natural beauty of the area, John D. Rockefeller, Jr. commissioned New York architect Grosvenor Atterbury to establish an architectural style for the park. Grosvenor Atterbury was the son of Charles Larned Atterbury, a successful New York lawyer, and had graduated from Yale in 1891. After that he studied at Columbia College, School of Architecture and during the same time period purportedly worked for McKim, Mead and White.[16] However, the Office Roll of McKim, Mead and White did not list Grosvenor Atterbury as an employee at any time between 1879

---

[12] Raymond B. Fosdick. *John D. Rockefeller, Jr.: A Portrait* (New York: Harper & Brothers, Publishers, 1956) p. 304.

[13] Rieley and Brouse, p. 72.

[14] http://www.nps.gov/acad/historyculture/historiccarriageroads.htm

[15] *Otter Cliffs Station, Acadia National Park, ME*. (Washington, DC: 72nd Congress, February, 1932; copy at ACAD Archive) Document No. 62, p. 2.

[16] Robert B. MacKay, Anthony K. Baker, and Carol A. Traynor. *Long Island Country Houses and Their Architects, 1860 – 1940* (New York: W.W. Norton & Company, 1997) pp. 49 – 57.

and 1909.[17] It was apparent that Grosvenor Atterbury was acquainted with McKim, Mead and White, because they had designed his father's home in Shinnecock on Long Island in 1888 and Stamford White was a neighbor and family friend.[18] So it seems possible that he worked with the firm, but that was not confirmed by the firm's payroll records.

Grosvenor Atterbury spent a year in Paris at the École des Beaux-Arts in 1894 through 1895. Upon returning to New York, Atterbury began his architectural practice, getting his first commission in 1896. His New York and Long Island connections garnered commissions to design mansions and summer cottages for wealthy clients on Long Island, as well as several commissions on Mount Desert Island. The Russell Sage Foundation hired Atterbury as lead architect for the design of some of the buildings at the model garden suburb of Forest Hills Gardens, Queens, New York, in 1909. Forest Hills allowed Atterbury to pursue his interest in the development of low-cost housing construction and the use of prefabricated building systems.[19]

Grosvenor Atterbury was first hired by John D. Rockefeller, Jr. to design a barn complex at his estate in Tarrytown, New York. In the late 1920s JDR Jr. commissioned Atterbury to create an architectural style for Acadia NP and design some of the structures for the park carriage road system. Prior to determining what style of architecture would be best for Acadia NP Atterbury traveled to the western national parks in August and September of 1929. His trip was sponsored by Mr. Rockefeller, Jr. with the purpose of studying the established park architecture and reporting his observations to Rockefeller.[20] During his survey of the western parks Atterbury developed an opinion of which architecture was appropriate for the parks and what was not. In general he was critical of buildings that did not harmonize with the natural beauty of the area and reserved higher praise for structures that were placed among the trees and had vines growing on the roofs. He was particularly concerned with the color of the structure including the roof and the exterior wall colors. Atterbury also devoted a section of his report to the consideration of roofs; he advocated high-pitched roofs as "the logical, practical, as well as the picturesque type,"[21] and recognized the importance of the proper material, texture, and color of the roofs, which was often dictated by the site.[22] Atterbury noted that "the type of Architectural development directly depends on what you most want to give the people who come to the national parks – education, inspiration or diversion – and the relative importance you give their other functions in scenic, historic, and monumental conservation."[23]

Grosvenor Atterbury did note in the foreword of the report that his observations were "to be taken rather as a point of departure – suggestive leads – rather than conclusions – such as may follow from their further consideration." In concluding his report, he offered the following points to be considered when handling "the Architecture problem in the National Parks:"[24]

---

[17] Charles Moore. *The Life and Times of Charles Follen McKim* (Boston & New York; Houghton Mifflin Company, 1929). Appendix II, pp. 327 – 337.
[18] MacKay, Baker, and Traynor. pp. 49 – 57.
[19] Ibid.
[20] Rieley and Brouse, p. 197.
[21] Grosvenor Atterbury. "Notes on the Architectural and Other Esthetic Problems Involved in the Development of Our Great National Parks," August and September 1929 (Technical Information Center, Denver Service Center, NPS).
[22] Ibid.
[23] Ibid.
[24] Ibid.

> First, by avoidance, where the structures are kept so small that they need not involve any question of architectural style. While this is frankly begging the question, it is better than a poor solution along definite and conventional lines.
>
> Second, and somewhat similarly, by keeping the buildings entirely outside the picture, placing them where the surroundings and background permit of normal treatment as to size and style: where there is no direct comparison or competition with the scenic marvels that have justified the establishment of the Park area.
>
> Third, by going back to ancient local traditions, where such exist – as, for example, in Mesa Verde and other places in the Pueblo region – and developing a style from these historic precedents that will also satisfy the modern practical requirements.
>
> Fourth, in cases where no such logical precedents exist, by adapting and acclimating some foreign style that has been produced under similar climactic and scenic conditions and which can be properly expressed in local materials.
>
> Lastly, it may be faced squarely, as a new problem, and fought out on its own merits – or, more properly speaking, on the merits of the designer. This means a solution along original or eclectic lines. But to a certain extent it may make use of one or more of the forgoing methods.[25]

Soon after his western trip, Atterbury traveled to Acadia NP and began planning an appropriate architecture for the park. His efforts at Acadia NP focused on the fourth point made in the conclusion of his report. Among Atterbury's first commissions in the park were the designs for the gate lodges at Brown Mountain and Jordan Pond. For those structures he chose a revival style that was influenced by French domestic architecture from the medieval period. The architectural style was approved by Superintendent George Dorr who noted that the French tradition was appropriate for the park because of the area's French Colonial associations.[26]

Grosvenor Atterbury was apparently influenced by his exposure to French architecture during his training at the École des Beaux-Arts and his subsequent work as supervising architect at the Army University at Beaune, France.[27] As described by Deborah Thompson, Ph.D., Atterbury's choice of architectural style for Acadia NP was a "creative interpretation of the Burgundian early Gothic" architecture.[28] Though she noted some differences, Thompson observed that "the Acadia gatehouse towers and the high tile-clad hipped roofs of

---

[25] Atterbury. "Notes on the Architectural and Other Esthetic Problems Involved in the Development of Our Great National Parks."

[26] Charles Peterson to Director of NPS, H. Albright, Oct. 27, 1931. Rockefeller Family Archives (RFA); Record Group: OMR; Series: Homes; Box: 84 (copy at ACAD Archives).

[27] Deborah Thompson, Ph.D., "National Register of Historic Places Continuation Sheet," for "Apartment Building, Building 1; Naval Security Group Activity, Winter Harbor, ME," September 2001, section 8, p. 3.

[28] Thompson, section 8, p. 1.

the lodge buildings and their masonry construction reflect the architect's exposure to French Romanesque and early Gothic buildings, particularly those of Beaune."[29]

The revival style employed by Atterbury at Acadia NP has been alternately described as French Romanesque, French Gothic, and/or French Renaissance style. NPS Landscape Architect Charles E. Peterson wrote that Atterbury told him the type of architecture employed for the gate lodges "originated in the Romanesque period" of France.[30] Current architectural terminology generally refers to this style as French Eclectic, which is a renaissance style that has its roots in French Romanesque traditions and is often influenced by other styles of medieval period architecture.[31]

Grosvenor Atterbury's designs for the gate lodges at Brown Mountain and Jordan Pond would become part of the Rockefeller legacy at Acadia NP and would influence the later development of the U.S. Naval Radio Station on Big Moose Island at Schoodic Peninsula.

Schoodic Peninsula

Schoodic Peninsula, located within Hancock County and situated across Frenchman Bay from Mount Desert Island, became part of Acadia National Park in 1929. Large tracts of land on Schoodic Peninsula had been bought by John G. Moore in the 1880s. Moore, a native of Steuben, Maine, who gained wealth as a Wall Street financier, was interested in developing the land for summer "cottage" residences in response to the high demand for such properties in the area. In 1897 he had a road constructed to the top of Schoodic Head so that visitors could survey the surrounding peninsula and islands. John G. Moore died in 1898 and, contrary to his plans for development, his heirs donated the land on Schoodic Peninsula to the Hancock County Trustees of Public Reservations (HCTPR) to preserve and conserve the natural resources of the area.[32]

The 1929 Act of Congress (45 Stat. 1083) that renamed Lafayette National Park also allowed the Secretary of the Interior "to accept in behalf of the United States lands, easements, and buildings, as may be donated for the extension of the Lafayette National Park, lying within the bounds of Hancock County within which the park is located, ...;"[33] that same year the HCTPR donated over 2,000 acres of land on Schoodic Peninsula formerly owned by John Moore to the National Park Service, which included Little Moose Island and Pond Island.[34] The land on Schoodic Peninsula included at the southern tip of the peninsula Big Moose Island and Schoodic Point. The NPS acquired Schoodic Island and Rolling Island in 1989 and 1999, respectively (fig. 4).

---

[29] Thompson, section 8, p. 4.
[30] Peterson to Albright, Oct. 27, 1931.
[31] Virginia & Lee McAlester. *A Field Guide to American Houses* (New York: Alfred A. Knopf Publishing, 1984) pp. 387 – 395.
Cyril M. Harris. *Dictionary of Architecture and Construction, Fourth Edition* (New York: McGraw-Hill Company, 2005) p. 441.
[32] *Schoodic General Management Plan Amendment*, p. 6.
[33] *General Management Plan, Acadia National Park, Maine.* Appendix A: Legislation.
[34] *Schoodic General Management Plan Amendment*, p. 6.

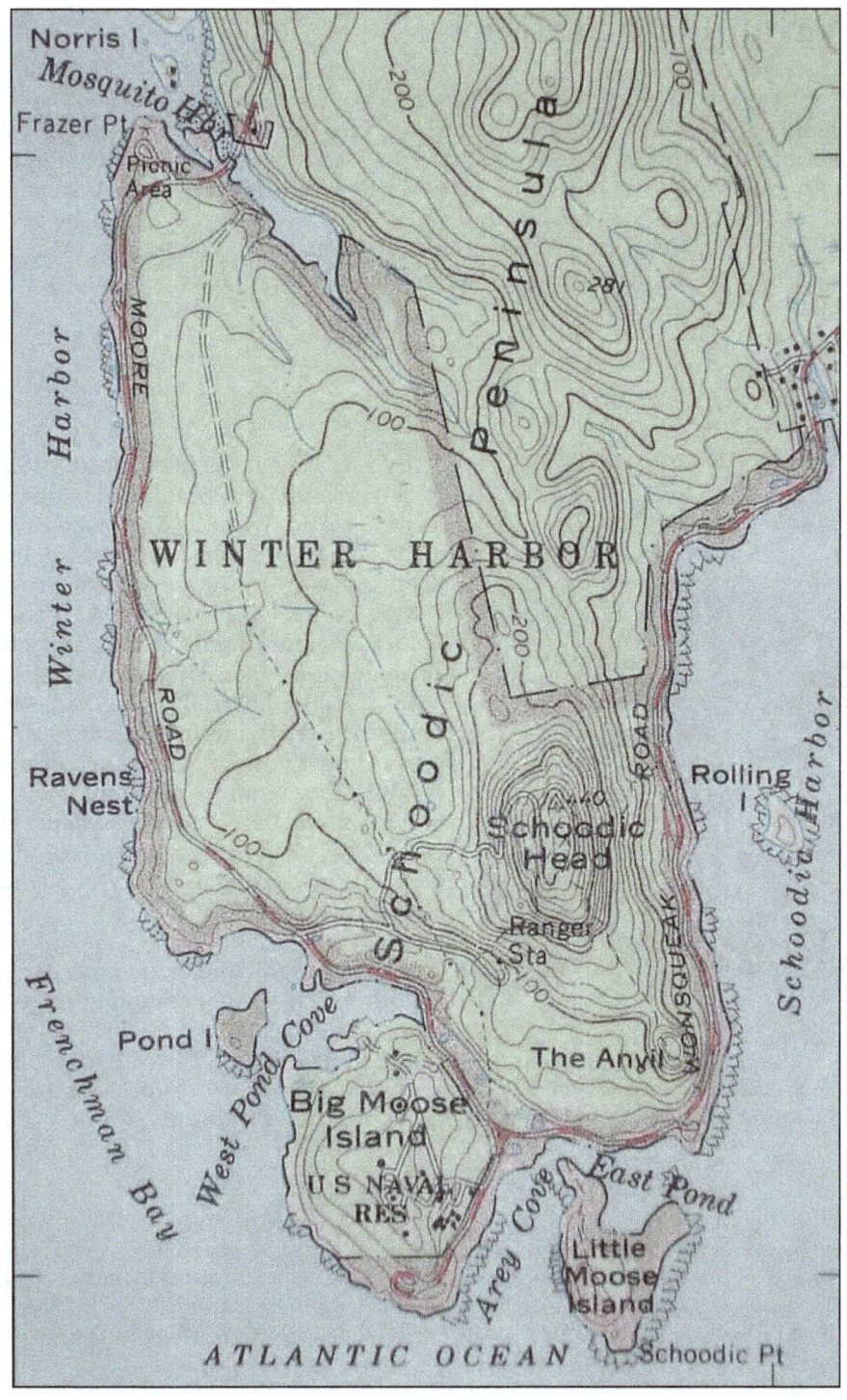

Figure 4. Current USGS Map of Schoodic Peninsula, Winter Harbor, Maine.

U.S. Naval Radio Station[35]

At the beginning of the twentieth century the U.S. Navy was responsible for the development of the government radio communications systems. The Navy set up a chain of radio stations along the Atlantic and Pacific coasts and by 1908 had established a system of communication capable of relaying between the two coasts. With the onset of World War I the government became interested in developing more secure overseas communication.[36] Mount Desert Island and Acadia NP would play an important role in transatlantic communication for the United States.

Otter Cliffs Radio Station

Figure 5. Lieutenant Alessandro Fabbri (front row, center) and his men at Otter Cliffs Radio Station, Bar Harbor, Maine, March 27, 1919.

The first U.S. Naval Radio Station on Mount Desert Island was established at Otter Cliffs during World War I. The radio station was made possible through the efforts of Alessandro Fabbri, a wealthy summer resident of Mount Desert Island. Fabbri had a keen interest in radio communications and held both an amateur radio operator's license and a station license. Fabbri had built a small radio station on Mount Desert Island in 1912 and his interests, coupled with the Navy's requirement for reliable transatlantic radio communications, led to the construction of the Naval Radio Station at Otter Cliffs. Fabbri agreed to lease the land and construct the station in return for a commission as an Ensign in the U.S. Navy.[37]

The Otter Cliffs Radio Station was completed in 1917 and went into operation in August of that year with Alessandro Fabbri as Officer-in-Charge (fig. 5).[38] The Otter Cliffs station operated as the Navy's primary transatlantic receiving station during WWI. The Navy operations on Mount Desert Island were

---

[35] The following section and subsections partly relied on primary documents compiled by Lee Terzis during previous research at the Rockefeller Archive Center, Sleepy Hollow, NY. Terzis's research was assembled in a binder of correspondence whose contents related to the transfer of the Naval Radio Station from Otter Cliffs to Schoodic Point. The binder is entitled "Rockefeller Family Archives, John D. Rockefeller, Jr. correspondence—Naval Radio Station, Schoodic Peninsula, Acadia National Park" and is housed at the ACAD Archives.

[36] *Navy Cold War Communication Context: Resources Associated with the Navy's Communication Program, 1946 – 1989* (Frederick, MD.: R. Christopher Goodwin & Associates, Inc., December, 1997).

[37] Brandon Wentworth. *The Fabulous Radio NBD, Otter Cliffs, Acadia National Park* (Southwest Harbor, ME: Beech Hill Publishing Co., 1984; copy ACAD Archives).

[38] Ibid.

expanded in 1918 with the addition of a radio station at Seawall near Southwest Harbor that was used for transmissions (fig. 6). Both stations were active during the war and through most of the 1920s. During the latter period the Otter Cliffs station provided radio direction-finding services to mariners, and broadcast services.[39] However, by 1927 some of the facilities at Seawall were in poor condition and the Navy was determining whether to dispose of that site.[40] The site was abandoned in November of that year.[41] The Seawall site was later transferred to the Department of the Interior in 1930 and became part of Acadia NP.[42] After Seawall was vacated, Otter Cliffs Radio Station remained as the only U.S. Naval Radio Station on Mount Desert Island.

Figure 6. The remote transmitter site at Seawall Station, near Southwest Harbor, Maine, circa 1919.

The Disposition of the Otter Cliffs Radio Station

The Otter Cliffs Radio Station stood in the way of John D. Rockefeller, Jr.'s plans to expand the Ocean Drive section of the motor roads in Acadia NP. In particular JDR Jr. wanted to extend Ocean Drive beyond Otter Creek, but the roadway was obstructed by the Otter Cliffs station. In correspondence with Colonel Arthur H. Woods in 1926 Rockefeller expressed interest in the government's plans for the station. He was hopeful that he would have an opportunity to purchase the land if it became available.[43] From that point on JDR Jr. became very interested in the Otter Cliffs station and the fate of the Seawall Station. Colonel Woods

---

[39] *A History of the U.S. Navy at Schoodic Peninsula*, p. 2.
[40] Col. Arthur Woods to JDR Jr., Nov. 30, 1927; RFA; Record Group: OMR; Series: Homes; Box: 105 (copy ACAD Archives).
[41] J.Edgar Hoover to Col. Woods, Nov. 23, 1927; RFA; Record Group: OMR; Series: Homes; Box: 105 (copy ACAD Archives).
[42] *General Management Plan, Acadia National Park, Maine*. Appendix A: Legislation.
[43] JDR Jr. to Col. Woods, Sept. 16, 1926; RFA; Record Group: OMR; Series: Homes; Box: 105 (copy ACAD Archives).

wrote JDR Jr. in November 1927 that the Navy had decided to keep the Otter Cliffs station and had closed the Seawall station.[44] Additional correspondence between JDR Jr. and National Park Service and U.S. Navy personnel documented his continued interest in the future of the two radio stations on Mount Desert Island.

John D. Rockefeller, Jr. made an official inquiry into the matter on December 28, 1929. His letter to Charles Francis Adams, Secretary of the Navy, on that day discussed his desire to construct the road that would pass through the Otter Cliffs station and whether the Navy would consider relocating the station.[45] The official finding from the Judge Advocate General on February 5, 1930 was that "so long as the land comprising the Naval Radio Station, Bar Harbor, Me., is in the custody of the Navy Department, in the absence of specific legislation from the Congress, it is without authority of law to enter into a contract to relinquish the interest of the United States in exchange for a tract of land offered by Mr. Rockefeller."[46] In the meantime, however, the possibility of moving the station to Schoodic Point on Big Moose Island near Winter Harbor had surfaced. In a letter to Acadia NP Superintendent George Dorr, Rockefeller noted that he thought Schoodic Point would be the best permanent solution for relocating the station and he hoped the Navy's tests of the site would show that it was as good as Otter Cliffs. The tests that were scheduled for March 1930 would determine the future of the Naval Radio operations in the area.[47]

The Chairman of the Naval Affairs Committee of the House of Representatives, Congressman Britten, introduced the following legislation on June 11, 1930:

> A BILL TO provide for the Removal of the Otter Cliffs Radio Station.
>
> Be it enacted by the Senate and House of Representatives of the United States of America, in Congress assembled; that there is hereby authorized to be appropriated, out of any money in the Treasury not otherwise appropriated, not to exceed the sum of $350,000 for the complete removal of the present Otter Cliffs radio station on Mount Desert Island in the State of Maine and its reconstruction and relocation on Government land on Schoodic Peninsular [sic] opposite Mount Desert Island, within Acadia National Park, subject to the approval of both site and design by the Secretary of the Navy and the Secretary of the Interior, and upon relocation of said radio station the tract of land formerly occupied thereby shall be, and is hereby, added to and made part of the Acadia National Park.[48]

---

[44] Col. Woods to JDR Jr., Nov. 30, 1927; RFA; Record Group: OMR; Series: Homes; Box: 105 (copy ACAD Archives).

[45] JDR Jr. to Sec. of the Navy, Charles Francis Adams, Dec. 28, 1929; RFA; Record Group: OMR; Series: Homes; Box: 105 (copy ACAD Archives).

[46] The Judge Advocate General to Chief of Naval Operations, Feb. 5, 1930; RFA; Record Group: OMR; Series: Homes; Box: 105 (copy ACAD Archives).

[47] JDR Jr. to George B. Dorr, Feb. 10, 1930; RFA; Record Group: OMR; Series: Homes; Box: 105 (copy ACAD Archives).

[48] "Private Confidential Memorandum regarding the proposed removal to Schoodic Point of the Naval Radio Station at Otter Cliffs, Maine" to JDR Jr., no date (circa Dec. 1930); RFA; Record Group: OMR; Series: Homes; Box: 105; folder 1050 (copy ACAD Archives). This 11-page memo includes a transcript of the proposed legislation as well as further details regarding the transfer of the Naval Radio Station from Otter Cliffs to Schoodic Point.

The disposition of the Otter Cliffs station would entail extensive negotiation and correspondence between the Departments of the Navy and Interior, as well as other interested parties, including JDR Jr. The issues raised by the Navy Department included the following:

1. That the area and location of the new site shall be satisfactory from a technical standpoint for radio and compass operation.

2. That there shall be provided on said new site with cost to the United States in good operating condition for radio station purposes necessary buildings, appurtenances, improvements and equipment of a standard equal to those comprising the present station.

3. That the new station thus provided shall be of such character and workmanship as not to require a materially greater annual maintenance expense than the present one.

4. That there be provided with out cost to the United States proper and sufficient road connections to the new station where ever deemed necessary.

5. That there be provided with out cost to the United States necessary wire and telephone connections between the new station and the nearest exchanges; and

6. That living and recreation conditions are to be reasonably satisfactory.[49]

The recurring point in the Navy's objections was apparently the overall cost of relocating the radio station. In keeping with his generosity in support of Acadia NP, JDR Jr. offered to subsidize the cost of moving the Otter Cliffs station to some other location "to the extent of up to one-half of a sum not to exceed $500,000."[50] However, the Secretary of the Interior felt that, in light of all John D. Rockefeller, Jr. had done for the NPS and Acadia NP specifically, the appropriations for the relocation of the radio station should be covered by the government and could be part of the Department of the Interiors budget.[51] This proposal, if approved by Congress, would appear to have removed a significant roadblock in the relocation of the radio station. However, consent from the Navy and the removal of the Otter Cliffs station was not immediate.

The other issues raised by the Navy Department were addressed in an undated confidential memorandum presumably sent to JDR Jr. from one his confidants within the NPS. The memo cited a report by Admiral Andrews on the feasibility of the Schoodic Point site and suggested that the site met and even surpassed the Navy's requirements in almost every instance; the technical capabilities of the site surpassed the Otter Cliffs site; the land was suitable for the construction of the necessary buildings (and later tests indicated an adequate

---

[49] Private Confidential Memorandum to JDR Jr., no date (circa Dec. 1930).
[50] JDR Jr. to Arno Cammerer, Associate Director NPS, Feb. 11, 1932; RFA; Record Group: OMR; Series: Homes; Box: 105; folder 1050 (copy ACAD Archives). This letter refers to the original offer made on April 24, 1930.
[51] Private Confidential Memorandum to JDR Jr., no date (circa Dec. 1930).

water supply); the new facility would be modern and therefore more efficient and economical to operate; a new road to the site would be built and maintained by the NPS; installation of wire and telephone connections would be part of the appropriations for the new station; and lastly, the new station would include recreation and its proximity to Winter Harbor and Ellsworth would provide shopping and amusement.[52] The memo appeared to answer the concerns of the Navy, but the process of approving the new site was a slow one.

Negotiations for the removal of the Otter Cliffs Radio Station and the construction of the new station at Schoodic Point on Big Moose Island continued into 1932. In February of that year JDR Jr. withdrew his pledge to cover some of the cost of relocation, noting the elapsed time since the offer and that the Secretary of the Interior had told him that the expense should be provided by the NPS. JDR Jr. did note his continued support of the objective and that he would be ready to help out if needed.[53] Though his financial assistance was not required for the direct costs of relocating the radio station, JDR Jr. did contribute resources that would make the location at Schoodic Point a viable one (see subsequent section "Schoodic Point").

Based on the Navy's reconnaissance report, the initial costs for the relocation of the Naval Radio Station to Schoodic Point were estimated at $350,000, which was reflected in Congressman Britten's legislation. Documents indicated that as the project developed the Department of the Interior (DOI) sought an estimated $250,000 for the relocation of the radio station.[54] The reduced estimate appeared to be due to revised estimates, budgetary pressures, and the creation of a separate allocation for road construction to Schoodic Point (see subsequent section "The Road to Schoodic Point"). Congressional records documented that the funds for the relocation were an amendment to the DOI "Roads, and trails, National Parks, 1933" appropriation. The amendments included the following language:

> *Provided*, That not to exceed $250,000 of this appropriation may, in the discretion of the Secretary of the Interior, be transferred to the Navy Department for direct expenditure for the removal of the present Otter Cliffs radio station on Mount Desert Island, Me., and the reconstruction of the station within the Acadia National Park, Me.
>
> The present Otter Cliffs radio station on Mount Desert Island occupies land required for the proper location of a proposed road to be constructed at private expense at an estimated cost of $4,000,000, and to be donated to the Government as the principal highway in Acadia National Park.[55]

The relocation of the Otter Cliffs Radio Station "on lands within Acadia National Park" was authorized by an Act of Congress April 22, 1932.[56] The legislation and consideration of Schoodic Point by the Navy gave Mr. Rockefeller, Jr. the advantage he was looking for and paved the way to the construction of the Naval Radio Station at Schoodic Point.

---

[52] Private Confidential Memorandum to JDR Jr., no date (circa Dec. 1930).

[53] JDR Jr. to Arno Cammerer, Associate Director NPS, Feb. 11, 1932; RFA; Record Group: OMR; Series: Homes; Box: 105; folder 1050 (copy ACAD Archives).

[54] Horace Albright, Director NPS, to JDR Jr, Feb. 26, 1932 with attachment Document No. 62, 72nd Congress, Feb. 1932; RFA; Record Group: OMR; Series: Homes; Box: 105; folder 1050 (copy ACAD Archives).

[55] Ibid, Document No. 62, 72nd Congress, Feb. 1932.

[56] *General Management Plan, Acadia National Park, Maine*. Appendix A: Legislation.

Schoodic Point

Though other sites within Acadia NP were considered for the new radio station, it was determined by October 1932 that the Schoodic Point site on Big Moose Island near Winter Harbor would be the best choice. A telegram from Bar Harbor Attorney Albert Lyman on October 25, 1932 informed John D. Rockefeller, Jr. that the "Secretary of the Navy and Chief of Operations have approved recommendation of Captain Hooper to transfer station to Schoodic on condition that a road giving access be built by the Interior Department."[57] In a handwritten letter to Arno B. Cammerer, Associate Director of the NPS, JDR Jr. expressed his pleasure at this news:

> Lyman wires Schoodic is the site being recommended. This seems to me the only wholly satisfactory solution and infinitely better than Cranberry (Island). Hope any physical difficulties can be overcome even if at some added cost and this site finally adopted. Am deeply interested and immensely pleased.
>
> JDR Jr.[58]

The "physical difficulties" mentioned by JDR Jr. apparently referred to some of the issues outlined in the confidential correspondence previously cited, including the construction of sufficient buildings, the availability of a fresh water supply, and the presence of an adequate road. JDR Jr. did not specifically say that he would cover the additional cost of overcoming such difficulties, but his willingness to assist in the past was a good indication that he would help financially if necessary.

The Road to Schoodic Point

When John G. Moore had first purchased property on Schoodic Peninsula, he constructed a road to the top of Schoodic Head. The road extended along the west coast of the peninsula but was apparently an unimproved road that was only passable at certain times of the year. In planning an improved road from Winter Harbor to Big Moose Island and Schoodic Point, Superintendent Dorr determined that additional land on Schoodic Peninsula should be acquired. On October 28, 1932 Albert Lyman sent JDR Jr. a map of the private land on both sides of Frazer Creek where the NPS planned to build a bridge for the new road.[59]

Once again JDR Jr. offered his financial support, eventually contributing over $13,000 toward the purchase of land on either side of Frazer Creek. In this case JDR Jr. apparently worked behind the scene, with Albert Lyman and his partners at Deasy, Lyman, Rodick, and Rodick acting as his agents to purchase the land beyond the park boundaries. With some additional financial support from certain wealthy residents of Winter Harbor, JDR Jr. and his agents pursued the purchase of the Schoodic Peninsula land throughout 1932 and into 1933.

---

[57] A.H. Lyman telegram to JDR Jr., Oct. 25, 1932; RFA; Record Group: OMR; Series: Homes; Box: 105; folder 1050 (copy ACAD Archives).

[58] JDR Jr. to Cammerer, Oct. 1932; RFA; Record Group: OMR; Series: Homes; Box: 105; folder 1050 (copy ACAD Archives).

[59] A.H. Lyman to JDR Jr., Oct. 28, 1932; RFA; Record Group: OMR; Series: Homes; Box: 105; folder 1050 (copy ACAD Archives).

The purchase of the property between the park land and Frazer Creek was of great concern to Samuel Henderson, who was organizing the Winter Harbor residents for financial support of the land acquisition. In a letter to Lyman he noted that he was anxious about the matter and was worried that "when the road is finished this little strip (of land) might be used for the purpose of hot dog stands and other unsightly things."[60] On the south side of Frazer Creek the Sargent lot totaled 18 acres and was the largest tract of land to be bought. Mr. Sargent was initially offered $10,000 for his property but he refused the offer, holding out for $13,000.[61] Apparently Lyman's partner Serenus Rodick was able to get Sargent to accept $12,000. On January 10, 1933 JDR Jr. wrote that he was sending Albert Lyman a cashier's check for $13,000 toward the purchase of the Sargent lot and other land at Frazer Creek.[62] In the meantime Rodick determined who owned the smaller lots near Frazer Creek and began negotiations to purchase that land as well. Records indicated that a total 25 acres plus a 100-square-foot lot were purchased by Deasy, Lyman, Rodick, and Rodick, and deeded to Serenus Rodick and in one case David Rodick.[63] The total purchase price for the property was $14,232.46, of which JDR Jr. had contributed $13,000 as well as an additional $607.46 for the Bragg and Andrews lot. JDR Jr. later received a check from Rodick for $450.25, which was the remaining balance from all the funds collected to buy the land.[64] That reduced JDR Jr.'s contribution to that portion of the project to $13,157.21. Correspondence from Serenus Rodick on March 11, 1933 indicated that the land had been transferred to the NPS securing the property near Frazer Creek for the road project and allaying Mr. Henderson's anxiety over unsightly roadside stands.[65]

Once the property was deeded to the federal government, planning for the road and the new radio station could begin in earnest. NPS Director Horace Albright wrote JDR Jr. on February 10, 1933 that there was an agreement to purchase the final lot near Frazer Creek and that bids for the road would be opened by February 28.[66] The Kelleher Corporation of Turners Falls, Massachusetts, was awarded the contract for the road on Schoodic Peninsula for $52,024.[67] Work on the structures for the radio station would begin as soon as the road was completed or was at least passable for the trucks bringing materials.

The road from Winter Harbor to Big Moose Island was constructed between March and November 1933. The road to Schoodic Point would combine improvements to one-and-a half miles of the approach road from Winter Harbor to the park, the construction of three-and-a-half miles of road on Schoodic Peninsula to Big Moose Island, and one mile of road to

---

[60] Samuel J. Henderson to A.H. Lyman, Dec. 23, 1932; RFA; Record Group: OMR; Series: Homes; Box: 105; folder 1052 (copy ACAD Archives).

[61] A.H. Lyman to Henderson, Dec. 27, 1932; RFA; Record Group: OMR; Series: Homes; Box: 105; folder 1052 (copy ACAD Archives).

[62] JDR Jr. to A.H. Lyman, Jan. 10, 1933; RFA; Record Group: OMR; Series: Homes; Box: 105; folder 1052 (copy ACAD Archives).

[63] Serenus Rodick to JDR Jr., Feb. 24, 1933; RFA; Record Group: OMR; Series: Homes; Box: 105; folder 1052 (copy ACAD Archives).

[64] Robert Gumbel Memo to JDR Jr., Dec. 5, 1933; RFA; Record Group: OMR; Series: Homes; Box: 105; folder 1052 (copy ACAD Archives).

[65] Serenus Rodick to Rbt. Gumbel, March 11, 1933; RFA; Record Group: OMR; Series: Homes; Box: 105; folder 1052 (copy ACAD Archives).

[66] Albright to JDR Jr., Feb. 10, 1933; RFA; Record Group: OMR; Series: Homes; Box: 105; folder 1052 (copy ACAD Archives).

[67] *The Bangor Daily News*, August 3, 1933; RFA; Record Group: OMR; Series: Homes; Box: 105; folder 1053 (copy ACAD Archives).

the point.⁶⁸ The Town of Winter Harbor had authorized the expenditure of $5,000 to assist in improving the approach road to the park. A progress report on the project from NPS Engineer Oliver Taylor to Director Albright documented that the State of Maine approved a bond issue of $22,000 by Hancock County to help build the approach road to the park.⁶⁹ The remainder of the road construction cost to Schoodic Point was apparently provided by the Department of the Interior under an appropriation that was separate from the funds for the relocation of the radio station.⁷⁰ The report from Taylor also indicated that the bridge at Frazer Creek was problematic. The existing trestle bridge was insufficient and there were not enough funds to pay for the construction of a causeway. Taylor's report included a photograph of the old trestle with the following caption:

> Old trestle across Frazer Creek. For even a temporary crossing this trestle is inadequate and must be entirely rebuilt. A rock-fill with a small bridged opening to allow the tide to ebb and flow is proposed to the right of present trestle as the permanent causeway. However, it is doubtful that it can be constructed at this time.⁷¹

The report suggested building the causeway with rocks excavated from the State portion of the roadway and providing a temporary bridge over the opening. Though no further documentation of this portion of the road construction was reviewed, apparently Taylor's solution was constructed.

The project report for surfacing of the new road indicated that it was constructed in three phases. The first phase by Kelleher Corporation "consisted of the grading and gravel surfacing of a road from Frazer's Creek to and about the U.S. Naval Radio Station Buildings on Big Moose Island."⁷² That project was completed by the end of November 1933 and cost $67,019.63.⁷³ A progress report filed by Oliver Taylor on December 28, 1933 noted that the new road had a solid surface suitable for all weather use.⁷⁴ The new road provided access to the radio station site and allowed for the commencement of construction there. The second phase "consisted of the grading and gravel surfacing of a road from the spur road leading to the U.S. Naval Radio Station to the extreme end of Big Moose Island where a three level parking area was constructed."⁷⁵ The second phase was constructed between May 5, 1934 and July 31, 1934 and cost $31,478.01.⁷⁶ The third and final phase of the road work was the surfacing of the roads built during the first two projects. The surfacing project was undertaken after the radio station was constructed. The new roads were surfaced with bituminous macadam pavement as specified in the bid documents. The road work was

---

⁶⁸ Arthur B. Miller, Walter Kidde Construction, Inc., to Raymond Fosdick, Feb. 5, 1931; RFA; Record Group: OMR; Series: Homes; Box: 105; folder 1050 (copy ACAD Archives).

⁶⁹ Oliver Taylor, NPS Engineer, to Albright, Jan. 31, 1933; RFA; Record Group: OMR; Series: Homes; Box: 105; folder 1053 (copy ACAD Archives).

⁷⁰ Albright to Sec. of the Interior, Nov. 3, 1932. RFA; Record Group: OMR; Series: Homes; Box: 105; folder 1053 (copy ACAD Archives).

⁷¹ Taylor to Albright, Jan. 31, 1933.

⁷² Leo Grossman. "Final Construction Report—1935, Acadia National Park, Frazer's Creek—Big Moose Island, Hancock County, Maine, Project No. 2A4" (Technical Information Center, Denver Service Center, NPS; Feb. 17, 1936) p. 4 of 42.

⁷³ Ibid.

⁷⁴ Taylor to Cammerer, Dec. 28, 1933; RFA; Record Group: OMR; Series: Homes; Box: 105; folder 1053; p. 1. (copy courtesy of Rockefeller Archive Center).

⁷⁵ Grossman, p. 4 of 42.

⁷⁶ Ibid., p. 5 of 42.

started on May 1, 1935 and completed on September 7, 1935 and was done by the Warren Brothers Roads Company, Cambridge, Massachusetts, at a cost of to the government of $41,741.97.[77] Though the construction projects were carried out by private firms, the documents indicated that the Civilian Conservation Corps (CCC) camp located near Ellsworth, Maine, assisted with roadside cleanup after the first phase of the project and was most likely involved in future projects for roadside cleanup and beautification.[78] The three-phase road construction project completed the access from the Winter Harbor approach road to Schoodic Point.

The newspaper articles and correspondence from JDR Jr. to Arno Cammerer indicated that the road would "ultimately" continue along the east shore of Schoodic Peninsula to Wonsqueak Harbor and then to Birch Harbor where it would rejoin the coastal highway.[79] Taylor's reports and some historic plans suggested that there was an old road from Big Moose Island to Birch Harbor. The road project report and site plans of Schoodic Peninsula prepared in June 1935 indicated that the finished road surface was completed to Schoodic Point but had not yet continued up to Wonsqueak and Birch Harbors.[80] In a letter to Arno Cammerer in August 1935, JDR Jr. did note that the road on the "east side of the mountain" was under construction.[81] However, the documentation reviewed did not indicate the extent of that road or whether it was completed. Historic photographs document CCC workers helping with road construction on Schoodic Peninsula in March 1937.[82] This was probably related to the continuation of the loop road to Birch Harbor. Historic maps of Schoodic Peninsula indicated that the continuation of the road forming the present loop road was completed by June 1939.

U.S. Naval Radio Station, Winter Harbor, Maine

Documentation regarding the relocation of the U.S. Naval Radio Station from Otter Cliffs to Schoodic Peninsula clearly indicated that there was a certain amount of planning for the site prior to the design of the buildings. When Big Moose Island was being considered, JDR Jr. arranged for and financed the drilling of a 240-foot-deep well on Schoodic Point to determine if there was the fresh water supply required by the Navy. Correspondence from the Secretary of the Navy to the Secretary of the Interior in January 1931 noted that the well only yielded 5 gallons per minute while the minimum requirement was 7 gallons per minute.[83] However, the previously cited confidential memo from the same period noted that three

---

[77] Grossman, pp. 11 – 13 of 42.
[78] Taylor to Cammerer, Dec. 28, 1933; p. 1.
Foulds, p. 17.
[79] *The Bangor Daily News*, Dec. 15, 1934 (copy ACAD Archives).
JDR Jr. to Cammerer, Jan. 8, 1934; RFA; Record Group: OMR; Series: Homes; Box: 105; folder 1053 (copy ACAD Archives).
[80] Grossman, p. 2.
[81] JDR Jr. to Cammerer, August 22, 1935; RFA; Record Group: OMR; Series: Homes; Box: 105; folder 1053 (copy courtesy of Rockefeller Archive Center).
[82] http://www.nps.gov/acad/historyculture/ccc.htm.
[83] C.F. Adams, Sec. of the Navy to the Sec. of the Interior, Jan. 22, 1931; RFA; Record Group: OMR; Series: Homes; Box: 105; folder 1050 (copy ACAD Archives)

additional wells were drilled and that one, well no. 4, yielded 12 gallons per minute.[84] These wells were also apparently drilled at the expense of Mr. Rockefeller, Jr. Well no. 4 was retained for use at the new radio station.[85] Additional correspondence discussed the accessibility of the site, the financing of the project, and the condition of the roads, as well as other issues confronted during the relocation of the radio station.

Before proceeding with the comprehensive plans for the Naval Radio Station, the Navy Department required a topographical map of Big Moose Island. Engineer Oliver Taylor's report dated January 31, 1933 noted that, with the assistance of Engineer Walters Hill and Chief Ranger Hadley, he had completed the field work for the maps and would soon make copies available to the Navy. Taylor indicated that the maps would be used to make general plans and that, once those had been checked, more detailed plans of the radio station would be started.[86]

The initial site plans prepared by the NPS in February 1932 included two schemes for the radio station complex. One scheme placed the buildings on the northeast side of Big Moose Island and the other had one building along the shore and the others at the interior of the island. Both schemes included a large apartment building for Navy personnel that had been specified by the Navy for the new radio station complex.[87] Neither plan would end up being the final solution, but the site plan labeled "Scheme B" came closest to the final layout. Soon after the preliminary plans were made, the Navy Department decided to move all the buildings to the interior of the island.[88]

The first structures erected at the site of the Schoodic Point Naval Radio Station were the two steel radio towers. Early in the planning process the height requirements of the proposed radio towers to be installed on the site were an issue. Initially the Navy proposed that the towers should be 300 feet tall.[89] However, negotiations between the Navy and the NPS reduced the height to approximately 200 feet.[90] The contract for the towers had been awarded to McClintic and Marshall (representing Bethlehem Steel Corporation), Washington, D.C., for $8,027. On April 12, 1933 the *Bar Harbor Times* announced that the contract for the towers had been let earlier in the week and that bids for other structures on the site would soon follow.[91] The foundations for the towers were laid in August 1933, and

---

[84] "Private Confidential Memorandum regarding the proposed removal to Schoodic Point of the Naval Radio Station at Otter Cliffs, Maine" to JDR Jr., no date (circa Dec. 1930); RFA; Record Group: OMR; Series: Homes; Box: 105; folder 1050 (copy ACAD Archives).

[85] Richard Sherman, NPS Engineer, & George Gordon, NPS Assistant Landscape Architect, "Statement of Cost, Buildings, Equipment, Service Facilities, etc., Schoodic Naval Radio Station," April 1, 1935 (copy ACAD Archives).

[86] Taylor to Albright, Jan. 31, 1933; RFA; Record Group: OMR; Series: Homes; Box: 105; folder 1053 (copy ACAD Archives).

[87] "Preliminary Sketch, Schoodic Radio Station, Big Moose Island, Acadia National Park, Scheme A" and "Scheme B" (Technical Information Center, Denver Service Center, NPS; Feb. 1933).

[88] Albright to JDR Jr., March 11, 1933 (copy ACAD Archives).

[89] Albright to JDR Jr., Nov. 15, 1932: RFA; Record Group: OMR; Series: Homes; Box: 105; folder 1053 (copy ACAD Archives).

[90] Albright to JDR Jr., Nov. 25, 1932: RFA; Record Group: OMR; Series: Homes; Box: 105; folder 1053 (copy ACAD Archives).

[91] *Bar Harbor Times*, April 12, 1933 (copy courtesy of Rockefeller Archive Center).

the towers were completed on October 28, 1933.[92] The progress report filed by Engineer Oliver Taylor on December 28, 1933 noted the following:

> Radio Towers
>
> The erection of two 210 foot steel radio towers, 600 feet apart, centering over the radio station operating room which occupies a portion of the apartment building, was completed in November.[93]

While the radio towers were being erected, work on the radio station buildings had begun. As reported by *The Bangor Daily News* the contract for the other structures at the radio station complex, including the eleven-unit Apartment Building, went to Central Engineering and Construction Company, Pawtucket, Rhode Island, for $123,760.[94] Presumably, the construction of the buildings began soon after the contract was signed, and documents indicated that the primary focus of the construction was the Apartment Building.

The construction of the original complex of structures began in the fall of 1933, and the five original buildings were evidently completed by December 1934. The primary buildings on the site were designed by Grosvenor Atterbury's firm and included the Apartment Building, Power House, Pump House, Intercept Building, and Radio Compass Station (Appendix A). Since it was the largest of the structures, the focus of the construction appeared to be on the Apartment Building, which was designed and built in the French Eclectic style (see subsequent section "Chronology of Development and Use" and subsections "Planning," "Construction," and "Original Appearance"). Historic photographs and progress reports documented that all of the original buildings at the radio station complex were constructed during the same period.[95]

The U.S. Naval Radio Station, Winter Harbor, Maine, was formally commissioned on February 28, 1935.[96] When the site was commissioned, 26 acres of the Acadia NP land at Schoodic Peninsula were transferred to the U.S. Navy Department. A map of the U.S. Naval Radio Station on Big Moose Island dated June 30, 1935 depicted the arrangement of the original structures on the site (fig. 7).

The Navy operated the radio station on Big Moose Island during World War II and into the Cold War. During that period additional buildings were constructed on the site to serve the U.S. Navy. The Apartment Building continued to serve as housing for Navy personnel and as a base for the radio operations. By the end of World War II, the U.S. Naval Radio Station, Winter Harbor, Maine, included ten buildings on Big Moose Island and an operation that was apparently expanding (fig. 8). Maps of Big Moose Island during that period depicted the buildings on site, as well as the construction of additional antenna arrays on the island. In

---

[92] Sherman & Gordon, "Statement of Cost, ..." April 1, 1935.
[93] Taylor to Albright, Dec. 28, 1933; RFA; Record Group: OMR; Series: Homes; Box: 105; folder 1053 (copy courtesy of Rockefeller Archive Center).
[94] *The Bangor Daily News*, August 3, 1933; RFA; Record Group: OMR; Series: Homes; Box: 105; folder 1053 (copy ACAD Archives).
[95] "Naval Radio Station, Schoodic Point, Me., Progress Photos" 1933 – 1935; NPS Technical Information System, Denver Services Center, Denver, CO. (copies ACAD Archives, Bar Harbor, ME).
Taylor to Albright, Dec. 28, 1933.
Sherman & Gordon, "Statement of Cost, ..." April 1, 1935.
[96] *A History of the U.S. Navy at Schoodic Peninsula*; p. 5.

1947 the National Park Service transferred an additional 152 acres to the U.S. Navy for the further development of the Navy base at Winter Harbor.[97]

The growth of the Navy's activities during the Cold War further increased operations in Winter Harbor, and in 1950 the radio station was redesignated U.S. Naval Security Group Detachment, U.S. Naval Radio Station, Winter Harbor, Maine, and became part of the Naval Security Group Detachment. The radio station remained vital during the early 1950s as the Navy presence near Winter Harbor continued to expand. More buildings were added to the compound at Big Moose Island, and the site around the Apartment Building was littered with Quonset huts to house the additional personnel.[98]

With the escalation of the Cold War through the 1950s and 1960s, additional sites were acquired by the Navy including a site at Corea, east of Schoodic Peninsula. During this expansion the radio station was renamed the Naval Security Group Activity, Winter Harbor, in 1957. A new array of high-frequency antennae was constructed at Corea in 1962 and all communications operations were eventually moved from Big Moose Island to the new site.[99] The Navy continued to utilize the facilities at Big Moose Island, which at that point primarily served administration, housing, and recreational purposes. The U.S. Navy returned 81 acres of shoreline land to Acadia NP in 1977. More recent additions to the site at Schoodic Peninsula have been related to housing for Navy personnel. During all of this activity the Apartment Building remained a distinctive structure on the compound and was continuously occupied by Navy personnel. Some features of the building were rehabilitated over the years, but the structure was not significantly altered. In 2001 the Navy determined that it would close the base, and on July 1, 2002 the property was transferred to the National Park Service and once again became part of Acadia National Park.[100]

Since the acquisition of the site, the NPS and its nonprofit partner, APSL, have used the former Navy base to support park operations and the SERC. The Apartment Building has been used for some of these educational programs and currently has a laundry facility in the basement for SERC housekeeping operations. The housekeeping operation also uses Apartment No. 1 on the first story as an office and for storage. One of the apartments was renovated in the 1990s and used as an office but is now vacant. Otherwise the building has remained unoccupied.

---

[97] *Schoodic General Management Plan Amendment*; p. 8.
[98] *A History of the U.S. Navy at Schoodic Peninsula*; pp. 6 & 7.
[99] Ibid, pp. 7 & 8.
[100] *Schoodic General Management Plan Amendment*; pp. 2 & 8.

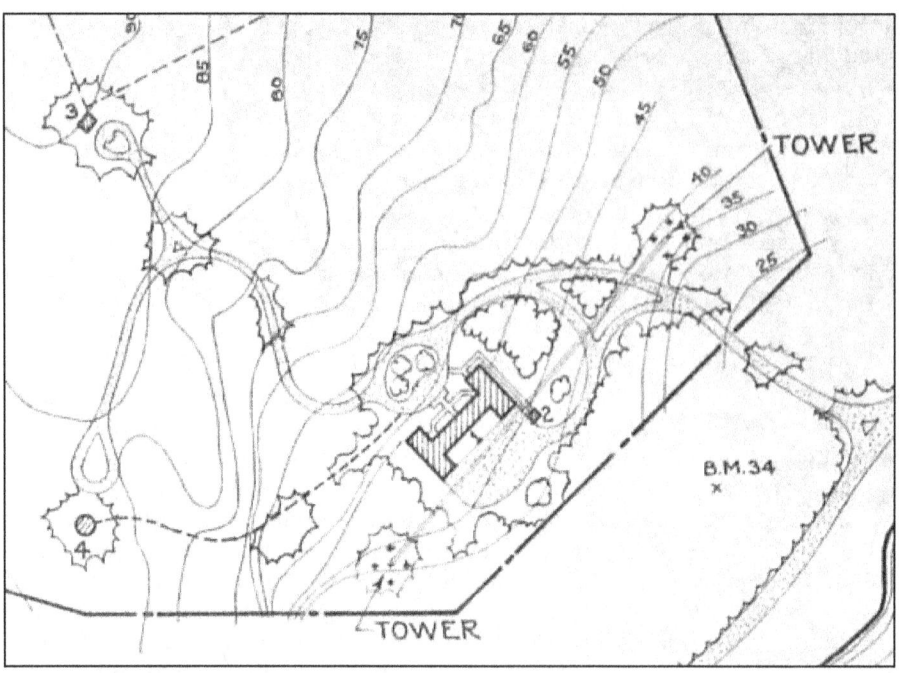

Figure 7. Detail of Naval Radio Station depicting the Apartment Building (1), Power House (2), Intercept Building (3), and Radio Compass Station (4); from Map of U.S. Naval Radio Station, Winter Harbor, Maine, June 30, 1935.

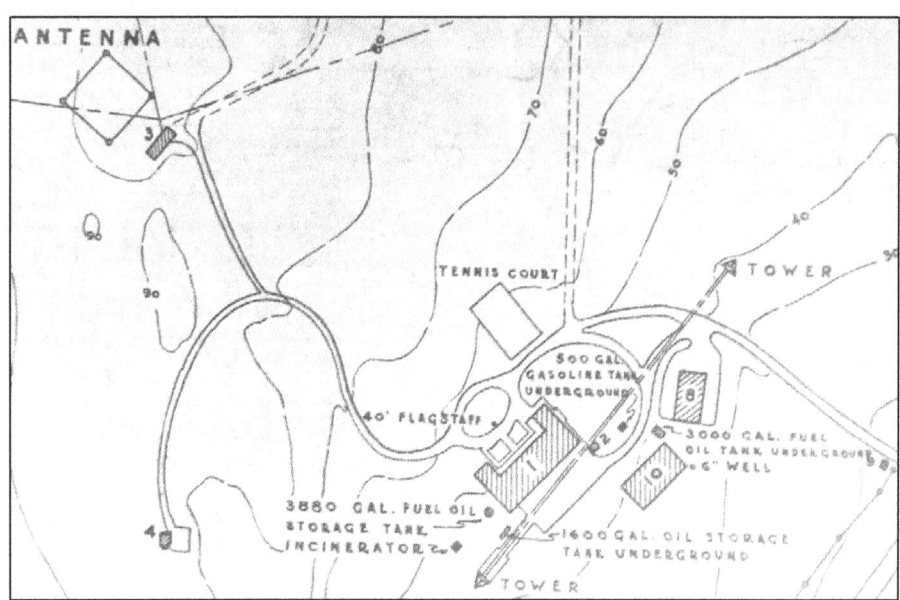

Figure 8. Detail of Naval Radio Station depicting the Apartment Building (1), Power House (2), Intercept Building (3), Radio Compass Station (4); Garage (8), and Barracks (10), as well as other structures from Map of U.S. Naval Radio Station, Winter Harbor, Maine, June 30, 1944.

CHRONOLOGY OF DEVELOPMENT AND USE

Introduction

The following sections on Planning and Construction are based on evaluation of primary resource documents including correspondence, progress reports, historic photographs, architectural plans, and maps. The documentation pertained primarily to the Apartment Building but also included information about other structures on the site. The evidence is generally presented in chronological order.

Planning

Correspondence suggested that planning for the Schoodic Point Radio Station was a balancing act between the requirements of the Navy, the wishes of the Department of the Interior, and the concerns of the Winter Harbor residents. The interested parties, including NPS personnel and JDR Jr., were determined to build a station that would be architecturally appealing. In a letter to NPS Director Albright, George Dorr expressed his opinion about the buildings for the station:

> To answer your question with regard to building, I think the Service should take an active interest in it and in all exterior planning, working with the Navy Department to satisfy its practical needs. That the Navy Department be thoroughly satisfied and that no room be left for complaint or dissatisfaction hereafter, it seems to me desirable that some architect of recognized standing and satisfactory to both be employed who shall submit to both Departments his plans for what is of interest to each, to be approved by each. And that he, when decided on, should enter into consultation from the beginning, as to site and all, being made acquainted equally with the Navy's needs and the desires of the Park Service from the landscape and public point of view.[101]

The resolve of the NPS to have control over the exterior appearance of the buildings was communicated to the Secretary of the Interior, who in correspondence with the Secretary of the Navy noted that the NPS would execute the plans and designs of the station based on the

---

[101] Dorr to Albright, undated (circa Nov. 1932); RFA; Record Group: OMR; Series: Homes; Box: 105; folder 1053 (copy ACAD Archives).

requirements and specifications of the Navy.[102] This course of action was approved by the Secretary of the Navy, and the NPS began the initial site plans and building plans.

Horace Albright had first discussed the Schoodic Point project with Grosvenor Atterbury in December 1932. At the time Albright explained to Atterbury that the radio station was being moved and that the NPS wanted to design the new buildings to harmonize with his designs for Mount Desert Island. Indeed, given Atterbury's association with building projects on Mount Desert Island, it seemed apparent that Dorr's letter to Albright was insinuating that Atterbury should be the "architect of recognized standing" for the project. Atterbury was apparently interested in the project and, in light of limited funds, was willing to provide his services gratis, as long as the project didn't interrupt his professional work.[103]

Preliminary designs for the radio station Apartment Building were dated February 25, 1933. These plans were drawn by NPS architects to meet the requirements of the Navy, as well as address aesthetic issues of the NPS: the eleven-unit Apartment Building was a large masonry structure that was designed in the Georgian Revival style. It had a main block that was three stories high topped with a dormered gable roof, flanked by two one-and-a-half-story pavilions with hipped roofs, and connected by one-and-a-half-story hyphens (fig. 9).[104] These preliminary plans were probably the plans sent by NPS Director Albright to JDR Jr. for review and were also presented by NPS architects to Grosvenor Atterbury for his consultation in March 1933.

Figure 9. Preliminary Study, Apartment House, Schoodic Radio Station, Big Moose Island, Acadia National Park, February 25, 1933.

---

[102] Ray Lyman Wilbur, Sec. of the Interior to Sec. of the Navy, Nov. 21, 1932; RFA; Record Group: OMR; Series: Homes; Box: 105; folder 1053 (copy ACAD Archives).

[103] Albright to JDR Jr., March 11, 1933; RFA; Record Group: OMR; Series: Homes; Box: 105; folder 1053 (copy ACAD Archives). The letter describes Albright's meeting with Atterbury in Dec. 1932.

[104] "Preliminary Study, Apartment House, Schoodic Radio Station, Big Moose Island, Acadia National Park," Feb. 25, 1933 (Technical Information Center, Denver Service Center, NPS).

After the first meeting between Atterbury and the NPS architects, it seemed that the vague gentlemen's agreement of the previous December between Horace Albright and Mr. Atterbury was not sufficient. JDR Jr. wrote Albright that Atterbury was eager to help but felt unclear about his position with regard to the project. JDR Jr. also noted that Atterbury "would be loath to be regarded as in any way responsible for the final outcome of the plans unless he has commensurate authority in directing what that outcome shall be."[105] Horace Albright's letter to JDR Jr. on March 11, 1933 agreed that there seemed to be some confusion on Atterbury's part as to his relation to the project and that both Albright and Dorr felt it was "desirable to have a more definite arrangement with Mr. Atterbury."[106] In a subsequent meeting in New York, Horace Albright and Grosvenor Atterbury apparently came to some understanding that gave control of the design to Atterbury and his associates. Albright's correspondence to JDR Jr. dated March 25, 1933 noted the following:

> I have now arranged with Mr. Atterbury to assume the preparation of all the plans and specifications for the radio station. I have arranged to appoint Mr. Atterbury and his own associates, Tompkins and Devorak, as consulting architects to the Director of the Park Service under a certain provision of the Civil Service Rules and Regulations which permits employment of this type of service provided the cost thereof for any one individual does not exceed $540 per annum. In other words, three of the Atterbury organization will receive $540 per annum.[107]

Although, as JDR Jr. would later point out, the amount of funds available for Atterbury's contributions were remarkably low, Atterbury assured Director Albright that the design of the radio station buildings would get his personal attention.

Grosvenor Atterbury and his associates worked on the plans for the radio station buildings over the next month. Albright wrote JDR Jr. on April 8, 1933 that Atterbury had submitted new floor plans and elevations for the buildings and that the architects could begin the working drawings for the project.[108] The working drawings submitted by Grosvenor Atterbury's firm on May 26, 1933 depicted five radio station buildings that were approved by both the NPS and the Navy Department upon submission. The plans were primarily for the eleven-unit Apartment Building that would house the Navy personnel and radio operations rooms but also included drawings of the Power House, Pump House, Intercept Building, and Radio Compass Station (Appendix A). The approvals of both the NPS and the Navy indicated that the plans met the specifications of the Navy and the desire of the NPS for designs that were in keeping with buildings on Mount Desert Island (fig. 6).[109]

---

[105] JDR Jr. to Albright, March 10, 1933: RFA; Record Group: OMR; Series: Homes; Box: 105; folder 1053 (copy ACAD Archives).

[106] Albright to JDR Jr., March 11, 1933 (copy ACAD Archives).

[107] Albright to JDR Jr., March 25, 1933; RFA; Record Group: OMR; Series: Homes; Box: 105; folder 1053 (copy ACAD Archives).

[108] Albright to JDR Jr., April 8, 1933; RFA; Record Group: OMR; Series: Homes; Box: 105; folder 1053 (copy ACAD Archives).

[109] Sheet 1 of 37 sheets (this originally read 1 of 31, and the 31 was struck out with 37 penciled in), Grosvenor Atterbury Architect, John Tompkins, May 26, 1933 and Navy Dept., Bureau of Yards & Docks, June 1933. "Acadia National Park, Apartment Building, Naval Radio Station, Schoodic Point, Hancock County, Maine" (Acadia NP, Winter Harbor, ME; Map Case C, drawer 5, folder 1, with a total 37 drawings including additional drawings revised in June 1933).

Grosvenor Atterbury's redesign of the Apartment Building lowered the height of the preliminary design by removing the third story; it retained the flanking pavilions and masonry exterior walls and steep roofs while introducing a distinctly French Eclectic style to the exterior (fig. 10). Atterbury's plans sited the building on a gently sloping site with the façade of the building oriented to the northwest and the flanking wings on the northeast and southwest sides (fig. 10). The drawings were revised in June 1933, presumably adding details to the working plans and including the Navy Department, Bureau of Yards and Docks drawings for the contractor. Albright informed JDR Jr. on June 20th that bids for the buildings at the new radio station complex had been received,[110] and on August 3, 1933 *The Bangor Daily News* reported that the contract for the construction of the buildings at the U.S. Naval Radio Station at Schoodic Point had been awarded.[111]

Figure 10. Sheet 5 of 37, Apartment Building, Acadia National Park, Naval Radio Station, Schoodic Point, Hancock County, Maine.

---

[110] JDR Jr. to Albright, July 6, 1933: RFA; Record Group: OMR; Series: Homes; Box: 105; folder 1053 (copy courtesy of Rockefeller Archive Center). Letter references Albright's letter of June 20th.

[111] *The Bangor Daily News*, August 3, 1933; RFA; Record Group: OMR; Series: Homes; Box: 105; folder 1053 (copy ACAD Archives).

Construction

Construction of the eleven-unit Apartment Building and the other structures at the radio station complex by Central Engineering and Construction Company, Pawtucket, Rhode Island, began in the fall of 1933 soon after the contract was signed. A collection of historic photographs taken during various phases of the project documented the construction of the Apartment Building and other structures on the site (Appendix B). Photographs taken of the Apartment Building on November 13 and 16, 1933 showed that the masonry foundation and first-story masonry exterior walls had been completed. The photographs also illustrated that some of the steel framing for the second-story ceiling had been installed, including a central I-beam and some of the steel ceiling joists. The building was at least partially staged at that time. Photographs dated November 22 and 23, 1933, depicted the progress of the steel roof framing of the Southwest Pavilion and the second-story concrete slab floor. The staging of the Apartment Building appeared to be complete in those photographs and included a staging tower on the southeast elevation for conveying materials to the upper stories.

Figure 11. View of the SW elevation and roof framing from SW radio tower, December 9, 1933.

Work on the second-story framing and roof framing continued into December and appeared to be complete in photographs taken on December 9 and 12, 1933. In a December 9th photograph (fig. 11) it appeared that the cinder-block masonry walls of the second story had been started and that some of the steel window sashes had been installed.

The "Progress Report on Naval Radio Station, Acadia Nation Park, Maine" submitted by Oliver Taylor on December 28, 1933 provided the following details on the site work at Schoodic Point:

Apartment Building

The exterior and rough interior is completed to above the second floor. The frame work for the second floor and roof is in place and much of the exterior wall masonry is completed above the second floor.

The heating plant has been installed and radiators are being placed on the first floor. This will afford protection for casting the nailcrete slabs which are to be used in the roof construction.

It is expected that the building will be completely inclosed [sic] in January and that work on the building will continue throughout the winter.

Power House

    This is a stone building near the apartment. It is completed except for the roofing.

Intercept Building and Compass Building

    Foundations completed and building materials on hand.

Pump House

    This is to be a very small building. No work has been started.[112]

Mr. Taylor's report included updates on the water and sewer systems, the electrical system, and the telephone service to the new station. He noted that the contractor was making good progress and was scheduled to complete the job by mid – August 1934. He further noted that work would continue through the winter, and he appeared optimistic that the work would be complete before schedule.

The further progress at Schoodic Point from December 1933 through June 1935 was also documented by the collection of historic photographs. On January 15, 1934 the cinder-block walls of the second story were apparently complete and the steel window sashes on all levels had been installed. This was consistent with Taylor's report that the building would be enclosed by January. Upon enclosing the first story, the contractors evidently started casting the "nailcrete" slabs for the roof in the heated first-story rooms.

One of the March 8, 1934 photographs depicted the "nailcrete" panels being installed on the roof of the Apartment Building (fig. 12). The photograph also showed that work was being done on the north chimney. It is possible that the south chimney was complete by that time since it would have been needed for the heating system Taylor indicated was installed in December and operating in January. In addition, the Intercept Building had been framed by March 8th.

Figure 12. Apartment Building, SW elevation, March 8, 1934.

---

[112] Taylor to Albright, Dec. 28, 1933; (copy courtesy of Rockefeller Archive Center).

The subsequent set of progress photographs was dated April 14, 1934 and entitled "Nailcrete Roof Slab Construction Nearing Completion." On that page four photographs documented the installation of the panels and included a view from the attic of the steel roof framing and the wire ties, which secured the panels to the steel purlins. The north chimney was also depicted in those photographs and was complete (fig. 13).

Figure 13. Apartment Building, SE elevation, April 14, 1934.

Historic photographs taken for the April 28th progress report indicated that the "nailcrete" roof panels were in place. Those photographs also showed that the brick panels between the half timbers in the gables of the apartment building had been installed. Photographs of the Radio Compass Station indicated that masonry work was being done at the foundation level of that building.

When the May 10, 1934 progress photographs were submitted, the 30-pound felt roof underlayment had been installed and the installation of the clay roof tiles had begun.[113] It was also evident from the photographs that the construction of the brick panels at the second story level had begun by this time. Photographs from the following week dated May 16th illustrated that the work had continued on both the tile roof and the brick panels. The May 16th photographs also recorded progress on the exterior walls and roof of the Intercept Building and the framing of the Radio Compass Station.

By June 2, 1934 the roof of the Apartment Building appeared to be almost complete with the exception of the tiles on the dormers. The progress photographs for that date also documented work on the Intercept Building, the Pump House, and the Radio Compass Station. At that time the Radio Compass Station had been enclosed, and by the end of the month it was sided with wood shingles and had a wood shingle roof.

The documentary photographs dated June 30, 1934 recorded that the exterior of the Apartment Building was practically completed. The staging had been removed from around the building and the exterior walls appeared finished. During the month of June the roof had been completed and the gutters had been installed. On the southeast elevation the garage

---

[113] Sheet 7 of 37 sheets, Grosvenor Atterbury Architect, John Tompkins, May 26, 1933.

doors had not been installed and it appears that the center doorway on the Terrace had not been installed. By this time the Power House had been roofed and appeared to be complete except for the southwest elevation garage doors. The photographs show a large amount of building debris around the site, and no obvious attempts had been made to landscape the site.

The next set of photographs was dated September 15, 1934 and depicted the exterior of the Apartment Building as complete. Views of the SE elevation showed the garage doors installed, gutters hung, exterior electrical fixtures in place, and exterior doors installed with automatic closers (fig. 14). The debris on the southeast side of the building was being removed in preparation for landscaping around the building. Photographs of the Intercept Building and the Radio Compass Station from the same date illustrated that the exteriors of those buildings were complete as well.

Figure 14. Apartment Building, SE elevation depicting completed exterior of building and debris removal, September 15, 1934.

Subsequent photographs taken in October and November 1934 recorded the site prior to landscaping (fig. 15) and the initial efforts of the landscaping around the Apartment Building in the fall of 1934 (see subsequent section "Landscaping"). A sequence of two photographs depicted a panoramic view of the northwest elevation of the Apartment Building (fig. 20). The panorama showed the completed building exterior, the sublevel of the driveway and pathways, and some preliminary landscaping.

Both *The Bangor Daily News* and the *Bar Harbor Times* announced in December 1934 that the Naval Radio Station would be moving from Otter Cliffs to Schoodic Point in January 1935.[114] The newspaper articles indicated that the apartment building was complete and awaiting the removal of equipment from Otter Cliffs to Schoodic Point.

---

[114] *The Bangor Daily News*, Dec. 15, 1934 (copy ACAD Archives).
Bar Harbor Times, Dec. 26, 1934; RFA; Record Group: OMR; Series: Homes; Box: 105; folder 1053 (copy ACAD Archives).

After reviewing photographs of the radio station buildings, JDR Jr. wrote Grosvenor Atterbury on January 7, 1935 congratulating him on his accomplishments and noting that the new buildings were attractive and appropriate for the site and Acadia NP.[115]

The U.S. Naval Radio Station, Winter Harbor, Maine was formally commissioned on February 28, 1935.[116] The "Statement of Cost, Buildings, Equipment, Service Facilities, etc., Schoodic Naval Radio Station" dated April 1, 1935 documented the cost of the project and provided some details regarding the construction.[117] Though the report did not discuss the construction of the Apartment Building, it did list the following costs associated with the project:[118]

Apartment Building	$122,257.60
Receiving (Intercept) Building	4,039.64
Direction Finding Building (Radio Compass Station)	3,850.59
Pump House	304.68
Power House	1,533.00
Power Transmission Line	7,784.28
Telephone Line	431.39
Auxiliary Power Plant	11,937.00
Electrical Service Lines including main switchboard	3,387.00
Water Supply Lines	1,607.72
Radio Towers	8,233.80
Water and Sewer System, force account work, National Park Service	21,000.00
Landscaping, including the installation of storm drains, walks, shrub and tree planting, grading, and installing the counterpoise grounding system	13,342.33
Total	$199,709.03

The radio station equipment and personnel were presumably moved to the new Radio Station between January and February. Though no documentation of the exact dates was found, the sequence of events suggested that most, if not all, of the move occurred prior to May 1935 when legislation to transfer the Otter Cliffs Radio Station to the NPS was introduced. Photographs of the exterior of the Apartment Building from June 1935 depicted the completed building and improved grounds (fig. 16).

A bill to authorize the transfer of the Otter Cliffs Radio Station, including 12 acres, to the Secretary of the Interior for inclusion in Acadia NP was introduced on May 7, 1935.[119] As with the previous legislation, this bill took some time to make its way through Congress. On August 19, 1935 Arno B. Cammerer wrote JDR Jr. that the bill had passed both branches of

---

[115] JDR Jr. to Atterbury, Jan. 7, 1935: RFA; Record Group: OMR; Series: Homes; Box: 105; folder 1053 (copy ACAD Archives).

[116] *A History of the U.S. Navy at Schoodic Peninsula*, p. 5.

[117] Sherman & Gordon, "Statement of Cost, Buildings, Equipment, Service Facilities, etc., Schoodic Naval Radio Station," April 1, 1935 (copy ACAD Archives).

[118] Sherman & Gordon, "Statement of Cost, ..." April 1, 1935.

[119] H.R. 7938 [Report No. 881], 74th Congress, 1st Session; May, 1935; RFA; Record Group: OMR; Series: Homes; Box: 105; folder 1053 (copy courtesy of Rockefeller Archive Center).

the Congress and was awaiting the President's signature.[120] The bill was signed into law on August 24, 1935 (49 Stat. 795), which allowed for the continuation of the road projects on Mount Desert Island and finalized the transfer of the U.S. Naval Radio Station from Otter Cliffs to Winter Harbor.

Mr. and Mrs. Rockefeller, Jr. visited Schoodic Point in August 1935. Following the visit, JDR Jr. wrote both Grosvenor Atterbury and NPS Assistant Director Arno Cammerer that he and Mrs. Rockefeller were both delighted with the accomplishments at the site. In his letter congratulating Atterbury on his accomplishment, JDR Jr. wrote that they "were charmed with the building and thought it delightful, attractive, well arranged and eminently successful."[121] JDR Jr. wrote Cammerer that the drive along the west coast of Schoodic Peninsula was much improved and that the parking lot at Schoodic Point was "of the best designed and most charmingly constructed areas of the kind that I have ever seen."[122] He continued with the following observations of the radio station building, which apparently referred to the Apartment Building since it did house the operations rooms for the radio station complex:

> As for the Radio Station building itself, it is all and more than I hoped and expected it would be from the plans. Mr. Atterbury has done a splendid piece of work and the Park is under great obligation to him for what he has accomplished. I saw nothing to criticize from start to finish and viewing things with as critical an eye as you know I do that is saying a great deal. It gives me much satisfaction to speak thus unqualifiedly of this splendid accomplishment.[123]

The letter to Cammerer suggested that JDR Jr. had kept abreast of the development of the site at Schoodic Point. He certainly had a vested interest in the transfer of the U.S. Naval Radio Station, and it was evident from the documentation that he had been involved in that process since he first expressed interest in the Otter Cliffs site in 1926. The completion of the U.S. Naval Radio Station complex at Schoodic Point was apparently to JDR Jr.'s great satisfaction, which he noted was doubled since it also cleared the way for the continuation of Ocean Drive through the former U.S. Naval Radio Station at Otter Cliffs on Mount Desert Island.[124]

---

[120] Cammerer to JDR Jr., August 19, 1935; RFA; Record Group: OMR; Series: Homes; Box: 105; folder 1053 (copy courtesy of Rockefeller Archive Center).

[121] JDR Jr. to Atterbury, August 19, 1935: RFA; Record Group: OMR; Series: Homes; Box: 105; folder 1053 (copy ACAD Archives).

[122] JDR Jr. to Cammerer, August 22, 1935: RFA; Record Group: OMR; Series: Homes; Box: 105; folder 1053 (copy courtesy of Rockefeller Archive Center).

[123] JDR Jr. to Cammerer, August 22, 1935. Note: None of the other structures on the site was referred to as the "Radio Station building" and it was evident that JDR Jr. was describing the Apartment Building in his letter Arno Cammerer.

[124] JDR Jr. to Cammerer, August 22, 1935.

Figure 15. Apartment Building, NW elevation and courtyard, looking NE, before selective tree cutting and landscaping, October 1934.

Figure 16. Apartment Building, SE elevation, looking SW. Power House in the right hand foreground, June 1935.

Landscaping

Historic photographs taken in October and November 1934 recorded the landscaping of the Apartment Building. In the "Statement of Cost" report of April 1935 Assistant Landscape Architect George B. Gordon provided a description of the landscaping around the building.[125] It noted that the work was undertaken between October 10 and November 15, 1934. During that period the service court on the southeast side of the building had been graded and covered with gravel; paths around the apartment building were laid out and graveled; approximately 900 yards of topsoil had been deposited; and trees and shrubs had been planted. The report noted that "plant material was by necessity confined to collected wild trees and shrubs" and listed the following specimens that were planted in the shaded areas on the plans:[126]

White spruce, 8 to 10 feet	23
Viburnum cassinoides, 3 to 8 feet	125
Ilex verticillata, 3 to 8 feet	21
Nemopanthus, 3 to 6 feet	29
Rhodora, 2 to 3 feet	65
Blueberry and Lambkill Sod	1, 265 sq. ft.

The landscape plan that accompanied the report indicated that the planting that fall had been concentrated on the northwest and northeast elevations of the apartment building (fig. 19). The cost associated with the landscaping in 1934 was given as $4,645.40. The landscaping work was stopped in mid-November due to cold weather but had not been completed. An estimate cost of $3,207 for the remainder of the landscaping included an additional 400 yards of loam; 450 small shrubs and trees; an additional 2,000 square feet of blueberry and lambkill sod; and 5,000 square feet of seeding, as well as cleanup and vista cutting.[127]

Progress photographs taken in June 1935 were contrasted with the site photos from fall 1934 and clearly demonstrated the site improvements (figs. 17 and 18). On the northwest side of the Apartment Building some of the scrub growth was cleared out and new plant materials introduced; and the driveway and paths were established but not yet surfaced. It was evident from the photographs and the plans that some of the existing trees were kept, most notably some of the mature birch trees near the northwest façade and in the driveway circle. The southeast side of the building was dominated by the large service court with a yard to the southwest. Between October 1934 and June 1935 drainage was installed and curbing was placed around the service court, which was graded and graveled in preparation for surfacing. Large trees in the yard southwest of the service court were removed and smaller spruces were planted to screen the drying yard that was placed at the end of the yard. Though some site cleanup was still required, the overall landscape was improved and appeared more complete and neater.

The surfacing of the driveways and service court was completed by September 1935.[128] This was the final piece of the site work around the apartment building and marked the completion of the Naval Radio Station at Schoodic Point.

---

[125] Sherman & Gordon, "Statement of Cost,..." April 1, 1935.
[126] Ibid.
[127] Ibid.
[128] Grossman. "Final Construction Report—1935, Project No. 2A4;" p. 10 of 42.

Figure 17. Apartment Building, NW elevation courtyard before grading and topsoil was deposited, November 1934.

Figure 18. Apartment Building, NW elevation courtyard depicting some scrub cleared, shrub planting completed, driveway and paths graded, and graveled, seeding and cleanup still required, June 1935.

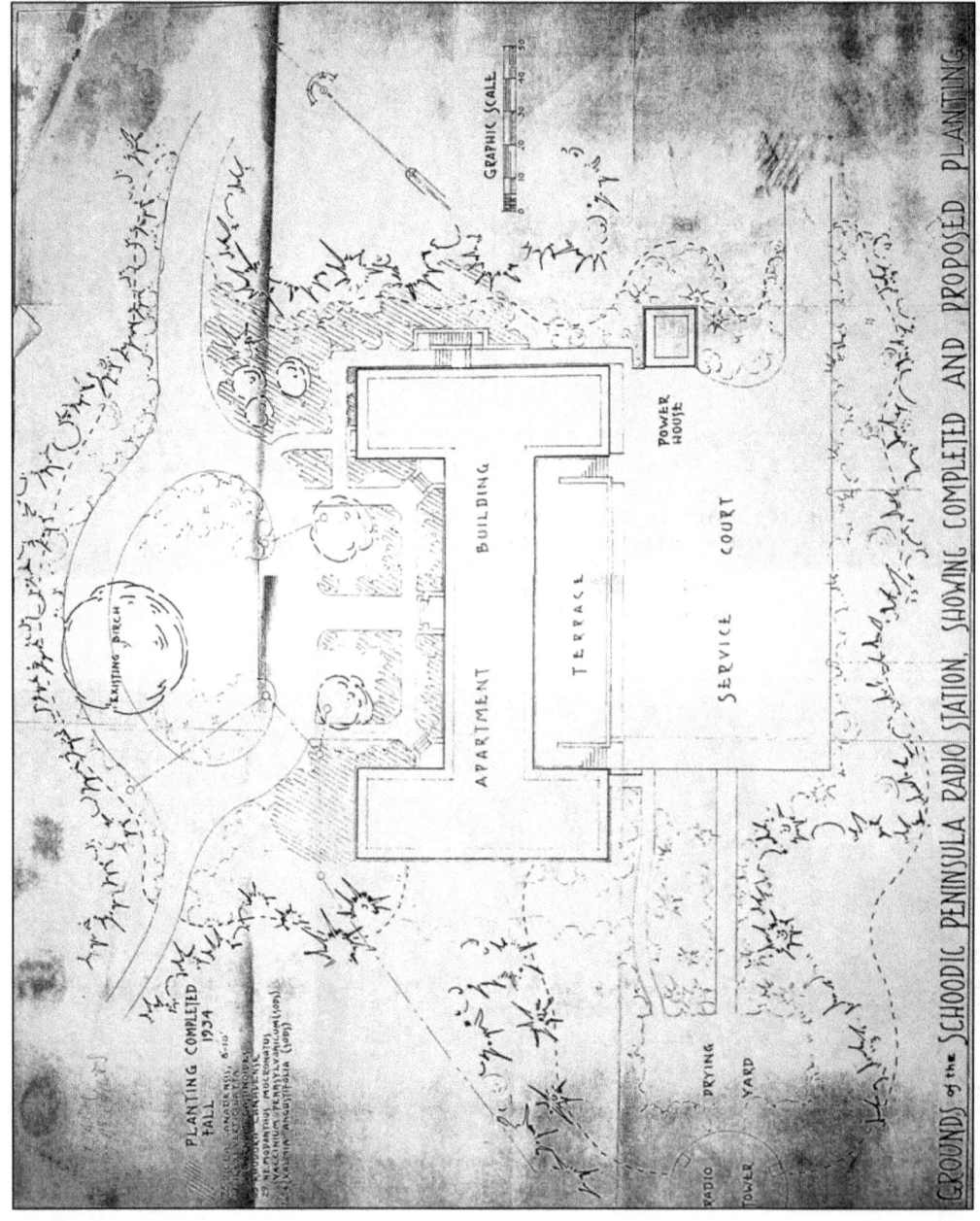

Figure 19. Apartment Building, Landscape Plan depicting planting completed in fall 1934 and proposed planting for spring 1935.

Original Appearance

Figure 20. Panoramic view of Apartment Building, NW elevation, November 1934 after some landscaping had been completed.

Introduction

The following description of original appearance is based on extant elements, historic photographs, and original architectural drawings of the Apartment Building prepared by Grosvenor Atterbury's firm and the Navy Department, Bureau of Yards and Docks in 1933 (Appendix A). Though some construction details are specified on the architectural drawings, the research efforts did not unearth the written specifications for the Apartment Building. However, the specifications for the Lodge at the Brown Mountain Gatehouse were available for research at Acadia NP archives. The similarities between the Lodge and the Apartment Building made it plausible that similar materials and sources were used for some of the building elements. Review of the Brown Mountain Lodge specifications did contribute to the understanding of the construction of the Apartment Building. That information combined, with the documentary and physical evidence, provided an understanding of the Apartment Building's original appearance.

The architectural drawings of the Apartment Building included several drawings that detailed the doorways and window openings and their associated elements (Appendix A).[129] The drawings showed details of the structural framing of the doorways and window openings, as well as cross-sections of the door leaves detailing materials and molding profiles. Since some elements of the exterior doorways and window openings are not extant, the information provided in these drawings was of particular importance to understanding and describing those elements (see subsequent sections "Doorways" and "Window Openings").

---

[129] Drawing Numbers 8, 9, 10, 12, 13, & 34 of 37 sheets, Grosvenor Atterbury Architect, John Tompkins, and Navy Dept., Bureau of Yards & Docks, May and June 1933.

Likewise, alterations to several of the basement rooms made it more difficult to observe original elements in those rooms. However, the basement floor plan and some of the detail drawings did provide a better understanding of the original appearance.

In addition to the 1933 architectural drawings for the Apartment Building, more recent drawings of the building and the apartments have been included to help illustrate the interior spaces and room arrangements (Appendix C). The current room numbers were designated according to the apartment numbers. The subsequent section "Interior Elements" uses the original room designations from Atterbury's plans but also references the room, doorway, and window opening numbers that were assigned during the current project.

Exterior Elements

Design

The Apartment Building was designed by Grosvenor Atterbury and his associates to harmonize with the Acadia NP architectural style previously used by Atterbury on Mount Desert Island. The building was a large masonry building with steeply pitched hipped roofs and courtyards that evoked the same French influence Atterbury had successfully employed at the Brown Mountain Gate Lodge and the Jordan Pond Gatehouse. Architectural Historian Deborah Thompson, Ph.D., has pointed out the similarities between the Apartment Building and the Hôtel-Dieu Hospices de Beaune (a charity hospital built in Beaune, France, 1443). Among these are the "adjacent wings with high hipped roofs enclosing a courtyard" and "the half-timbering of roof gables" also used on the Beaune hospital.[130]

The Apartment Building was a symmetrically designed building of the French Eclectic style. The exterior was characterized by masonry walls of granite and brick, half-timbered upper-story walls with brick panels, half-timbered cross gables with brick panels, varied yet symmetrical fenestration, and steeply pitched terra-cotta tiled roofs. The interior was designed to be sufficiently functional to serve the requirements of the Navy. It included eleven apartments and two operations rooms on the first and second stories, and utility rooms, storage, and garage bays on the basement story. All of the first- and second-story rooms were finished with similar materials that were typical of the period. The overall effect was a building that met Atterbury's tenets for adapting a foreign style where no local precedent existed and a structure that fulfilled the needs of the U.S. Naval Radio Station.

Atterbury's adaptation of the French Eclectic style of architecture for Acadia NP was carried out on a large scale at the Apartment Building. The overall length of the building was 153 feet 8 inches. It had a rectangular Main Block that measured 29 feet wide (NW to SE) by 95 feet 8 inches long (NE to SW); the Main Block was flanked by pavilions or wings that were 29 feet wide (NE to SW) and 80 feet long (NW to SE); and at either end of the Main Block hyphens connected the pavilions to the Main Block.

In plan the arrangement of the Main Block and flanking pavilions formed an H. The façade of the building was oriented northwest (NW) and was bracketed by the flanking pavilions to the northeast (NE) and southwest (SW). The layout of the building formed a courtyard on

---

[130] Thompson, section 8, p. 4.

the NW elevation that was defined by the Main Block and flanking pavilions. The courtyard had pathways to the building entrances and was landscaped with grass, shrubs, and trees, including mature birches. At the back of the building (SE elevation) an expansive terrace was built between the pavilions at the first story. The topography of the site sloped from front (NW) to back (SE), which created an accessible basement level at the back half of the building. Thus the rear Terrace had a staircase at either end (NE and SW) leading down to the ground level.

The NW façade of the Apartment Building was two stories high with two cross-gable bays that flanked the center entrance doorway (fig. 20). Each cross-gable bay had three window openings on the first and second stories and a single window opening in the gable. The gable projected approximately six-inches beyond the plane of the façade. At either end of the Main Block were two additional bays:[131] on the first story those bays had a window opening and a doorway, and on the second story there were window openings.

Figure 21. Apartment Building, SE elevation, center bay and cross-gable bay, September 1934.

Due to the slope of the site, the southeast (SE) elevation was three stories high. The basement story was at ground level and was dominated by eight garage bays under the Terrace of the Main Block, two additional garage bays under the Northeast Pavilion, and a service entrance to the utility rooms in the basement of the Southwest Pavilion. Exterior staircases were constructed along the inside elevation of each pavilion and led to the first-story Terrace. The SE elevation of the Main Block was also built with cross-gable bays flanking the center entrance. On that elevation the cross-gable bays were narrower than the façade bays and had three-window bays of a different configuration than the façade (fig. 21). In addition, both the second-story window openings and the third-story gable projected about 6 inches beyond the wall plane as a shallow medieval oriel window. The center bay on the SE elevation projected 3 feet beyond the main plane of the building (fig. 21). It was two stories high with a shed roof that extended from the main roof. The first story of the center bay had a doorway and a window opening, and the second story had a single window opening with two sets of casement sashes. To either side of the cross-gable bays were three bays. On the first story the bays at either end had doorways to the first-story hallways. The other first-story and second-story bays had window openings.

---

[131] For the exterior descriptions the term "bay" generally refers to vertical section of the building that contains one opening per story (either window openings or doorways). However, a "bay" could also be a distinct section of the building (i.e. the cross-gable bay). The text will explain when that term refers to a different building section or feature.

The flanking pavilions were designed to be symmetrical with slight variations to accommodate the different uses of the interior spaces. Each of the pavilions had two bays on the courtyard and Terrace sides of the building. The NW elevation of each pavilion had two bays, including a doorway on the Northeast Pavilion. The other elevations were varied based on the functions within the Apartment Building.

The NE elevation of the Northeast Pavilion had eight bays on the first and second stories, as well as openings at the basement story. On the first story the fourth bay from the right (NW) had a doorway to the Bachelors' Apartment. The basement story had an asymmetrically placed doorway near the center of the elevation with an adjacent window opening and a window opening that lined up with the end bay on the left (SE). The SE elevation of the Northeast Pavilion had two garage bays at the basement level, two window openings at the first story, and three window openings at the second story.

The SW elevation of the Southwest Pavilion had seven bays on the first and second stories all of which held window openings. The basement story had three window openings that lined up with bays on the first and second stories. The SE elevation of the Southwest Pavilion had three bays on all three stories. At the basement story the right (NE) bay had a doorway and all other bays on that elevation had window openings.

Foundation

The architectural drawings indicated that below grade the foundation was constructed with poured concrete at the base and in some sections granite stones set in mortar above the concrete. However, all of the above-grade foundation material was constructed with granite and brick set in mortar and laid in alternating bands. The granite stones were irregular in size and shape and laid in horizontal bands that were approximately 2 feet high. The granite was most likely quarried from local sources, but some may have come from Massachusetts quarries, as in the case of the Brown Mountain Gate Lodge.[132] The brick courses were laid with whole and broken bricks and were one brick width high. The brick were probably local hand-burned brick[133] and were varying shades of red. The granite and brick were set in a mortar composed of cement, sand, and hydrated lime. The proportions used at the Brown Mountain Gate Lodge were one part cement, three parts sand, and hydrated lime at 10% by volume.[134] A similar mix was probably used at the Apartment Building. In all cases the pattern of the masonry foundation was continued on the exterior walls.

Walls

The exterior wall elements combined granite, brick, and half-timbering to achieve Atterbury's design. At the basement and first stories the exterior walls were constructed with horizontal bands of granite stones separated by alternating bands of red brick as previously

---

[132] Grosvenor Atterbury Architect, "Acadia Park, Brown Mountain Lodge Specifications for John D. Rockefeller, Jr. Esq." (copy at ACAD Archives) p. 21. The specifications for "Stone Work" called for "Local Stone" as well as "Seam Face Granite shall be Miller Quarries or Eastern Quarries, Inc., East Weymouth, Mass." And "Chelmsford Gray Granite" from W.E. Fletcher Co., West Chelmsford, Mass.
[133] Ibid, p. 17. The common brick for Brown Mountain Gate Lodge was hand-burned local brick.
[134] Ibid

described for the foundation. The masonry walls on the first story were 1 foot 4 inches thick. On the first story, half-timbering was used to frame the window openings. Half-timbering was infilled with brick panels, also installed above all first-story window openings except those with single sashes (see subsequent section "Window Openings"). At the second story half-timbering continued at the windowsill level and was carried around the building. The masonry walls on the second story, including the brick and the interior cinder block, were 1 foot thick. The exterior cross gables on both the NW and SE elevations were also constructed with half timbers and brick panels. The half-timber sections of the exterior walls were constructed with pecky cypress timbers.[135] Pecky cypress was also used at the Brown Mountain Gate Lodge, and in that case Atterbury called for the wood to be "hand hewn and all exterior trim shall be burnt with a torch on all exposed faces and edges and thoroughly brushed with a steel wire brush to remove all charred wood."[136] This was apparently done to give the pecky cypress an aged look and may have also been done at the Apartment Building.

The more detailed drawings of the exterior walls illustrated that the half timbers were chamfered along the exposed edges and had decorative pegs at both ends of the timber. They also detailed the pecky cypress wooden brackets that supported the projecting cross gables and window openings on the NW and SE elevations (fig. 22).[137] The brackets were approximately 1 foot 5 inches long and were composed of a beveled ovolo, fillet, covetto, and cyma reversa profile. They were fastened to the wall framing with lag screws. The architectural drawings also indicated that some of the timbers were fastened to the steel frame of the building with lag screws. This was depicted for the horizontal timbers used to frame the window opening and the horizontal timber at the base of the cross gable.[138] Other half-timbering was probably lagged to interior framing, and the vertical timbers framing the window openings were fastened to the masonry.[139]

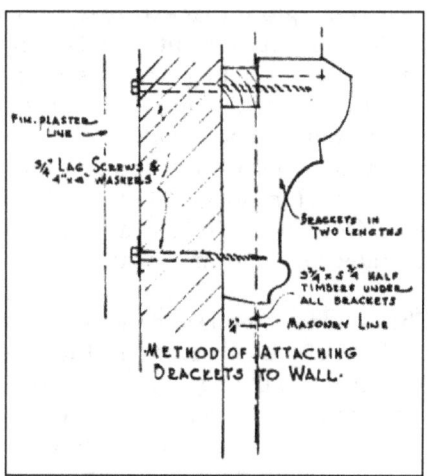

Figure 22. Apartment Building, bracket detail, Grosvenor Atterbury, drawing number 8 of 37 sheets.

The panels between the half timbers were in-filled with face brick that was generally a red color and in some cases a darker tone. The brick veneer was laid in varying patterns including chevrons, zigzags, and basket-weave. The architectural drawings indicated that the brick panels were constructed with an air space between the back of the brick and the interior portion of the wall. The same plans showed that flashing was installed at the base of each panel between the brick and the half timbers.[140] At the Brown Mountain Gate Lodge the brick veneering was secured to the wall with galvanized iron straps.[141] One of the plans for the Apartment Building depicted an anchor between the brick mortar joint and the joint of

---

[135] Pecky cypress is cypress that was attacked by a fungus that leaves holes in the wood. The fungus dies after the tree is cut down. Harris, p. 710.

[136] Atterbury, "Brown Mountain Lodge Specifications," p. 38.

[137] Drawing Number 8 of 37 sheets and Drawing Number 34 of 37 sheets, Grosvenor Atterbury Architect, John Tompkins, May 26, 1933.

[138] Drawing Number 8 of 37 sheets, Grosvenor Atterbury Architect, John Tompkins, May 26, 1933.

[139] Drawing Number 9 of 37 sheets, Grosvenor Atterbury Architect, John Tompkins, May 26, 1933.

[140] Drawing Number 8 of 37 sheets, Grosvenor Atterbury Architect, John Tompkins, May 26, 1933.

[141] Atterbury, "Brown Mountain Lodge Specifications," p. 23.

the concrete block wall.[142] This was probably a galvanized strap, and a similar system was probably repeated at regular intervals throughout the brick veneer. The brick was probably laid with a mortar similar to the mix previously described for the foundation, and the joints were probably "struck weathered joints" as used at the Brown Mountain Gate Lodge.[143]

Entrance Stoops and Terrace

The NW elevation of the Main Block had a center entrance, as well as an entrance at either end. All three entrances had masonry stoops of a similar design that were partially covered by cantilevered doorway hoods (see subsequent section "Doorways"). The basement floor plan of the Apartment Building indicated that the foundations for the entrance stoops were constructed with poured concrete.[144] The center entrance stoop was built with granite knee walls above grade that extended from either side of the doorway and turned at right angles to partially enclose the entrance landing. The granite was similar to that used on the exterior walls of the building and was capped with bluestone coping. A blueprint detailing the construction of the entrances illustrated that the walls were 1 foot 4 inches thick and the coping was 1 foot 6 inches wide, overhanging each side of the wall by 1 inch.[145] Three bluestone steps ascended to a small landing that was also constructed with granite and had bluestone along the outer edges. The bottom step was terraced, and the risers of the staircase were faced with brick headers. All masonry elements were set in a cement, sand, and hydrated lime mortar similar to the mix used for the exterior walls of the building.

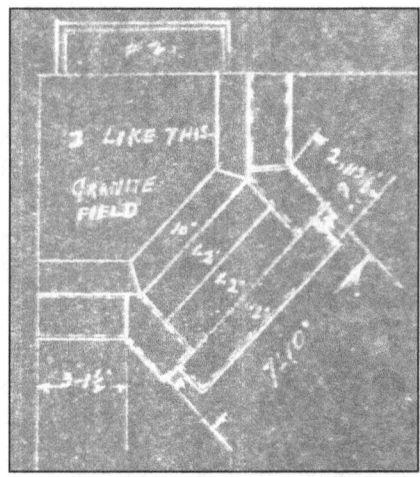

Figure 23. Apartment Building, NW elevation, entrance stoop and steps, August 1933.

The entrance stoops at either end of the NW elevation of the Main Block accessed the side hallways of the Apartment Building. These were both constructed with similar materials to the center entrance including concrete foundations, above-grade granite knee walls, bluestone coping, and bluestone steps with brick risers. The entrances were built at opposite inside corners of the façade where the Main Block was connected to the pavilions, and mirrored each other. The granite walls of the stoops extended at right angles from the adjacent walls of the building and were angled at the entrance steps. The steps of the side entrance stoops came out from the corner of the building at 45-degree angles as depicted by the construction blueprint (fig. 23). The bottom step was longer than the others and extended beyond the inside edges of the stoop sidewalls. Thick bluestone thresholds were installed at the entrance doorway as depicted in the blueprint (see subsequent section "Doorways").

---

[142] Drawing Number 14 of 37 sheets, Grosvenor Atterbury Architect, John Tompkins, May 26, 1933.
[143] Atterbury, "Brown Mountain Lodge Specifications," p. 23.
[144] Drawing Number 1 of 37 sheets, Grosvenor Atterbury Architect, John Tompkins, May 26, 1933.
[145] Construction blueprint stamped "Alexander Thompson, Inc., Naval Radio Station, Schoodic Point, Hancock County, ME, Department of Interior, G. Atterbury, Central Engineering and Construction Co., 8/23/33" (ACAD Archives, Winter Harbor, ME; Map Case C, Drawer 5, Folder 1).

An entrance to the first-story Office and Operations Room in the Northeast Pavilion was located on the NW elevation of that wing. That entrance was constructed with brick risers and two bluestone steps that were terraced. The architectural drawings indicated that the steps originally led to a vestibule that had a doorway to the Office.[146] The entrance was covered by a cantilevered metal hood supported by ornate metal brackets (see subsequent section "Doorways").

The Northeast Pavilion had another entrance on the NE elevation that led to the Bachelors' Apartment. This entrance was constructed in a similar manner to those on the façade of the Main Block but due to the sloping grade had four steps up to the landing (fig. 24). The change in grade from the front to the back of the building also required that the granite wall on SE side of the entrance be carried down to the basement story, with the NE wall following the slope of the grade, and the staircase constructed in that location. Unlike the front entrances, the top of the side wall (NE) was sloped from the bottom of the steps up to the landing. A thick bluestone threshold was installed at the doorway, and a cantilevered hood that partially covered the entrance was constructed above the doorway (see subsequent section "Doorways").

A staircase leading from the first-story level down to the basement story was constructed on the NE side of the Northeast Pavilion adjacent to the entrance steps (fig. 24). The staircase was constructed with a granite retaining wall with bluestone coping and had ten bluestone steps with brick risers leading down to a lower granite landing. At the lower landing the staircase turned SW and continued down one step to the basement-story grade. From there a pathway continued along the NE elevation toward the back of the building. The granite retaining wall with bluestone coping was continued along NE side of the pathway for approximately 14 feet where it was terminated.

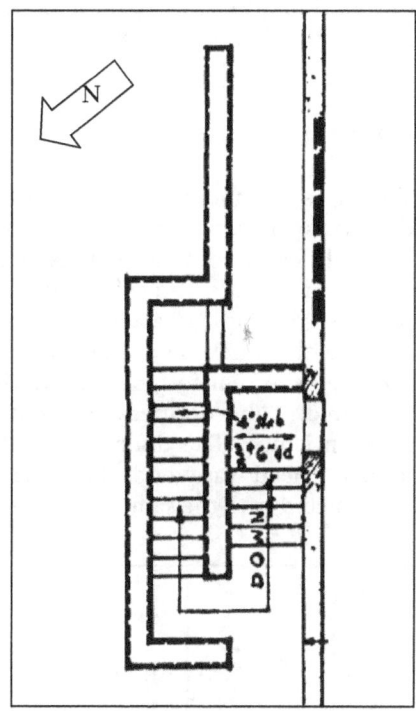

Figure 24. Apartment Building, NE elevation of Northeast Pavilion, steps to NE entrance and staircase to the back of the building. Sheet 21 of 37, Drawing No. 116387, Navy Dept. Bureau of Yards & Docks, June 1933.

The first story terrace that was constructed on the SE elevation filled the area between the Northeast and Southwest Pavilions. It was built above eight garage bays on the basement story and formed the roof over that section of the basement. The Terrace measured 23 feet wide and 83 feet 8 inches long. It was enclosed with a masonry parapet wall that was built with granite and brick bands following the pattern of the exterior walls of the building. The parapet wall was capped with bluestone coping. The architectural plans noted that the Terrace floor should have a "cement finish scored [in] 2'-0" squares as shown."[147] The cement floor was slightly pitched toward two drains that ran down through the basement

---

[146] Drawing Numbers 2 & 12 of 37 sheets, Grosvenor Atterbury Architect, John Tompkins, May 26, 1933.

[147] Drawing Number 2 of 37 sheets, Grosvenor Atterbury Architect, John Tompkins, May 26, 1933.

garage. The Terrace was accessed through doorways from the first-story hallways at either end of the Main Block and the doorway in the projecting center bay (see subsequent section "Doorways"). On both sides of the Terrace were 6-foot-wide staircases that led from the Terrace to the ground level. The staircases were constructed with sixteen bluestone steps and brick risers. The construction blueprint indicated that the bottom step of both staircases was made up of three stones and was slightly rounded.[148] Two historic photographs depicted an iron handrail along the SW side of the SW staircase.[149] A similar railing on the NE side of the NE staircase was evident in other historic photographs. The SE Terrace was a prominent feature of the Apartment Building and had views of the Atlantic Ocean and nearby islands.

Doorways

The three entrances on the NW elevation of the Main Block were constructed with similar doorways. The center entrance doorway (D103) had double wooden doors; each door leaf had eight lights above a single panel; the stiles and rails were constructed with wooden cores and wood veneers; and the lower panel was a three-ply wood panel. The molding around the panel was a simple quarter-round bead, and the muntin profiles for the lights were quarter-round with a fillet. The left door leaf had a molded astragal attached to the meeting stile that provided the seal for the double doors. The doorway was constructed with a bluestone threshold. The doorway was enframed with a 12-inch-wide brick reveal and a simple wooden jamb. The doorway lintel was constructed with a pecky cypress beam, and the doorway head was wood. The side entrance doorways on the façade (D102 and D104) were constructed with the same materials and details as the center doorway.

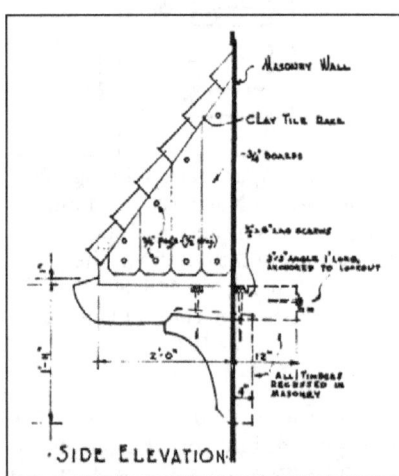

Figure 25. Apartment Building, typical doorway hood, depicting brackets, cladding, and clay tile rake, drawing number 12 of 37.

The three doorways on the façade were capped with cantilevered hoods. The hoods were constructed with brackets on either side of the doorway that supported a wooden hood covered with clay roof tiles (fig. 25). Each bracket was composed of a lower vertical member with a coved profile, which supported an upper horizontal piece with a beveled quarter-rounded end. The brackets were probably constructed with cypress, and the sides had a hand-hewn appearance and were lagged together. The bracket members were housed in the masonry wall and the upper piece was lagged to the interior steel frame. The shed roof was framed with 3-inch-by-5-inch pecky cypress plates and 2¾-inch-by-3¾-inch rafters and sheathed with 1⅜-inch ship-lapped boards. The sheathing was covered with 30-pound roofing felt and the clay roof tiles were fastened on top of that. The tiles along the rake edges of the roof were specifically made with a right angle for that application and overlapped the side walls of the hood. The top edge of the roof joined the exterior wall at the second-story half timber and was flashed at that joint. The side walls of the hood were clad with

---

[148] Construction blueprint, 8/23/33.
[149] Photographs 47 and 48 of 73, October 1934 and June 1935, Naval Radio Station, Schoodic, Me. Progress Photos (ACAD Archives; see Appendix B).

boards that were notched at the bottom corners and had decorative pegs at the top and bottom. The entrance-doorway hoods at either end of the façade abutted the flanking pavilions and were constructed with step flashing at the junction of the exterior wall and the rake.

The NW entrance of the Northeast Pavilion (D101) was unique to the Apartment Building. The two steps previously described led to an opening in the exterior wall that opened into a vestibule. The architectural drawing of the Apartment Building indicated that when the building was originally constructed, this opening had no door and the vestibule was partially open.[150] Like the façade doorways, the exterior opening was framed by brick and had a bluestone threshold and a pecky cypress lintel. The opening inside the brick reveal was approximately 3 feet wide and the jamb was framed with 5¾-inch-by-7¾-inch timbers. The hood covering this doorway was constructed with a lead-covered hipped roof with an integral gutter and a scalloped cornice. The soffit of the hood was constructed with V-grooved six-inch-wide boards and had a circular hole for a light fixture. The hood was supported by decorative wrought-iron brackets and was framed with dimensional lumber that was covered with standing-seam lead roofing. The joints between the hood and the exterior wall materials were flashed. Also unique to this doorway was the sign for the operations room. The sign was attached to the right of the doorway and hung from an overhead wrought-iron bracket with decorative scrollwork. The sign had a metal plate framed with wrought iron and was to be lettered by the Navy Department.

The drawings suggested that the doorway inside the vestibule served as the exterior doorway. The interior walls of the vestibule were covered with V-grooved ship-lapped siding, and the ceiling was plastered. There was a 6-inch step up to the doorway threshold, which was constructed with bluestone and had a bronze saddle. The doorway was apparently framed with pecky cypress and had a plain wooden jamb. The drawings indicated that the doorway had a vertical plank door with splines and was mounted on a stile and rail frame. Two fixed lights, one-over-one, were cut into the top half of the door. This doorway originally led from the vestibule to the Office in the Northeast Pavilion.

The entrance doorway on the NE elevation of the Northeast Pavilion (D108) was constructed in a similar manner as the façade doorways. It was framed by brick and a wooden lintel with a bluestone threshold. Within the brick reveal was a plain wooden jamb and header. The doorway held a single door that hung on three butt hinges from the SE jamb. The doorway had a double-thick door with splined vertical planks on the exterior and two panels with stiles and rails on the interior. A single glazed light was installed in the top panel of the door. Three reproduction strap hinges with heart-shaped points were mounted on the exterior of the door. The hinges were brass and consisted of only the strap part of a Colonial-style wrought-iron strap hinge and were purely decorative. The door had a reproduction brass Suffolk-style handle and latch with a separate deadbolt lock mounted above, which had a heart-shaped escutcheon. The handle and latch copied a well-known Colonial-style wrought-iron Suffolk latch. The Suffolk-style latches were used in several other doorways and were probably used on the façade doors. This doorway originally opened into the vestibule of the Bachelors' Apartment.

---

[150] Drawing Numbers 2, 12, & 37 of 37 sheets, Grosvenor Atterbury Architect, John Tompkins, May and June 1933.

The basement doorway on the NE elevation (D012) was installed next to a basement window opening. The doorway was framed with brick and had a wooden lintel. The lintel extended over a window opening to the left of the doorway, and the half-timber frame on the right side of window opening was incorporated into the doorway frame. Visually the arrangement of the doorway and window opening in that location created a single unit. The doorway had a double-thick door with vertical planks on the exterior similar to the door on the first story of that same elevation. The door was hung from the right jamb with three butt hinges and had the same decorative hardware as the first-story door. When the Apartment Building was first built, this doorway provided access to the Battery-Machine and Generator Room.

The SE elevation of the Main Block had three doorways on the first story leading to the Terrace. The projecting center bay had a doorway that was framed with brick and had a pecky cypress lintel (D106, fig. 21). The doorway threshold was bluestone, and inside the brick reveal was a plain wooden door jamb and head. A wooden door with twelve glass lights over one wood panel was hung from the right door jamb. Evidence of extant doors of the same design suggested that the door handle was a brass Suffolk-style handle and latch with a separate deadbolt lock above that had a heart-shaped escutcheon. The door had an automatic closer and was hung with butt hinges. That doorway led to the back vestibule of the Center Hallway.

At both ends of the SE elevation of the Main Block were the doorways to the respective hallways (D105, SW Hallway and D107, NE Hallway). Both doorways were constructed in the same manner with as the façade doorways for the side hallways. Typical of all exterior doorways, they were framed with brick surrounds and pecky cypress lintels; they had bluestone thresholds and plain wooden jambs. Within each doorway was a set of double wooden doors. Each door leaf was constructed with a wood core under a wood veneer and had eight glass lights over one wood panel. Based on historic photographs and extant examples of similar original doorway elements, the doors probably had Suffolk-style handles and separate deadbolt locks with heart-shaped escutcheons. Both of these doorways were covered with cantilevered hoods similar to those on the façade. The hoods were supported by wooden brackets, were wood framed, and had clay-tile roofs. The doorways opened into the back vestibules of their respective hallways.

The basement story doorway on the SE elevation of the Southwest Pavilion (D001) was framed with brick and had a pecky cypress lintel. The doorway had a wooden jamb inside the masonry frame and a wooden door hung from the left side of the doorway. The door was similar to the basement door on the NE elevation with vertical planks on the exterior and two panels on the interior. The door hardware included three ornamental strap hinges and a Suffolk-style latch. This doorway led to the basement storage rooms and boiler room.

Eight garage doorways for the Apartment Building (D002 through D009) were constructed under the SE Terrace (fig. 26). The garage doorways were framed with brick and had pecky cypress lintels. The wooden lintels were constructed with 8-inch-by-10-inch timbers that spanned each doorway and were supported on brick piers that separated the doorways. The construction drawings indicated that the lintels were fastened to a steel L-bracket that was in turn anchored to an interior reinforced-concrete lintel that spanned the entire length of the eight-bay garage. Each doorway had a concrete ramp and an angled steel edge at the lip of the garage floor. The inner frame of each doorway was constructed with a plain wooden jamb and head that were attached to wood framing that was anchored to the masonry walls. Each doorway had a set of wooden double doors that were constructed with vertical-splined planks with V-groove joints attached to a Z-braced frame. A two-light window opening with a squared muntin was installed in the top portion of every door leaf. Each door leaf was hinged with three Colonial-style strap hinges and swung out. Each door leaf had a Suffolk-style handle, and the left leaf of each set of double doors had a separate deadbolt lock with a heart-shaped escutcheon installed above the door handle. Every doorway had a barn-door-style keeper with a sliding wooden bar that secured the double doors. The garage doorways led to an open garage space on the basement level that was not partitioned.

The SE elevation of the Northeast Pavilion held two additional garage doorways (D010 and D011). The doorways were framed like the other garage doorways and were separated by a wide pier of brick and granite. All other exterior doorway elements were constructed in a similar manner as the other garage doorways on the SE elevation. The doorways opened into a non-partitioned two- car garage under the Bachelors'/Commanding Officer's Apartment.

Window Openings

Figure 26. Apartment Building, SE elevation depicting window openings with original multi-light steel sashes, September 1934.

The exterior fenestration, including doorways and window openings, of the Apartment Building was part of the overall symmetry of the building and was best depicted in the original architectural drawings and the historic photographs (fig. 26). With few exceptions, the window openings were symmetrically placed, and the corresponding sashes in the first- and second-story bays were the same type. The notable exceptions were the projecting bay on the SE elevation, and the Northeast Pavilion. As previously described, the projecting bay had a doorway and single window opening on the first story below a wide window opening with four sashes on the second story. Overall the exterior symmetry was maintained on the Northeast Pavilion, but, due to the different functions of the interior rooms, some of the window openings varied from the first story to the second story (see subsequent section "Interior Elements"). The following section on window openings will provide a general description of the types of historic window openings and the associated elements. The subsequent section on "Current Physical Description" will include specific window opening locations and will reference the historic window elements, as well as existing features.

The original multi-light steel sashes of the Apartment Building had a clearly defined grid of glazed lights that was part of the exterior pattern of materials and contributed to the overall appearance of the Apartment Building. The original appearance of the window openings was captured in the historic photographs of the building, which aptly illustrated the effect of the multi-light sashes (figs. 14, 18, 20, 21, and 26).

The Apartment Building had a variety of window types that were used throughout the building and arranged to maintain the building's symmetry. The 1933 floor plans for the basement story, the first story, and the second story all included window schedules that provided a letter code for each type of window opening and described sashes in the respective window openings. The window openings on the elevation drawings were also keyed to the window schedule that was included in those drawings. The following table was reproduced from the window schedule on the first-story floor plan and included all of the window opening types for the Apartment Building.[151]

WINDOW SCHEDULE

Type	Size (width by height)	Number of Lights	Remarks
A	1'-8" x 3'-1"	6	Steel Sash
B	5'-0" x 3'-1"	18	
C	3'-4" x 3'-1"	12	
D	3'-4" x 4'-0"	16	Transom
E	3'-4" x 5'-0"	20	Transom
F	1'-8" x 5'-0"	10	Transom
G	5'-0" x 5'-0"	30	Transom
H	6'-7" x 3'-1"	24	
I	1'-6" x 1'-6"	1	Special Plate Glass Fixed
J	3'-4" x 2'-2"	8	Wood Sash - bot. hinged i. o. [bottom hinged inside opening]

The different window types were used throughout the Apartment Building and were marked on both the floor plans and the elevation drawings (Appendix A). A majority of the window openings were framed with wooden timbers, and some were framed either partially or entirely with masonry. All of the window openings were constructed with plain wooden jambs and heads, and beveled wooden sills. The architectural drawings indicated that the jambs were fastened to an interior wooden framework that appeared to be tied to the exterior timbers. The exterior timbers were in turn anchored to the structural masonry walls of the building. In the case of the masonry frames, the framing for the jambs was anchored to the masonry. Likewise the drawings indicated that the heads of the window openings were fastened to the exterior lintels. The lintels were tied to steel I-beams that were installed as the

---

[151] Drawing Number 1 of 37 sheets, Grosvenor Atterbury Architect, John Tompkins, May 26, 1933.

structural headers for all of the window openings. The drawings depicted a steel plate that was fastened to the I-beams and then lag-screwed into the exterior lintel.[152] The variation in the window types and sizes, as well as the symmetrical arrangement of the window openings contributed to the overall design of the building.

With the exception of the type J, all of the window sashes were steel. The type-A window openings had one casement sash with six lights. The type-A sashes were casement sashes with six lights. The type-A window openings on the first story were framed with brick and a granite lintel, and had a lower sill of dressed granite and an upper wooden windowsill. On the second story and the cross gables, the type-A openings were framed with pecky cypress timbers and had wooden sills. The type-A windows were generally installed in bathrooms and in the attic gables.

Only one type-B window was installed, and that was located on the NE elevation of the Northeast Pavilion on the basement story (W007). The window opening was adjacent with the basement doorway (D012) and was visually grouped with that opening. The window opening held three steel casement sashes, each with six glazed lights. The left side of the opening was framed with brick and the right side was separated from the doorway by a timber mullion. A pecky cypress lintel spanned both the window opening and the doorway, thus creating the visual connection. The window opening had a lower dressed granite sill and an upper wooden sill, both of which were slanted outward. The type-B window was unique and originally opened into the basement Battery-Machine and Generator Room.

The type-C windows were constructed on the basement level and first and second stories. The type-C window sashes were composed of two steel casement sashes, with six lights in each sash. On the basement story the window openings were framed with brick and had pecky cypress lintels, and dressed granite sills. On the first and second stories the window openings were framed on all four sides with pecky cypress timbers. As with the other window types, the jambs, heads, and sills surrounding the sashes were wooden. The type-C windows were used in the basement storage rooms, and were installed in the upper stories on the courtyard and Terrace sides of the pavilions, which, with the exception of the Bachelors' Apartment, correlated with the kitchens and dining rooms of the apartments.

One extant example of the type-C window exists on the SE elevation of the Power House (figs. 35 and 36). Based on that example, the steel casement sashes were hinged at the top and bottom with steel L-hinges and the sashes were separated by a steel mullion in the center of the window opening. Each sash had a curved locking interior handle that was surface mounted on the inside stile and a casement adjuster attached to the bottom rail that would keep the sash in an open position. Though this was the only extant example of the type-C sash, it is likely that the other specified steel casement sashes, type C, in the Apartment Building were of a similar basic design and used similar hardware.

The type-D windows had two steel casement sashes and a steel transom above each casement. Each casement sash had six glazed lights, and each transom sash had two lights. It was evident from the historic photographs that the transoms had awning sashes that were hinged at the top and opened out. Like the type-C windows, the basement-story window openings were framed with brick and had pecky cypress lintels, and dressed granite sills; and the first-story window openings were framed on all four sides with pecky cypress timbers.

---

[152] Drawing Number 9 of 37 sheets, Grosvenor Atterbury Architect, John Tompkins, May 26, 1933.

There were only three type-D windows in the building: two in the basement of the Southwest Pavilion and one in the first story of the Northeast Pavilion.

The type-E windows were used throughout the first and second stories. These windows were composed of two casement sashes and two transoms. Each casement sash had eight glazed lights, and each transom had an awning sash with two lights. In all cases except the SE elevation cross gables, the type-E windows were surrounded by pecky cypress timbers. On the SE elevation cross gables, the type-E window was combined with a single casement on either side (type F) and the windows were separated by pecky cypress mullions. The type-E window openings were often installed above the exterior doorways. On the NW elevation both the first and second stories of the cross-gable bays contained a row of three type-E windows. That formed a group of windows, which helped define the cross-gable bays.

The type-F windows held a single steel casement with transom and were only used in combination with the type-E windows. Each casement had eight lights and the transoms had a two-light awning sash. The two window types were grouped in an F–E–F (1–2–1) combination, and the window types were separated by mullions. The group of windows essentially formed one large window opening with four casement sashes and transoms. This was particularly evident on the interior where the group of windows did constitute one window opening. The combination of the type-E and type-F windows was used on the SE cross gables and the courtyard side of the Northeast Pavilion.

The type-G windows had three steel casement sashes with transoms. All three casement sashes were operable, and each had eight lights. The transoms above each casement had two-light awning sashes. The type-G window openings were framed with pecky cypress timbers and had wooden jambs, heads, and sills. This type of window was used on the first and second stories throughout the building.

There was only one type-H window opening used in the Apartment Building, and that was located in the second story of the SE elevation projecting bay. The window opening had two sets of steel casement sashes, which totaled four sashes, each with six glazed lights (fig. 21). The window opening was framed with pecky cypress and flanked by brick panels framed with cypress. The four casements formed a band of windows on the second story of the projecting bay. That window opened onto the Center Hallway staircase.

The type-I window was also unique to one location in the Apartment Building. In this case the type-I window sash was installed on either side of a type-G window on the NE elevation of the Northeast Pavilion. Each of the type-I window openings had a one-light fixed sash, which the schedule noted was "special plate glass."[153] The tops of the type-I window openings were aligned with the top of the type-G window opening, and the sashes were separated by pecky cypress mullions. The window opening was framed with pecky cypress and had a wooden sill. This particular window opened into the original Simplex Traffic Room, and the arrangement of the two window types was reflected in the design of the interior elements as well (see subsequent section "Interior Elements").

The type-J windows were located in the four shed dormers of the pavilion roofs. The shed dormers were framed with steel to which a wooden casing and sill were fastened. These window openings contained wooden sashes with eight lights. The sashes were hinged at the

---

[153] Drawing Number 1 of 37 sheets, Grosvenor Atterbury Architect, John Tompkins, May 26, 1933.

bottom and tilted into the attic space. The wooden framework around the window opening was covered with copper, as were the side walls of the dormer. The type-J window sashes opened into the unfinished attic space of the Northeast and Southwest Pavilions.

The various types of window openings constructed for the Apartment Building and the sashes contained therein were in response to both the aesthetics and the functional requirements for the building. The original window openings remain extant, and the overall window placement from Atterbury's design was retained. However, the window sashes have been replaced with modern sashes that do not have distinctly divided lights, and some of the original texture of the windows in relation to the other building materials has been lost (see subsequent section "Current Physical Description").

Roofs and Related Elements

Figure 27. Apartment Building roofs, looking north with Southwest Pavilion in foreground, photograph taken from south radio tower, June 2, 1934.

The various roof surfaces of the Apartment Building continued the French-influenced design theme and maintained the symmetry of the building. The roofs were covered with terra-cotta clay tile that was generally orange-red in color with a blend of darker tiles. The Main Block and the pavilions had hipped roofs with a slight flare at the eaves. The appearance of the roofs complemented the exterior masonry and contributed to the overall character of the Apartment Building.

The roof covering the Main Block was a one-and-a-half-story-high hipped roof. The main slope of that roof on the NW and SE elevations included a one-story-high roof section over the hyphens and continued to the pavilion roofs where valleys marked the intersection. The NE and SW slopes of the Main Block hipped roof sloped down to the flat portions of the roofs that covered the connecting hyphens on either side of the Main Block. The decks of both flat roofs had a slight pitch and were covered with standing-seam copper roofing. Both pavilions had one-and-a-half-story-high hipped roofs with two shed dormers on the NE and SW slopes of the respective pavilions.

The roofs of the Apartment Building were framed with steel rafters, purlins, and a steel ridge beam (see subsequent section "Structural Elements"). The purlins were bolted to the tops of the rafters and were inverted T-shaped pieces. The steel structure was covered with 2½-inch-thick nailable concrete or "nailcrete" panels that were laid between the purlins with the top and bottom of each slab resting on the edge of the inverted T-shaped purlin. The panels were then secured to the purlins with wire ties. "Nailcrete" panels were also installed under the copper roofing on the flat roof decks. The progress report by Engineer Oliver Taylor indicated that the "nailcrete slabs" were made on site.[154] The architectural drawings of the Apartment Building indicated that a 30-pound felt underlayment was installed between the "nailcrete" and the clay tiles.

The terra-cotta clay tiles installed on the roofs were "Imperial" tile made by Ludowici-Celadon Company, Chicago, Illinois. The clay tiles were produced in varying shades of orange-red. The field tiles were rectangular and were laid in even courses. The edges of the shingles overlapped and two holes at the top of each shingle were used to fasten it to the roof. The field tiles were probably fastened to the "nailcrete" with 2-inch copper nails, which had been specified for the clay tile roof of the Brown Mountain Gate Lodge.[155] The roof valleys were flashed with copper and the valley shingles were miter cut and butted up to one another. Copper flashing was also installed on all of the hips and ridges, which were then covered with clay tile.

Beyond the field tiles the design of the roofs required special tiles for various applications. These included tiles for the ridges, ends of ridges, hips, tops of hips, ends of hips, and rakes of cross gables. The specifications for the Brown Mountain Gate Lodge also called for specially made tiles by the same company including "Top Fixtures, End Bends, #275 Ridge made to conform to the pitch of the roof, #275 special closed Ridge Ends and Cut Hip Tile."[156] The installation of clay tiles at the Brown Mountain Gate Lodge indicated that the ridge and hip tiles were installed with elastic cement and the gable-end tiles were pointed with Portland cement.[157] Although not all the characteristics of the roofs on the Apartment Building and the Gate Lodge are the same, it seemed likely that certain aspects of the installation followed the same specification. The extant examples indicated that the hip tiles were cemented in place. The gable rake tiles, like the rake tiles on the doorway hoods, were face nailed but did not appear to be pointed with Portland cement. With the exception of the flat roof decks, all roof surfaces at the Apartment Building were covered with tile.

Ventilation pipes for the apartment bathrooms pierced the tile roof on practically every elevation. Above the roof level the pipes were covered with a copper boot with a rounded copper flange. The roof tiles were cut around the boot and the flange of the boot extended under the adjacent tiles.

The Apartment Building was constructed with a simple cornice at the junction of the roofs and walls. An elliptical quarter-round wooden cornice was installed at the top of the wall and

---

[154] Taylor to Albright, Dec. 28, 1933; (copy courtesy of Rockefeller Archive Center).
[155] Atterbury, "Brown Mountain Lodge Specifications," p. 36.
[156] Ibid, p. 33.
[157] Ibid, p. 36.

a plain-board fascia was installed above that. Copper gutters were installed along the fascia of the building. The gutters were 6 inches wide and had copper hangers that extended up under the roof tiles and were fastened to the "nailcrete" sheathing. The gutters were connected to copper downspouts that were connected to a drainage system for the building.

Chimneys

The Apartment Building was built with two large chimneys situated at the NE and SW ends of the Main Block. The chimney masses were actually constructed within the respective flanking pavilions and pierced the flat roofs previously described. The NE chimney had a single flue and served the fireplace on the first story of the Bachelors' Apartment. The SW chimney had two flues that served the boiler and the hot water heater in the basement Boiler Room of the Southwest Pavilion.

Above the roof line both chimneys were constructed with granite stones and brick matching the materials used on the exterior walls. The corners of the each stack were built with the granite stones, and the face of the chimney was brick. Both chimneys were topped with pitched concrete caps that had hipped slopes. Terra-cotta chimney pots were installed at the top of all flues, and the large flues extended 3 feet above the highest roof ridge line (the smaller flue for the hot water heater was slightly shorter).

Detailed drawings of the two chimneys provided additional information about their construction.[158] The SW double-flue chimney had a concrete base at the basement level that rose 3 feet 4 inches to where the flues started. The rest of the chimney stack was constructed with brick and measured 4 feet by 4 feet 2 inches. Clean outs for both flues were located just above the concrete base, and the circular flues were lined with terra-cotta pipe. At the attic level the chimney was corbelled out over seven courses. The brick chimney extended to the roof level where it was flashed on all sides and transitioned to granite and brick. The size of the chimney above the roof line was 5 feet by 5 feet 6 inches.

The NE chimney was constructed in a similar manner. However, the concrete base of that chimney extended to the first story and was constructed with a hollow section for an ash pit and cleanout door in the basement. The chimney was brick from the first story fireplace to the roof level. Like the SW chimney, the NE chimney stack was corbelled at the attic level. The chimney was flashed at the roof level and transitioned to granite and brick above the flashing. Since this chimney had one flue it was slightly smaller, measuring 5 feet by 4 feet above the roof line.

The construction of the chimneys at the Apartment Building fulfilled the functional needs of the building and was also part of the overall design of the building. The placement of the two chimneys continued the symmetry of the exterior design, and the exterior materials were compatible with the exterior wall and roofing materials.

---

[158] Drawing Number 16 of 37 sheets, Grosvenor Atterbury Architect, John Tompkins, May 26, 1933.

Utilities and Fixtures

The Apartment Building had exterior lighting at all primary doorways, as well as two light fixtures on the SE elevations of the pavilions near the basement entrances and garage bays. As with other exterior elements, the design of the exterior light fixtures was part of the overall aesthetic appearance of the building and harmonized with the design.

Each of the façade doorways (D102, D103, and D104) had a single overhead light fixture above the doorway. The fixture was wired through the masonry above the doorway lintel and was covered by the doorway hood. The drawing of the electrical work for the Apartment Building indicated that all three fixtures were wired to switches in the Center Hallway. The original lighting fixtures over the façade doorways are not extant. They were most likely lantern-style brass fixtures with glass globes and a single light bulb. Similar light fixtures were installed over the doorways that had the same type of doorway hood (D105, D107, and D108).

The light fixture for the doorway to the Northeast Pavilion operations rooms (D101) was recessed into the ceiling of the doorway hood. In that case the ceiling was covered with 6-inch boards and the fixture was cut into the middle of the ceiling. The fixture had a metal dome-shaped can with a single light bulb and a glass lens. That light was wired to a switch just inside the vestibule.

The center bay on the SE elevation was not covered by a hood, and the light fixture for that doorway (D107) was attached to a bracket mounted on the masonry wall (fig. 17). The bracket consisted of a pipe extending horizontally from the wall to which a lantern-style light fixture was attached. A brass strap was attached to the wall above the pipe and extended down at an angle to the end of the pipe. The center of the strap was decorated with a brass star. Historic photographs and extant fixtures indicated that the lamps were six-sided brass lanterns with domed tops (fig. 17).

The same style lantern and bracket was installed on the basement story of the SE elevation of both pavilions. The lantern on the Southwest Pavilion hung near the basement doorway (D001) and the one on the Northeast Pavilion hung near the garage doorways. The lamps were symmetrically placed on the SE elevation and provided light for the nearby doorways and the staircases to the Terrace.

Structural Elements

The structural elements of the Apartment Building were detailed in the architectural drawings by Atterbury's firm and the Navy Department, Bureau of Yards & Docks (Appendix A, drawing numbers 7, 21, 22, and 23 of 37). The materials and engineering used in the construction of the Apartment Building followed Atterbury's desire to utilize modern materials and building techniques to improve the overall function of the building. Moreover, the building had to meet the institutional needs of a large Navy personnel residence while maintaining the aesthetic desired by the NPS. By using concrete materials and steel as the main structural elements and combining them with the exterior granite, brick, and half-timbered walls, Atterbury was able to achieve the goals of an attractive and functional institutional building that served the Navy from 1935 through 2002.

The below-grade sections of the foundation were constructed with reinforced poured concrete. At the basement story the SE wall of the Main Block was also constructed with reinforced concrete. This wall separated the basement of the Main Block from the garage. The SE wall of the garage was constructed with brick piers that were constructed between the doorways, as previously described. Other exterior walls at the basement story were constructed with granite and brick laid in mortar. These masonry walls formed the supporting structure for the exterior walls on the upper stories.

In the basement of the Main Block and the two flanking pavilions, reinforced concrete piers were constructed to support the interior structure of the upper stories. The piers were aligned along the center axis of each section of the building and were generally spaced between 10 and 14 feet apart (Appendix A, drawing number 21 of 37 sheets). The piers in the Main Block and the Southwest Pavilion were 12 inches by 20 inches, and the piers in the Northeast Pavilion were 16 inches by 16 inches. The architectural drawings of the framing plans indicated that the piers should be either carried down to bedrock or be constructed with spread footings.[159] Each pier supported a steel Lally column on the first story, which in turn supported another steel Lally column on the second story that supported the steel framing for the roofs. For the most part the rest of the steel and masonry structural system was tied into the column system. Thus the concrete piers were essentially the building blocks for the structural system of the upper stories of the Apartment Building.

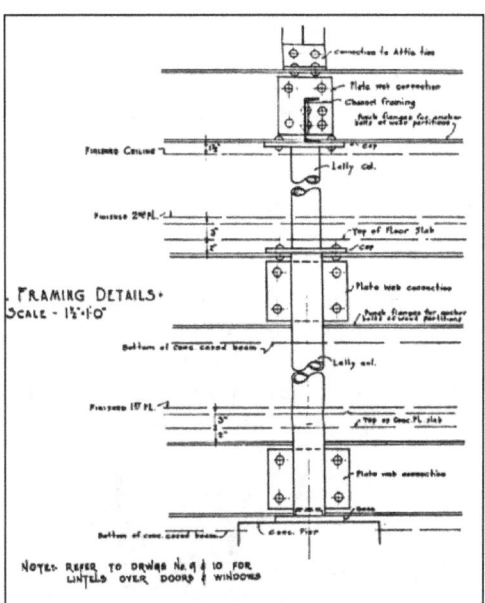

Figure 28. Steel framing details depicting steel Lally columns and beams, drawing number 21 of 37 sheets.

The system of concrete piers and steel Lally columns carried the horizontal steel I-beams that were installed between each column at the center of each section of the building and extended the length of each section. This framing system was used on the first and second stories of the building except in the Northeast Pavilion where the second story was framed with the beams extending from the center columns to the side walls (Appendix A, drawing number 22 of 37 sheets). On the first and second stories the beams were covered with concrete, but at the attic story the beams were not covered. The framing plans indicated that at both ends of the Main Block, steel beams were installed from the center columns to the NW and SE walls. That framing would have supported the staircases in the NE and SW Hallways. Likewise at the center of the Main Block, steel beams extended from the center beam to the SE wall where the Center Hallway staircases were constructed. Steel beams were also used to frame the chimney openings on the first and second stories. This system of

---

[159] Sheet 21 of 37, Drawing No. 116387, Navy Dept., Bureau of Yards & Docks, June 1933.

center columns and beams formed the primary supporting structure for the interior of the building and the roof framing.

The framing of the garage that supported the Terrace was independent of the main system of columns and beams but used similar framing techniques. The concrete wall on the SE side of the Main Block formed the interior wall of the garage and the brick piers between each garage bay provided the structural support for the exterior SE wall. Concrete-covered steel beams were installed between each pier and the interior wall creating the supporting structure for the garage roof and Terrace floor. The side walls of the garage were the concrete walls of the flanking pavilions and inside those were the staircase walls on either side of the Terrace. A reinforced-concrete slab deck was constructed above the grid of beams and supported the finished deck of the Terrace.

On the first and second stories the steel framing supported a structural floor constructed with reinforced-concrete slabs. The architectural drawings indicated that the slab floor was supported at the center of the building by the columns and beams and that the ends rested on a shelf on the exterior masonry walls. The drawings did not detail additional steel support structure for the concrete floors, but that may have been installed as part of the reinforcing of the structure.

At the attic story, the framing appeared to be more complex. The large I-beam supported by Lally columns spanned the center of each section of the building and steel channel beams were installed from the center beam to the exterior walls where they were fastened to the steel rafters of the building. The second-story ceiling was attached to the channel beams and the catwalk in the attic was installed over the steel framing.

Figure 29. Apartment Building roof framing, view from SW tower.

The roofs of the Apartment Building were framed with steel beams, rafters, and purlins (fig. 29). The roof framing was supported by the column system at the lower stories, which supported T-shaped columns in the attic. The attic columns carried the ridge for each section of the building to which the rafters were attached. The ridges were constructed with 10-inch I-beams, and the rafters were constructed with 8-inch channel beams, which were also used to frame the roofs of the cross gables. The plans indicated that the steel rafters were installed approximately 3 feet on center. Corresponding rafters on opposite slopes of the roof were connected at the peak of the roof with metal plates that were apparently fastened to the ridge beam. The framing plans indicated that the hip and valley rafters were 12-inch I-beams. L-shaped collar ties were bolted to the attic columns and to the rafters. The flat roofs at both ends of the Main Block were framed with 12-inch channel beams around the perimeter of the roof deck and channel beam rafters. The openings for the chimneys were also framed with channel beams. The inverted T-shaped purlins were bolted to the rafters and spaced approximately 4 feet 8 inches on center, and the "nailcrete" panels for the roof sheathing were attached to the purlins with wire ties. The plates installed at the tops of the exterior walls for the roof framing were L-shaped steel beams that were 6 inches wide on both sides. The plate was anchored to the concrete block walls, and the rafters were fastened to the plate. A caption with one of the progress photographs included the following note:

> All of roof framing supported on shores, the masonry walls being built under afterwards. This allowed all steel to be bolted without stress in anchor bolts or masonry.[160]

The cross gables appeared to be the only exterior walls that were partially wood framed. The cross-gable ends on both the NW and SE elevations were framed with 2-inch-by-4-inch studs that were fastened to a 4-inch-by-4-inch plate. The drawings indicated that the plate was bolted to the steel joists that framed the attic floor and the studs were fastened to the steel roof rafters.

The historic photographs documented the erection of the roof framing during November and December 1933 (Appendix B). Upon completion, the roof framing was an expansive web of steel that supported the "nailcrete" roof sheathing and terra-cotta roof tiles.

The interior walls were constructed in a traditional manner that also suited the function of the building. The original partition walls in the basement were constructed with concrete blocks. These walls were erected for the Battery-Machine and Generator Room, the adjacent Storage Room, the Boiler Room, and the Coal Storage Room. The partition walls in the first- and second-story apartment rooms were constructed with dimensional lumber that typically measured 2 inches by 4 inches. However, all of the interior walls of the NE, SW and Center Hallways were constructed with concrete that was 4 to 6 inches thick and enclosed the steel framing previously described. These concrete walls evidently served as structural interior walls and also provided fire walls between the hallways and the apartments.

The window openings were typically framed with masonry and/or wood exteriors that were supported by steel beams and steel anchors. The architectural drawings illustrated that the smaller window openings on the basement and first stories were framed on the sides by the masonry walls and wooden side jambs were anchored to the masonry.[161] The exterior lintels appeared to be tied to the structural lintels that were constructed with two 4-inch steel I-beams. Steel I-beams were also used as the structural lintels for the other first-story window openings, which were typically constructed with three beams. In effect, the steel lintels carried the load of the exterior masonry walls, and the exterior timber and granite lintels were decorative. The drawings indicated that the exterior wooden lintels on the second-story window openings were tied to an L-shaped steel beam, but the exact connection was not illustrated. The half timbers that framed the sides of the window openings were anchored to the masonry walls, and the wooden window jambs were fastened to the half-timber frames. The sides of the second-story window openings were framed in a similar manner with the half timbers being anchored to the concrete block walls. Some of the smaller window openings had granite sills that were mortared to the masonry wall and an upper wooden sill that rested on the granite. All other window openings had wooden sills

---

[160] Caption with photograph 41 of 73, October 1934 and June 1935, Naval Radio Station, Schoodic, Me. Progress Photos (ACAD Archives; see Appendix B).

[161] Drawing Number 9 of 37 sheets, Grosvenor Atterbury Architect, John Tompkins, May 26, 1933.

that were fastened to the horizontal half timbers below the sills that were in turn anchored to the masonry walls. The single window openings in the cross gables were framed with wood. The drawings showed that additional interior wood framing around the window openings typically consisted of 2-inch-by-2-inch furring to which the interior wall elements were attached. The extant elements at the Apartment Building suggested that the window openings were constructed in accordance to the plans developed by Atterbury's firm and the Navy Department.

The structural framing of the doorways was similar to the window openings, with masonry reveals and timber lintels on the exterior that were supported by an interior steel and wood structural system.[162] The sides of the doorways were supported by the exterior masonry walls and wooden jambs within the doorway. The masonry walls carried the timber lintel that was anchored to two 4-inch steel I- beams above the doorway. Unlike the window openings, the interior structure of the doorways was constructed with a more substantial framing. The drawings depicted that the interior of the doorway frame was constructed with 3-inch-by-4-inch studs and headers. The 3-inch-by-4-inch framing was apparently fastened to the doorway jambs and heads and also supported the interior wall elements. The basement doorways were constructed to similar specifications, but the two I-beams used for the structural lintels were 8 inches high.

The garage doorways were constructed with a continuous structural lintel that was made of reinforced concrete. A 6-inch L-bracket was anchored to the concrete and the exterior timber lintels above each doorway were fastened to that. The garage doorway jambs and heads were attached to an interior framework of 3-inch-by-4-inch studs and 2-inch-by-4 – inch headers. The drawings indicated that the wooden frame work was anchored to the masonry piers and lintel, all of which created the structural framing for the garage doorways.

The framing of the window openings and doorways were further examples of Atterbury's use of modern structural materials and aesthetically appropriate exterior elements that were combined to achieve the overall design goals of the Apartment Building.

Interior Elements

Basement Story

The basement story of the Apartment Building was comprised of utilitarian spaces that served the intended function of the building (Appendix A, drawing number 1 of 37 sheets and fig. 31). The basement plan included utility rooms, storage rooms, garage bays, and open areas that were constructed with minimal finishes.

Northeast Pavilion

The basement of the Northeast Pavilion had two garage bays at the SE end of the building that were accessed through two doorways on the SE elevation. The floor of the garage was poured concrete, and the ceiling was constructed with concrete slabs that formed the subfloor of the first-story rooms. There was a window opening on the NE elevation of the

---

[162] Drawing Number 10 of 37 sheets, Grosvenor Atterbury Architect, John Tompkins, May 26, 1933.

garage that had two casement sashes (type C). An interior concrete-block partition wall separated the garage from the adjacent room. The concrete walls were covered with concrete parging.

The Battery-Machine and Generator Room was near the center of the Northeast Pavilion. The room had poured concrete floors, and the interior walls were constructed with concrete block. The room was accessed through the NE basement doorway (D012) and had an interior doorway leading to a storage room under the Main Block. The interior doorway was framed with a metal surround and had a two-panel metal door that was hung on the SE jamb with three butt hinges. The drawing of the doorways and door schedule indicated that this door and other basement doors were "kalamein" doors, which had a wooden core and were covered with metal and had an automatic closer.[163] The "kalamein" door was developed as a fireproof door and was used throughout the basement of the Apartment Building.[164] The Battery-Machine and Generator Room had a window opening on the NE elevation that had three casement sashes (type B). The architectural drawings indicated that the window opening was trimmed with plain boards and quarter-round molding. The walls were apparently finished with wire lath and plaster and the ceilings were concrete.

At the NW end of the Northeast Pavilion the basement was excavated to a crawl space and was not finished. The crawl space had an earth floor, and the exterior walls were the masonry foundation. Concrete support piers were installed at the center of the area and carried the concrete-covered I-beam supporting the first story. The concrete slab subfloor for the first story formed the ceiling for the crawl space.

Main Block

The basement of the Main Block consisted of storage rooms and a staircase with access to the first-story Center Hallway. The storage space adjacent to the Northeast Pavilion was partitioned from the rest of the basement by concrete-block walls and the SE concrete foundation wall of the Main Block. The floor was concrete and the ceiling was concrete slab. This storage space had three doorways. One led to the Battery-Machine and Generator Room and was previously described. A doorway in the SE wall led to the garage bays and had a metal frame and a two-panel metal-clad door. There was a single step down between the storage space and the garage. At the SW end of the room a single step up led to a doorway that accessed the basement staircase. The doorway was framed with a metal surround and had a metal door with nine wire-glass lights over one panel. The door was hinged on the NW side of the doorway and opened into the room.

The basement staircase was constructed at the center of the Main Block with masonry walls on either side of the stairwell. The interior walls of the stairwell were covered with metal lath and plaster. At the basement level the stairway had a raised concrete landing and two doorways leading to the adjacent storage rooms. The staircase was built with a steel stringers and risers, and cement treads. From the basement landing, the ten steps ascended SE to an intermediate landing near the top of the staircase and from that landing that stairs turned ninety degrees and two more steps led to a doorway and the Center Hallway vestibule. There was a window opening at the intermediate landing with a single casement sash (type A). A wooden rail held with three brackets was mounted on the NE wall of the staircase.

---

[163] Drawing Number 13 of 37 sheets, Grosvenor Atterbury Architect, John Tompkins, May 26, 1933.
[164] Harris, p. 559.

The remaining area of the Main Block basement was open for storage. The area had a concrete floor and a concrete ceiling. The area SW of the staircase was accessed by a doorway from the staircase basement landing. That doorway had a metal door with nine wire-glass lights over one panel and was hung on the NW side of the doorway. Another doorway from this section of the basement led to the garage. This particular opening in the concrete foundation wall had brick infill on both sides of a single doorway. The doorway had a two-panel metal-clad door that was hung on the SW jamb and opened into the basement storage area.

At the NW side of the Main Block basement the open space extended to the NE and the crawl space. A portion of the basement floor in this section was concrete, and the portion along the NW foundation wall was excavated down to earth and bedrock.

The basement-level garage was SE of the Main Block and could be accessed from the basement storage rooms on either side of the staircase. The garage had eight bays, each with a separate doorway with double-leaf doors. The floor was covered with poured concrete, and the walls were concrete. The interior surfaces of the piers separating the garage doorways were covered with cementitious parging. At the ceiling the concrete-covered beams supported the concrete slab that formed the subfloor of the Terrace. The two drains for the Terrace were cut into the garage ceiling and drained through connections in the garage floor. At the NE end of the garage the area under the NE staircase of the Terrace was open for storage. However, at the SW end of the garage the area under the SW staircase of the Terrace was partitioned by a concrete block wall and was only accessible from the hallway in the Southwest Pavilion basement.

Southwest Pavilion

The basement of the Southwest Pavilion was separated into three areas by concrete-block partitions. The exterior doorway on the SE elevation (D001) entered into a basement hallway. On the NE side of the hallway were two storage areas under the SW staircase of the Terrace. The drawing labeled one of the areas as the Pump Room. The room on the SW side of the hallway was the Coal Storage Room. As with other basement rooms, the floor was constructed with poured concrete and the ceiling was concrete slab. The masonry walls were probably finished with a cementitious parging. The room had two window openings on the SE elevation, each with two casement sashes with transoms (type D) and a window opening on the SW elevation that had two casement sashes (type C). The plans indicated that there was a doorway in the NW wall of the room that led to the Boiler Room.

The Boiler Room was located at the end of the SW basement hallway near the center of the Southwest Pavilion. It was an open room and originally had a coal boiler and coal-fired hot water heater. Both of these were vented through the chimney that was built on the NE wall of the Boiler Room. There was a doorway in the NE wall that led to the storage area in the basement of the Main Block. The doorway had a two-panel metal-clad door that hung from the NW jamb and opened into the adjacent storage room. The SW wall of the room had two window openings, each with two casement sashes (type C). Otherwise the Boiler Room was finished in a similar manner to the other basement rooms.

The area at the NW end of the Southwest Pavilion basement was not finished. The floor was excavated down to earth and bedrock; the walls were open to the foundation; and the ceiling was concrete slab that formed the subfloor of the first story. Concrete piers were constructed at the center of the room and supported the concrete-covered steel beam.

First-Story Plan

The room layout of the first story of the Apartment Building followed the plan formed by the Main Block and the two flanking pavilions. The first story had five apartments, two operations rooms, and three main hallways (Appendix A, drawing numbers 2 and 25 of 37 sheets and fig. 32). Primary access to the building was through the façade entrance doorways, and the entrance doorways on the Northeast Pavilion. The secondary egress was provided through the exterior doorways on the SE elevation, all of which were previously described.

The apartments at the Apartment Building followed three basic plans with slight variations. The first story of the Southwest Pavilion housed a one-bedroom apartment and one two-bedroom apartment. There were two two-bedroom apartments in the Main Block that also shared a similar design, which was different from the two-bedroom apartment in the pavilion. In addition to the three basic plans, there was also a three-bedroom apartment and a two-room operations suite that were unique to the first story of the Northeast Pavilion.

The following descriptions include dimensions for the first-story rooms that were included in the architectural drawings by Atterbury's firm and the Navy Department, Bureau of Yards and Docks dated June 1933 (Appendix A, drawing numbers 2, 3, and 25 of 37 sheets). There was a slight discrepancy between the room dimension in some original drawings and drawing number 25 in which the room measurements appeared to be rounded to the nearest 6 inches. Therefore the room measurements included in the following descriptions were approximations meant to provide an understanding of the overall layout and the general room size.

First-Story Northeast Pavilion

<u>Operations Rooms</u>

The original plan for the first story of the Northeast Pavilion included an eight-room apartment designated as the Bachelors' Apartment and a two-room operations area. The operations rooms were at the NW end of the pavilion and were accessed through the open vestibule previously described (see previous section "Exterior Elements, Doorways"). The doorway from the vestibule opened into the Office, which measured 7 feet by 11 feet. The room had a window opening on the SW wall with two casement sashes with transoms (type D). A doorway on the NE wall led to the Simplex Traffic Room (Room CO-10), which measured 15 feet by 18 feet. That room had a window opening on the NW elevation with three casement sashes with transoms (type G). The window opening on the NE elevation had three casement sashes with transoms (type G) that were flanked on both sides with a single fixed sash (type I). A small bathroom was situated in the NE corner of the room. Those two rooms and one bathroom completed the original suite of the operations rooms.

Bachelors'/Commanding Officer's Apartment

The remaining first story of the Northeast Pavilion was occupied by the Bachelors' Apartment. That apartment had eight rooms including an entry vestibule, Living Room, Kitchen, bathroom, and three bedrooms. The apartment was accessed through the first-story entrance doorway on the NE elevation of the pavilion, which opened into a vestibule (Room CO-01). The vestibule had a doorway on the SE wall leading to the adjacent Living Room (Room CO-02) and a doorway on the NW wall leading to the Kitchen (Room CO-11). At the SW end of the vestibule was a closet.

The Living Room (Room CO-02) was near the center of the pavilion. The room extended the full width of the pavilion and measured 15 feet by 22 feet 6 inches. There were two window openings on the NE wall, each with three casement sashes with transoms (type G). On the NW wall a doorway led to the vestibule and a wide doorway opened into the Dining Room (Room CO-07). Centered in the SW wall of the Living Room was a fireplace with a wooden surround and decoratively carved mantelpiece. To the right of the fireplace was a closet. A doorway in the center of the SE wall accessed a hallway, which led to the bedrooms and bathroom.

The first bedroom on the left side of the hallway (Room CO-03) was a rectangular room measuring 11 feet by 13 feet. The bedroom had a window opening on the NE wall that had three casement sashes with transoms (type G). A closet was situated in the south corner of the room, and a sink was installed at the center of the SE wall.

At the SE end of the hallway was a doorway to another bedroom (Room CO-04), which measured 11 feet by 15 feet. The bedroom was situated in the east corner of the pavilion and had window openings on the NE and SE walls. Both of those window openings had two casement sashes with transoms (type E). In the north corner of the NW wall was a closet, and a sink was installed at the center of that wall, which was opposite the sink in Room CO-03.

A third bedroom (Room CO-05) was located in the west corner of the pavilion. It was a rectangular room measuring 10 feet by 13 feet and had window openings on both the SE and SW elevations. The SE window opening had two casement sashes with transoms (type E). The SW window opening was smaller and had two casement sashes (type C). There was a closet on the NW wall, and a sink was installed in the west corner of the room next to the closet.

On the SW wall of the hallway to the bedrooms was a small closet, and adjacent to that was the doorway to a large bathroom that served the apartment (Room CO-06). The architectural drawings indicated that the bathroom had two toilet stalls and a shower stall along the NW wall and a single sink in the south corner of the room. There was a window opening on the SW wall that had two casement sashes (type C).

First-Story Main Block

Northeast (NE) Hallway

The first story of the Main Block had a hallway at both ends of the building, a Center Hallway, and two two-bedroom apartments. The NE Hallway was accessed through the NE entrance doorway on the façade of the building (D102). The hallway was 8 feet 2 inches wide by 21 feet long and had a steel staircase leading to the second story. Interior masonry walls separated the hallway from the first-story apartments. On the left side near the SE end of the hallway was a utility closet. At the SE end of the hallway was an interior doorway that led to a vestibule that measured 4 feet 6 inches by 8 feet. The SE Terrace was accessed from the vestibule through a double doorway (D107).

Center Hallway

The center entrance doorway (D103) on the façade of the Main Block led to the Center Hallway. The exterior doorway opened into a large vestibule that had a doorway with sidelights leading into the hallway. The hallway had a steel staircase to the second story and doorways to Apartments No. 1 and No. 2. At the SE end of the hallway was an interior doorway to the back vestibule. This vestibule had a doorway on the right leading to the basement staircase and an exterior doorway (D106) that accessed the Terrace.

Apartment No. 1

Apartment No. 1 was on the NE side of the Center Hallway. The doorway from the hallway was near the center of the NE wall and opened into a small foyer (Room 101) that led to the Living Room (Room 107). There was a closet on the SE side of the foyer and a doorway on the NW side of the room led to the Kitchen (Room 102). The Kitchen was 8 feet 6 inches by 12 feet 6 inches and was furnished with cabinets and appliances (see subsequent section "First-Story Elements"). The window opening on the NW wall of the Kitchen had two casement sashes with transoms (type E). A doorway on the NE wall with a swinging door led to the Dining Room (Room 103).

The Dining Room (Room 103) measured 11 feet by 12 feet 6 inches. It had two window openings on the NW elevation, and both window openings had two casement sashes with transoms (type E). On the exterior of the building, these two windows and the window in the Kitchen formed the three-window grouping on the façade cross gable. A 6-foot-wide doorway on the SE wall of the Dining Room led into the Living Room (Room 107).

The Living Room (Room 107) was a rectangular room that measured 12 feet 6 inches by 16 feet. The room had a large window opening on the SE elevation that had four casement sashes. The window opening was composed of three windows grouped together. At the center of the group were two casement sashes with transoms (type E), and on either side of that were windows with single casement sashes with transoms (type F). The entire window opening had a wide windowsill, and the window units were separated by 10-inch mullions. On the exterior of the building these three window openings were installed within the SE elevation cross gable. There was a closet in the south corner of the Living Room. The Living Room could be accessed from the entry foyer and a doorway at the NE end of the room led to the bedroom hallway.

The bedroom (Room 104) on the NW side of the bedroom hallway was a square room with a large window opening on the NW wall. The room was 12 feet by 12 feet 6 inches and had two closets on the NE wall. The window opening had three casement sashes with transoms (type G) and looked out onto the front courtyard.

On the SE side of the apartment was a smaller bedroom (Room 105) that was 9 feet by 12 feet 6 inches. Like the other bedroom, this room also had a window opening with three casement sashes with transoms (type G) that was installed in the SE wall. There was a closet in the north corner of the room, and the doorway to the hall was in the west corner of the SW wall.

Adjacent to the bedroom was a bathroom (Room 106) that was accessed from the bedroom hallway. The bathroom had a window opening on the SE wall that held one casement sash. The bathroom facilities for Apartment No. 1 were typical for the Apartment Building. On the NE wall it had a sink with a cabinet and mirror above and a bathtub and toilet along the SW wall.

Apartment No. 2

Apartment No. 2 was on the SW side of the Center Hallway and was accessed through a doorway near the center of the SW wall. Apartment No. 2 was a two-bedroom apartment that mirrored the layout of Apartment No. 1. The rooms were the same size as Apartment No. 1 and had the same window openings and sash types.

Southwest (SW) Hallway

At the SW end of the Main Block, the SW Hallway provided access to the first-story apartments in the Southwest Pavilion and had a stairway to the second story. The plan of SW Hallway mirrored that of the NE Hallway, except that it did have access to the first story of the adjacent pavilion. The SW Hallway was accessed through the SW entrance doorway (D104) on the façade. As with the NE Hallway, there was a vestibule at the SE end of the hallway that led to the exterior doorway (D105) and the SE Terrace. Along the SW wall of the hallway were doorways to Apartments No. 3 and No. 4, as well as a utility closet.

First-Story Southwest Pavilion

Apartment No. 3

The two first-story apartments in the Southwest Pavilion were accessed from the SW Hallway of the Main Block. Apartment No. 3 was a two-bedroom apartment that occupied the NW end of the pavilion. The doorway from the SW Hallway led into a large foyer (Room 301) that had a closet on the NW wall and a closet on the SE wall. At the NW end of the foyer was a doorway to the bedroom hallway. In the west corner of the foyer was a doorway to a hallway leading NW toward the living area. The first doorway on the NE wall of that hallway led to the Kitchen for the apartment.

The Kitchen (Room 302) was 8 feet 6 inches by 11 feet 6 inches and had a closet at the SE end of the room. There was a window opening on the NE wall of the Kitchen that had two casement sashes (type C). The Kitchen was equipped with appliances and a built-in cabinet. The NW wall of the room had a doorway with a swinging door that led to the Dining Room.

The Dining Room (Room 303) was situated in the north corner of the Southwest Pavilion and measured 11 feet by 12 feet 6 inches. It had window openings on both the NE and NW walls with steel casement sashes. The window opening on the NE wall had two casement sashes (type C), and the window opening on the NW wall had three casement sashes with transoms (type G). The SE wall of the Dining Room had a doorway to the Kitchen and a doorway to the hallway. The SW wall had a wide opening that connected the Dining Room to the Living Room (Room 304).

The Living Room (Room 304) was situated in the west corner of the pavilion. It was a rectangular room measuring 12 feet by 15 feet and had window openings on the NW and SW elevations. Both window openings had three steel casement sashes with transoms (type G). A doorway in the east corner of the NE wall led back into the hallway.

A small bedroom hallway was accessed through a doorway in the SW wall of the foyer. At the NW end of that hallway was a bedroom (Room 305) that measured 10 feet by 12 feet 6 inches. The bedroom had a window opening on the SW wall that had three casement sashes with transoms (type G). In the south corner of the SE wall was a small closet. The doorway to the hallway was in the east corner of the SE wall.

The doorway to the bathroom (Room 306) was in the SW wall of the bedroom hallway. The bathroom had an L plan, because the closet of the bedroom (Room 305) occupied the west corner of the room. The SW wall of the bathroom had a window opening with a single casement sash (type A). The bathroom was between the two bedrooms and equipped with standard utilities.

The second bedroom (Room 307) was on the SE side of the apartment and accessed through a doorway on the SE wall of the bedroom hallway. This bedroom was rectangular, measuring 10 feet by 16 feet 6 inches. It had a window opening on the SW wall that had three casement sashes with transoms (type G). At the NE end of the bedroom was a large closet. The doorway to the bedroom hallway was located in the NW wall.

Apartment No. 4

Apartment No. 4 was a one-bedroom apartment located at the SE end of the Southwest Pavilion. The doorway to the apartment was toward the SE end of the SW Hallway and opened into a large foyer (Room 401). The foyer had two closets; one on the SE wall; and one on the NW wall. At the SW end of the foyer was a hallway that led SE toward the living area. There was a small linen closet on the NE wall of that hallway.

The Kitchen (Room 402) was the first doorway on the NE side of the hallway. The Kitchen measured 8 feet 6 inches by 11 feet and was equipped with standard appliances. A narrow doorway at the NW end of the Kitchen opened into a closet. A doorway with a swinging door at the SE end of the Kitchen led to the Dining Alcove (Room 403).

The Dining Alcove (Room 403) was a feature of the one-bedroom apartments and measured 8 feet 6 inches by 12 feet. Since the room occupied the east corner of the pavilion, there were window openings on both the NE and SE walls. The NE window opening had two casement sashes (type C), and the SE window opening had two casement sashes with transoms (type E). A wide opening in the SW wall led to the Living Room (Room 404) and created an open plan for the living quarters of the one-bedroom apartment.

The Living Room (Room 404) was a rectangular room measuring 12 feet by 16 feet 6 inches. It was situated in the south corner of the pavilion and had two window openings on the SE wall and one window opening on the SW wall. Both window openings on the SE wall had two casement sashes with transoms (type E) and the window opening on the SW wall had three casement sashes with transoms (type G). The doorway from the Living Room to the hallway was located in the north corner of the NW wall.

A doorway in the SW wall of the hallway led to a small hallway with access to the bedroom and bathroom. That hallway had a small closet on the SE wall and the doorway to the bathroom (Room 405) was on the SW side of the hall.

The bathroom (Room 405) was typical for the building and had the standard amenities. There was a window opening on the SW wall with a single casement sash.

The bedroom (Room 406) was located in the west corner of the apartment and was accessed through a doorway in the NW wall of the hallway. The bedroom was 12 feet 6 inches by 14 feet 6 inches, which was standard for the one-bedroom apartments. There was a window opening on the SW wall that had three casement sashes with transoms (type G). Since there was no closet in the bedroom, the closet in the adjacent hallway would have served the bedroom.

Second-Story Plan

The second-story apartments at the Apartment Building followed three basic plans with slight variations (fig. 33). The second story was accessed from staircases in the three main hallways and included six apartments as well as the three hallways. Both the Northeast and Southwest Pavilions contained a one-bedroom apartment and one two-bedroom apartment. The two apartments in the Northeast Pavilion essentially mirrored those in the Southwest Pavilion. There were also two two-bed room apartments in the Main Block that followed a similar design as the first-story Main Block apartments.

The following descriptions include dimensions for the second-story rooms that were included in the architectural drawings by Atterbury's firm and the Navy Department, Bureau of Yards and Docks, dated June 1933 (Appendix A, drawing numbers 2, 3, and 25 of 37 sheets). As with the first story, there was a slight discrepancy between the room dimension in some original drawings and drawing number 25 in which the room measurements appeared to be rounded to the nearest 6 inches. In addition the rooms on the second story were slightly larger, because the exterior walls were not as thick. Therefore the room measurements included in the following descriptions were approximations meant to provide an understanding of the overall layout and the general room size.

Second-Story Northeast Pavilion

Apartment No. 5

The two second-story apartments in the Northeast Pavilion were accessed from the second story of the NE Hallway of the Main Block. Apartment No. 5 was a two-bedroom apartment that occupied the NW end of the pavilion. The doorway from the NE Hallway led into a large foyer (Room 501) that had a closet on the NW wall and a closet on the SE wall. At the NE end of the foyer was a doorway to the bedroom hallway. In the north corner of the foyer was a doorway to a hallway leading NW toward the living area. The first doorway on the SW wall of that hallway led to the Kitchen for the apartment.

The Kitchen (Room 502) was 9 feet by 11 feet 8 inches and had a closet at the SE end of the room. There was a window opening on the SW wall of the Kitchen that had two casement sashes (type C). The Kitchen was equipped with appliances and a built-in cabinet. The NW wall of the room had a doorway with a swinging door that led to the Dining Room (Room 503).

The Dining Room (Room 503) was situated in the west corner of the Northeast Pavilion and measured approximately 12 feet by 13 feet 3 inches. It had window openings on both the SW and NW walls with steel casement sashes. The window opening on the SW wall had two casement sashes (type C), and the window opening on the NW wall had three casement sashes with transoms (type G). The SE wall of the Dining Room had a doorway to the Kitchen and a doorway to the hallway. The NE wall had a wide opening that connected the Dining Room to the Living Room (Room 504).

The Living Room (Room 504) was situated in the north corner of the pavilion. It was a rectangular room measuring 13 feet 3 inches by 15 feet 4 inches and had window openings on the NW and NE elevations. Both window openings had three steel casement sashes with transoms (type G). A doorway in the east corner of the SW wall led back into the hallway.

A small bedroom hallway was accessed through a doorway in the NE wall of the foyer. At the NW end of that hallway was a bedroom (Room 505) that measured 10 feet 2 inches by 13 feet 3 inches. The bedroom had two window openings on the NE wall and both had two casement sashes with transoms (type E). In the east corner of the SE wall was a small closet. The doorway to the hallway was in the south corner of the SE wall.

The doorway to the bathroom (Room 506) was in the NE wall of the bedroom hallway. The bathroom had an L plan, because the closet of the bedroom (Room 505) occupied the north corner of the room. The NE wall of the bathroom had a window opening with a single casement sash (type A). The bathroom was situated between the two bedrooms and equipped with standard utilities.

The second bedroom (Room 507) was on the SE side of the apartment, accessed through a doorway on the SE wall of the bedroom hallway. This bedroom was rectangular, measuring 10 feet 2 inches by 17 feet 3 inches. It had a window opening on the SW wall that had three casement sashes with transoms (type G). At the NE end of the bedroom was a large closet. The doorway to the bedroom hallway was located in the NW wall.

Apartment No. 6

Apartment No. 6 was a one-bedroom apartment located at the SE end of the Northeast Pavilion. The doorway to the apartment was located near the center of the NE Hallway and opened into a large foyer (Room 601). The foyer had two closets: one on the SE wall, and one on the NW wall. At the NE end of the foyer was a hallway that led SE toward the living area. There was a small linen closet on the SW wall of that hallway.

The Kitchen (Room 602) was the first doorway on the SW side of the hallway. The Kitchen measured 9 feet 1 inch by 11 feet 2 inches and was equipped with standard appliances. A narrow doorway at the NW end of the Kitchen opened into a closet. A doorway with a swinging door at the SE end of the Kitchen led to the Dining Alcove (Room 603).

The Dining Alcove (Room 603) was a feature of the one-bedroom apartments and measured 9 feet 1 inch by 12 feet 9 inches. Since the room occupied the south corner of the pavilion, there were window openings on both the SE and SW walls. The SW window opening had two casement sashes (type C), and the SE window opening had two casement sashes with transoms (type E). A wide opening in the NE wall led to the Living Room (Room 604) and created an open plan for the living quarters of the one-bedroom apartment.

The Living Room (Room 604) was a rectangular room measuring 12 feet 9 inches by 17 feet 3 inches. It was situated in the east corner of the pavilion and had two window openings on the SE wall and one window opening on the NE wall. All three window openings had two casement sashes with transoms (type E). The doorway from the Living Room to the hallway was located in the west corner of the NW wall.

A doorway in the NE wall of the hallway led to a small hallway with access to the bedroom and bathroom. That hallway had a small closet on the SE wall and the doorway to the bathroom (Room 605) was on the NE side of the hall.

The bathroom (Room 605) was typical for the building and had the standard amenities. There was a window opening on the NE wall with a single casement sash (type A).

The bedroom (Room 606) was located in the north corner of the apartment and was accessed through a doorway in the NW wall of the hallway. The bedroom was 13 feet 3 inches by 14 feet 8 inches. There was a window opening on the NE wall that had three casement sashes with transoms (type G). Since there was no closet in the bedroom, the closet in the adjacent hallway would have served the bedroom.

Second-Story Main Block

Northeast (NE) Hallway

The second story of the NE Hallway was accessed by the steel staircase, which ascended to the SE end of the hallway. At the second story the NE Hallway extended the full width of the building (NW to SE). There was a window opening on both the NW and SE elevations of the hallway, and both window openings had two casement sashes with transoms (type E). In the ceiling at the NW end of the hallway was a pull-down staircase that provided access to the attic of the building. The second story of the NE Hallway had doorways to the two second-story apartments in the Northeast Pavilion (Apartments No. 5 and No. 6) and served as the primary egress to those apartments. Like the first story, the interior masonry walls separated the hallway from the adjacent apartments.

Center Hallway

The staircase on the first story of the Center Hallway began on the SW wall and climbed to a landing that was constructed in the SE elevation projecting bay. Two steps on the NE side of the landing led to a second landing, and two more steps led NW to the second story. At the double landing there was a window opening on the SE wall of the projecting bay. That window opening had four casement sashes that were grouped together to form a band of windows (type H, fig. 21). At the second story was an open landing that was approximately 3 feet 6 inches wide by 7 feet 6 inches long. On the NE wall was the doorway to Apartment No. 7, and at the NW end of the landing was the doorway to Apartment No. 8.

Apartments No. 7 and No. 8 followed the same basic layout as Apartments No. 1 and No. 2. Both second-story apartments had an entrance Foyer and were planned with the Kitchen, Dining Room, and one bedroom on the NW side of the apartment and the Living Room, bathroom, and second bedroom on the SE side. However, there were some variations in the second-story apartments.

Apartment No. 7

Apartment No. 7 had the same plan as Apartment No. 1. However, the entrance doorway to Apartment No. 7 was located nearer to the SE side of the building than the doorway to Apartment No. 1. This created a difference from Apartment No. 1 in the location of the foyer and the configuration of the closets adjacent to the foyer. The foyer (Room 701) was constructed with two closets on opposite sides of the entrance doorway. The Kitchen (Room 702) was accessed from the Living Room and had no doorway from the foyer, as in Apartment No. 1. In comparison to Apartment No. 1, the reconfiguration of the closet space in Apartment No. 7 added a closet to the Kitchen and eliminated a closet in the Living Room (Room 707). The layout of the other rooms and the placement of the doorways and window openings was the same in Apartment No. 7 and No. 1.

Apartment No. 8

Apartment No. 8 was constructed following the same two-bedroom design as Apartment No. 2, but since Apartment No. 8 included floor space above the first-story Center Hallway, the apartment was larger. The foyer (Room 801) had a doorway to the Kitchen (Room 802) directly opposite the entry doorway, and a doorway at the SW end of the foyer led to the Living Room (Room 807).

The Kitchen (Room 802) was constructed above the first-story Center Hallway. It was approximately the same size as Apartment No. 2 with a similar layout and appliances. The extra square footage in Apartment No. 8 was partially used to install a grouping of closets between the Kitchen and the Dining Room (Room 803). Two closets were accessed from a passage hallway between the Kitchen and Dining Room, and would have served as the pantry for the Kitchen. The other closet in that section of the apartment was accessed from the Living Room (Room 807). The doorway from the Kitchen passageway to the Dining Room (Room 803) had a swinging door.

The Dining Room (Room 803) was typical of the two-bedroom apartment with two window openings on the NW elevation and a large doorway leading to the Living Room.

The bedroom (Room 804) on the NW side of Apartment No. 8 was larger than the others, measuring approximately 13 feet by 17 feet 6 inches. Like the other apartments of this design, the bedroom had two closets, which in this case were located on the SW wall of the room. Apartment No. 8 had two window openings on the NW elevation. The northernmost window opening had two casement sashes with transoms (type E), and the window opening near the west corner of the room had three casement sashes with transoms (type G). A doorway near the center of the SE wall led to the bedroom hallway, which accessed the second bedroom, the bathroom, and the Living Room.

As with the other rooms, the bedroom (Room 805) on the SE side of Apartment No. 8 was slightly larger, measuring about 10 feet 6 inches by 13 feet 3 inches. It had a window opening on the SE elevation that had three casement sashes with transoms (type G). The doorway to the hallway was located in the north corner of the NE wall.

The bathroom (Room 806) was about a foot wider than bathrooms in the other apartments but was otherwise constructed with the same materials and utilities.

The Living Room (Room 807) was also larger compared to other apartments of the same design. It was a rectangular room that measured 13 feet 3 inches by 18 feet 4 inches. The larger size was due in part to the elimination of the closets on the NE wall, which was possible since extra closets were installed between the Kitchen and Dining Room. The Living Room had a large window opening on the SE wall that had four casement sashes with transoms. Like Apartments No. 1, No. 2, and No. 7, the window opening was composed of three windows grouped together. The group included two casement sashes with transoms (type E) at the center of the window opening, and on either side of that were single casement sashes with transoms (type F). The window opening had a wide windowsill, and the window units were separated by 10-inch mullions. On the exterior of the building these three window openings were installed within the SE elevation cross gable. The doorway from the Living Room to the foyer was located in the north corner of the NE wall.

Southwest (SW) Hallway

On the second story the interior masonry walls separated the SW Hallway from Apartment No. 8 and the apartments in the adjacent pavilion. Like the NE Hallway, the second story of the SW Hallway extended the full width of the building (NW to E). It was accessed by the steel staircase that ascended to the SE end of the hallway. There was a window opening on both the NW and SE elevations of the hallway, and both window openings had two casement sashes with transoms (type E). The second story of the NE Hallway had a doorway to Apartment No. 9 at the NW end of the Southwest Pavilion and Apartment No. 10 at the SE end of the pavilion. The hallway served as the primary egress to those apartments and had a pull-down staircase to the attic of the building at the NW end of the hallway.

Second-Story Southwest Pavilion

Apartment No. 9

The two second-story apartments in the Southwest Pavilion were accessed from the second story of the SW Hallway of the Main Block. Apartment No. 9 was accessed through a doorway near the NW end of the hallway. It was a two-bedroom apartment that occupied the NW end of the pavilion. Apartment No. 9 had the same room plan as the two-bedroom apartment below it (Apartment No. 3), with one exception: The closet on the SE side of the foyer (Room 901) was deeper than the closet in the first-story apartment. This was due to the fact that there was no utility closet in the second-story hallway and that space was used for the foyer closet. Otherwise the room layout and doorway and window opening locations were the same in Apartment No. 9 and Apartment No. 3.

Apartment No. 10

Likewise, the plan of Apartment No. 10 at the SE end of the pavilion was the same as the one-bedroom apartment on the first story (Apartment No. 4). In this case there were no differences; the room plan and doorway and window opening locations were the same in the first-story and second-story apartments.

First-Story and Second-Story Elements

The architectural drawings of the Apartment Building indicated that the rooms in the apartments were constructed with similar materials and finished in the same manner. This was also true of the hallways and was evident from the extant original elements in the building. The original interior elements were constructed with high-quality materials that served the functional needs of the building while maintaining the intent of Atterbury's design on the interior.

Floors

The floors of the Apartment Building were constructed on top of the reinforced-concrete slabs that spanned from the steel framework to the masonry exterior walls. The architectural drawings indicated that the finished flooring on the first and second stories were laid on top of a 2-inch layer of nailable concrete (Appendix A, drawing 7 of 37). The exceptions to this appeared to be in the main hallways and the first-story vestibules in the Northeast Pavilion, but there were no detailed drawings of the subfloor in those spaces.

The finished floors in the rooms of the apartments were constructed with 3-inch tongue-and-groove boards that were generally installed lengthwise in the rooms. The wood floors were presumably fastened to the "nailcrete" subfloor with a hidden nailing system. The only apartment rooms that did not have wooden floors were the bathrooms.

All of the bathroom floors were covered with ¾-inch-square ceramic tiles. Both white and gray colored tiles were used and were laid in three-by-three squares of the same color. The squares (nine tiles in each) were arranged in an alternating pattern to form a checkerboard floor. The floors in the NE and SW Hallway utility rooms were tiled in the same pattern as the bathrooms.

Based on the extant examples, the floors of the closets were finished with concrete that was probably painted.

The floors in the main hallways and in the vestibules of the Northeast Pavilion (Rooms CO-01 and CO-09) were covered with terrazzo that was white with black flecks. Terrazzo was a composite floor material composed of concrete and marble chips that were finely ground.[165] The terrazzo floors in the hallways of the Apartment Building were set in 2-foot squares and were polished to a high sheen. This was one more example of Atterbury's use of modern materials to achieve both the function and the aesthetics desired in the Apartment Building.

---

[165] Harris, p. 988.

Walls

The architectural drawings indicated that the interior sections of the masonry walls were furred out and plastered. Between the exterior masonry and the interior wall there was an airspace that was approximately 1 inch wide, and 2-inch-by-2-inch furring was installed at 16 inches on center to form the frame for the interior walls. The plaster was presumably applied over metal lath in a three-coat system.

The interior partition walls were framed with dimensional lumber and finished with plaster. The typical wall framing was constructed with 2-inch-by-4-inch studs set 16 inches on center. However, the architectural drawings indicated that the walls enclosing the steel Lally columns that were installed down the center of each section of the building were framed with 2-inch-by-6-inch studs. The drawings further indicated that the walls around the chimney masses were framed with "metal furring,"[166] and finished with metal lath and plaster.

The interior stud walls were finished with metal lath and three coats of plaster. Based on the extant materials, the texture of the top coat of plaster was evidently different for various rooms. The existing walls were finished with a rough texture in the apartment hallways, living rooms, and dining rooms and had a smooth finish in the kitchens, bedrooms, and on the upper portions of the bathroom walls. The interior masonry walls that were constructed on either side of the main hallways were finished with a plaster skim coat.

The lower 4 feet of the bathroom walls were finished with "Keene's Cement" that was scored into 6-inch squares to create a faux-tile wainscoting. Keene's Cement was a quick-setting, high-strength finishing plaster that could be polished.[167] All four walls were finished with the faux-tile wainscoting, which was capped with a 2½-inch-wide wooden chair rail. The upper portions of the bathroom walls were finished with smooth plaster. The walls in the utility closets of the NE and SW Hallways were finished in the same manner.

The extant materials and architectural drawings indicated that trim elements were installed along the base of all interior walls. The walls in the apartment living quarters were generally trimmed with 6-inch wooden baseboards that had a quarter-round molding along the bottom edge and another quarter-round molding capping the baseboard. The wooden baseboard was meant to complement the wood floors and was used in those rooms with wood floors. Extant examples of this baseboard were found in the apartment hallways, living rooms, dining rooms, bedrooms, and even the closets. In addition, the drawings indicated that wooden baseboards were originally installed in the kitchens. Similar to most of the interior trim elements, the wooden baseboard was a medium brown color with a slight greenish tint.

The base trim in the bathrooms and hallways also complemented the flooring materials in those spaces. The bathrooms were trimmed with 6-inch ceramic tile along the base of the walls, which complemented the faux-tile walls above the base trim. The main hallways and the vestibule to the Bachelors' Apartment (Room CO-01) were constructed with 6-inch terrazzo base trim, which matched the terrazzo floor. Due to alterations to the building, it was not known what base trim was used in the open vestibule of the Northeast Pavilion (Room CO-09), but the drawings indicated that the floor was terrazzo, which suggests that the base trim was also terrazzo.

---

[166] Drawing Number 16 of 37 sheets, Grosvenor Atterbury Architect, John Tompkins, May 26, 1933.
[167] Harris, p. 559.

Ceilings

Based on extant evidence, the ceilings in most of the first-story rooms were finished with a skim coat of plaster. The ceilings in the main hallways appeared to have a coat of plaster that was applied over the concrete slabs that formed the structural floor for the second story. Likewise, the ceilings in the apartments appeared to be skimmed with a coat of plaster over the concrete slabs. The ceiling texture in the rooms generally matched the wall texture. In some rooms the structural steel I-beams encased in concrete were evident in the ceiling. These elements also appeared to be finished with a coat of plaster. The ceiling height in most of the first-story rooms was approximately 8 feet 6 inches. The ceilings in the bathrooms were dropped down lower in order to conceal the plumbing. The bathroom ceilings were framed with dimensional lumber and covered with metal lath and plaster.

The ceilings in the second-story rooms were also finished with plaster and were approximately 8 feet high. As previously described, the structural ceiling on the second story was constructed with steel joists. The architectural drawings indicated that furring was installed below the steel joists and that metal lath and plaster were installed below the furring.

Doorways

The interior elements of the entry doorways consisted of plain board surrounds with a slightly rounded edge and a quarter-round molding applied to the outer edge of the trim. On the sides of the doorways the trim stopped at the top of the terrazzo base trim and did not continue to the floor. In this application the terrazzo base trim served as a plinth block for the doorway surround.

The main hallways had some doorways that were unique to those spaces. At the SE end of each of the hallways was a doorway that opened into the back vestibule of the respective hallway. All three doorways were constructed with the same materials that included a plain board surround with a quarter-round molding on the outer edge. Each doorway had a wooden door with twelve lights over a single panel. The panel was trimmed with a quarter-round bead, and the muntins between the lights had a simple profile that consisted of a filleted quarter-round molding. The doors were hung with three brass butt hinges and equipped with automatic closers. The door had a brass door knob on the hallway side and a reproduction Suffolk-style latch on the vestibule side. The Suffolk-style latches were similar to those used on certain exterior doors.

The Center Hallway had an additional interior doorway near the NW end of the hallway. This doorway was essentially a partition between it and the façade entrance doorway and created an entry vestibule at the NW end of the Center Hallway. The doorway was constructed with a single door that was flanked by sidelights. Typical of the other hallway doorways, this doorway had plain wooden trim with quarter-round molding. The mullions between the door jambs and the flanking sidelights were also constructed with similar trim elements. The door was constructed with a wood core under a wood veneer and had twelve lights over one panel. The sidelights on either side of the door were built with four lights over one panel. The panels and the lights of this doorway had the same trim as the hall doorways previously described. Based on the extant doorway, the door had a Suffolk-style handles and a separate deadbolt lock with heart-shaped escutcheon on the vestibule side and a brass handle on the hallway side.

The doorways into the utility closets in the NE and SW Hallways were constructed in the same manner. The doorways were trimmed with a plain board surround and quarter-round molding that terminated at the terrazzo base trim. The doorways had two-panel wood doors with quarter-round beads along the stiles and rails. Both doors were hung with three brass hinges and had brass knobs with separate dead bolt locks. The doorways to the utility closets were constructed with marble thresholds that transitioned from the hall terrazzo floor to the closet tile floor.

The elements of the interior doorways at the Apartment Building were kept consistent for the apartments. The entrance doorways from the main hallways to the apartments were cut through the interior masonry walls. All of the doorways were constructed with molded-steel surround and had a steel threshold. The doorways to the apartments were constructed with two-panel wooden core doors with a veneered finish. The door panels were trimmed with quarter-round molding similar to other interior doorways. The entry doors were hung with three brass hinges and had brass knobs and separate deadbolt locks.

All other interior doorways shared a similar design, and the woodwork was a similar medium brown color with a greenish tint. The doorways were typically trimmed with plain boards and quarter-round moldings and had wooden thresholds, except for the bathrooms, which had marble thresholds. All interior apartment doors were the same type of two-panel wooden door previously described. The doors were sized for the particular doorways but were otherwise the same, including the double-action or swinging doors from the doorways between the kitchens and dining rooms (Appendix A, drawing 10 of 37). The doors were typically hung with three brass hinges and had brass knobs. Most doors had a separate keyhole with a brass escutcheon set below the doorknob. The extant evidence indicated that the door hardware in the kitchens and bathrooms was chrome plated and that the swinging doors had glass push plates instead of knobs.

The doorways leading to the apartment hallways were trimmed with the typical surround but had no doors. However, the doorways to the bedroom hallways did have doors. The wide openings between the dining rooms and living rooms were also constructed with the typical wood trim but had no doors.

Window Openings

The window openings at the Apartment Building were constructed with steel casement sashes and although there were several different configurations of the sashes, the interior elements on the first and second stories were very similar. Due to the thickness of the exterior walls, the interiors of the window openings were deep: on the first story the window openings were approximately 11 inches deep from the jamb to the plane of the interior plaster wall; on the second story the window openings were approximately 8 inches deep. At approximately 6 inches deep, the type-A single-sash window openings were shallower, because the exterior was framed with masonry elements and the sash was set deeper in the masonry wall. The construction of the window openings was best illustrated by the architectural drawings by Grosvenor Atterbury's firm (Appendix A and fig. 30).

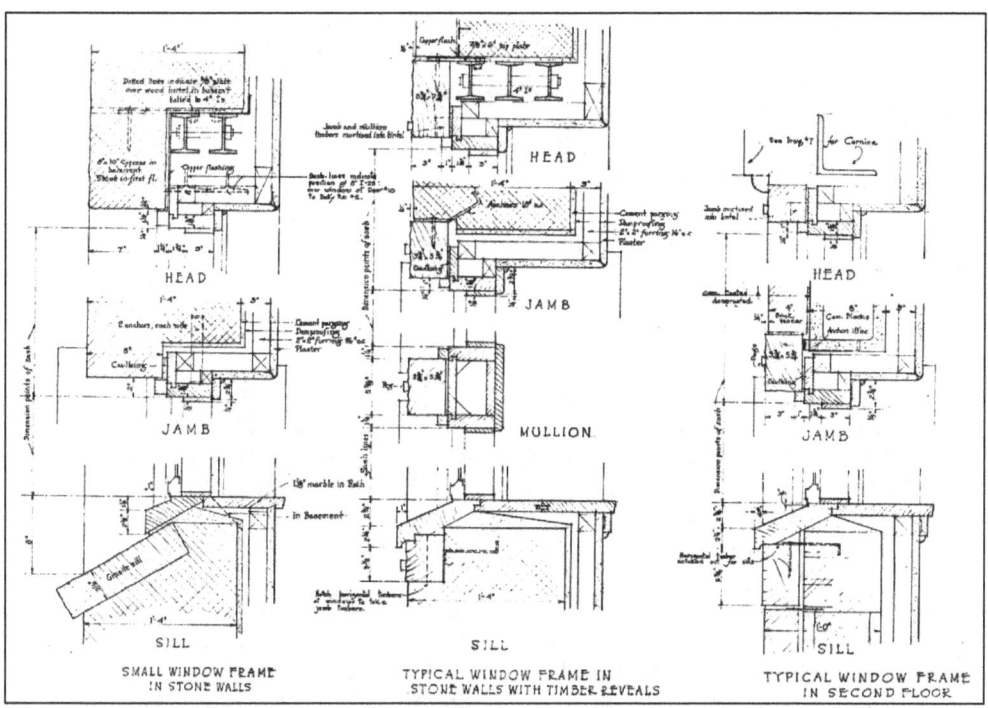

Figure 30. Apartment Building drawings depicting typical window opening elements, drawing number 9 of 37 sheets.

On both the first and second stories the interior window openings were generally constructed with wooden trim elements and plaster surrounds. The steel sashes were constructed with wooden jambs and heads that were face-trimmed with plain boards and quarter-round moldings encasing the sashes. The interiors of the window openings were framed out with 2-inch-by-2-inch furring like the interior walls. Between the quarter-round molding and the interior plaster walls the jambs and heads were finished with plaster. At both the jamb and head the transition from the plaster of the window opening and the plaster wall was constructed with a rounded edge. The windowsills were generally constructed with wood except in the bathrooms where they were constructed with marble. The front edges of the windowsills extended about 2 inches beyond the plain of the interior wall and were slightly rounded and beveled in profile. Likewise the sides of the windowsills overlapped the interior walls and had a slight bullnose. With the exception of the bathroom windows, a plain-board apron was installed below the windowsill with a quarter-round molding applied along the bottom edge of the apron to complete the window opening trim.

The original steel sashes are not extant and were not illustrated in detail in the architectural drawings. The one extant steel sash in the Power House would have been similar to some of the sashes in the Apartment Building and serves as a useful point of reference (fig. 36). Based on that example, the muntins in the steel sash most likely had a flat profile. In the typical window opening with two and three casement sashes, the mullions separating the sashes were probably flat. There was not enough evidence to determine whether the mullions had an applied interior wooden mullion. However, the window openings that had a grouping of type-F windows flanking a type-E window were constructed with wooden mullions between the center sashes and the flanking sashes. Locking handles were typically installed near the center of the inside stiles and would catch on the steel mullions. The casement adjusters were attached to the bottom rail and could be locked in position with an adjustable knob or wing nut. The steel transom bar separating the transom sashes from the casement sashes were probably flat on the interior, and the transom sashes most likely had a locking handle on the bottom rail. Like the casement sashes below them, each transom sash within a window opening was separated from the adjacent transom sash with a steel mullion.

The interior elements of the various types of windows were constructed in a similar manner and with similar materials.

Staircases

The staircases in the NE and SW Hallways were laid out in a similar manner and essentially mirrored each other. The Center Hallway staircase ascended along the SW wall of the hallway to the double landing and then returned along the NE wall to the second-story landing. The standard width of the staircases was 3 feet 7 inches and the Center Hallway staircase was 4 feet 1 inch wide at the double landing. All three staircases were constructed with the same types of materials and were open to the stairwell on the second story.

The main structure of the each staircase was steel that was apparently secured to the steel and masonry structure of the Apartment Building. The steel stringers extended from the first-story floor level to the second story, and angle brackets attached to the stringers carried the treads and risers. L-shaped pieces of steel that supported the treads and formed the risers were bolted to the angle brackets at each step. The treads were constructed with 1½-inch-thick terrazzo, and the steel support was bent to form the nose of the tread. The landings were also constructed with terrazzo that was 2½ inches thick. Steel molding with a cyma reversa profile was applied along the top and bottom flanges of the stringers. A steel base component with an applied cavetto molding ran along the inside wall of the staircase and leveled off at the second story where it terminated.

The staircase balustrades were constructed with ⅝-inch square balusters set 4 inches apart and 3½-inch square newel posts with rounded caps. The newel posts on the Center Hallway staircase landing and at the second story of all the staircases dropped down below the ceiling and had a rounded drop finial. The staircase railing was capped with a wooden handrail with a molded top. The top of the railing was set at 2 feet 8 inches above the stair treads and at 2 feet 10 inches above the floor level on the second story where the balustrade extended around the open stairwell.

Built-in Features

The architectural drawings of the Apartment Building indicated that all of the kitchens were constructed with one built-in cabinet unit. Though the kitchens have been altered since then and the original cabinets were not extant the drawings did provide some details (Appendix A, drawing number 13 of 37 sheets). The cabinets extended from floor to ceiling and were typically 3 feet 6 inches wide. The lower portion of the built-in had two cabinets with single-panel doors and a single drawer above each cabinet. The lower portion of the unit was 1 foot 9 inches deep and was topped with an ash shelf. The wall space between the lower and upper cabinets was covered with an ash backsplash. The upper portion of the unit had two cabinets that were 1 foot 3 inches deep. Each of the cabinet doors had a wooden frame and eight glass lights. The drawings indicated that the base and the top of the built-in cabinets were trimmed with simple wooden moldings.

The bathrooms were constructed with built-in medicine cabinets. Each cabinet was recessed into the wall above the bathroom sink and the base of the cabinet was flush with the top of the faux tile wainscoting. The drawings indicated that there was an open shelf below the cabinet that was also within the recess. The medicine cabinet presumably had a mirrored door with molded trim. Though the medicine cabinets have been replaced, some of the original recesses were extant in the bathrooms.

Fireplaces

The Apartment Building was constructed with one fireplace that was located on the SW wall of the Bachelors' Apartment Living Room. The fireplace was vented by the NE chimney that was constructed with a terra-cotta-lined flue. Detailed architectural drawings by Atterbury's firm and extant elements provided information on one of the few interior decorative details of the Apartment Building (Appendix A, drawing number 33 of 37 sheets).

The fireplace opening was 4 feet wide by 4 feet 8 inches high by 4 feet deep. Like the main structure of the chimney stack, the fireplace and the original hearth were also constructed with brick. Approximately 4 inches of the brick facing was exposed, and a wooden mantelpiece surrounded the brick work.

The mantelpiece was constructed with plain boards for the side elements and a decorative lintel and mantelshelf. The side elements were 7 inches wide and mortised into the lintel. Two pegs were installed in the lintel above each of the side elements but the detail drawings indicated that the pegs were decorative. The lintel and mantelshelf combined were 1 foot high. The lintel was decorated with a chamfer that started at the center of the lintel and was drawn out to a chamfer stop on either side. The center of the chamfer formed a point and both ends of the chamfer stopped near the respective side elements of the mantelpiece. The mantelpiece was completed with a narrow shelf with a decorative frieze and a molded cornice above the lintel. The mantelshelf frieze was carved in a scalloped design, which was capped with a cyma recta molding. The corners of the mantelshelf made a shallow return to the plaster wall. The wooden mantelpiece was stained to match the other wood trim in the apartment.

Utilities and Appliances

The extant elements indicated that many of the original utilities and appliances have been replaced over the past seventy-five years. Certainly the original appliances in the kitchens and most of the original bathroom fixtures have been upgraded. It appeared likely that a majority of the original plumbing and electrical utilities were still in place but that these were also upgraded with additional plumbing and wiring. The architectural drawings from 1933 depicted the kitchen appliances, bathroom fixtures, and included plumbing and electrical plans (Appendix A, drawing numbers 13, 25, 26 and 27 of 37 sheets).

The kitchens were typically equipped with a sink, a range, a refrigerator, and the built-in cabinet previously described. The sink was approximately 4 feet wide and combined a washboard with a deep tub. The kitchens had an electric range with three burners and a small oven on one side. The standard refrigerator was also electric and was small by modern standards. The drawings suggested that these four elements were generally located in the four corners of the kitchen, but in some cases two appliances were arranged on the same wall due to the configuration of the doorways and kitchen closets.

The standard bathroom utilities included a single sink, a bathtub, and a toilet. Other built-in elements included a soap dish above the bathtub and a toilet paper holder adjacent to the toilet. Every bathroom had a ceiling vent that was apparently connected to the vents that pierced roofs.

The NE and SW Hallway utility closets were constructed with deep sinks that remain extant. The lighting fixtures for the utility closets were wall mounted over the doorway.

The heating plan for the first and second stories indicated that the apartments were equipped with standard cast-iron steam radiators. The radiators were heated by the coal-fired steam boiler located in the basement of the Southwest Pavilion. The plans indicated that the steam pipes and returns were installed within the exterior walls, and within a pipe chase constructed on the SE side of the SW chimney. Most of the rooms had a single radiator sized for the square footage of the room, and a few of the larger living rooms had two radiators.

The main electrical panel for the Apartment Building was located in the Battery-Machine and Generator Room in the basement of the Northeast Pavilion. The wiring and lighting plans of the first and second stories depicted the locations of the ceiling and wall fixtures and the switches and outlets. The plans indicated that most rooms had a ceiling fixture mounted near the center of the room and that the bathrooms had wall-mounted fixtures above the sinks and medicine cabinets. Wall-mounted fixtures were also installed over the sinks in the bedrooms of the Bachelors' Apartment. The plans also suggested that two light fixtures, probably sconces, were mounted on the wall above the fireplace. Though the existing lighting fixtures, switches, and outlets appear to retain the original locations, additional wiring had been added and many of the original elements were removed and replaced with modern utilities.

Attic Story

The attic story of the Apartment Building was accessed via pull-down staircases located in the second story of the NE and SW Hallways. Both pull-down staircases were installed in the ceiling at the NW end of the respective hallways. They were wooden staircases that were hinged at one end and moved on counterweighted arms.

The attic of the Apartment Building was unfinished and open to the structural steel framing, which was covered with a protective red-orange paint. The brick chimney stacks that were corbelled below the roof line were evident at either end of the Main Block. The floor of the attic was open to the steel joists and insulation installed between the joists. An extensive catwalk that ran down the center of each section of the building and had branches to the window openings was installed on top of the floor joists. The wood framing and sheathing of the cross-gable ends was also exposed at the attic story, as was the rough framing of the gable-end window openings. The ceiling of the attic was also open to the steel framing elements and the underside of the "nailcrete" sheathing panel.

The steel framing and "nailcrete" sheathing of shed dormer windows openings were exposed at the attic story and unfinished. A beveled wooden shelf was constructed inside the dormer window opening, and a copper lining was installed over that. The copper-lined shelf would have kept any wind-driven rain from entering the interior of the building.

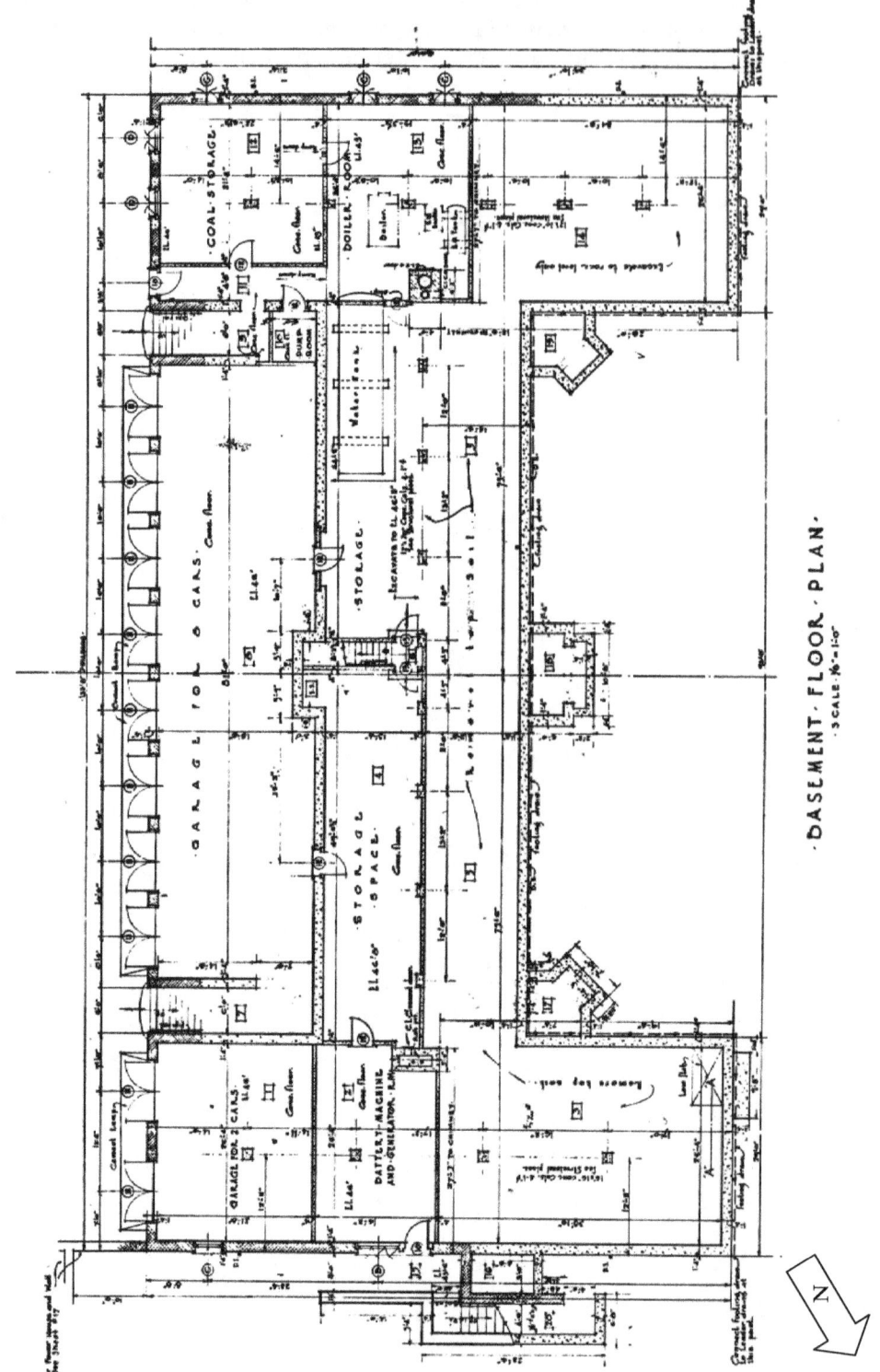

Figure 31. Apartment Building, Grosvenor Atterbury Architect, John Tompkins, Basement Floor Plan, May 26, 1933; (drawing number 1 of 37 sheets, this figure represents a portion of the original drawing reproduced at half-size, not to scale).

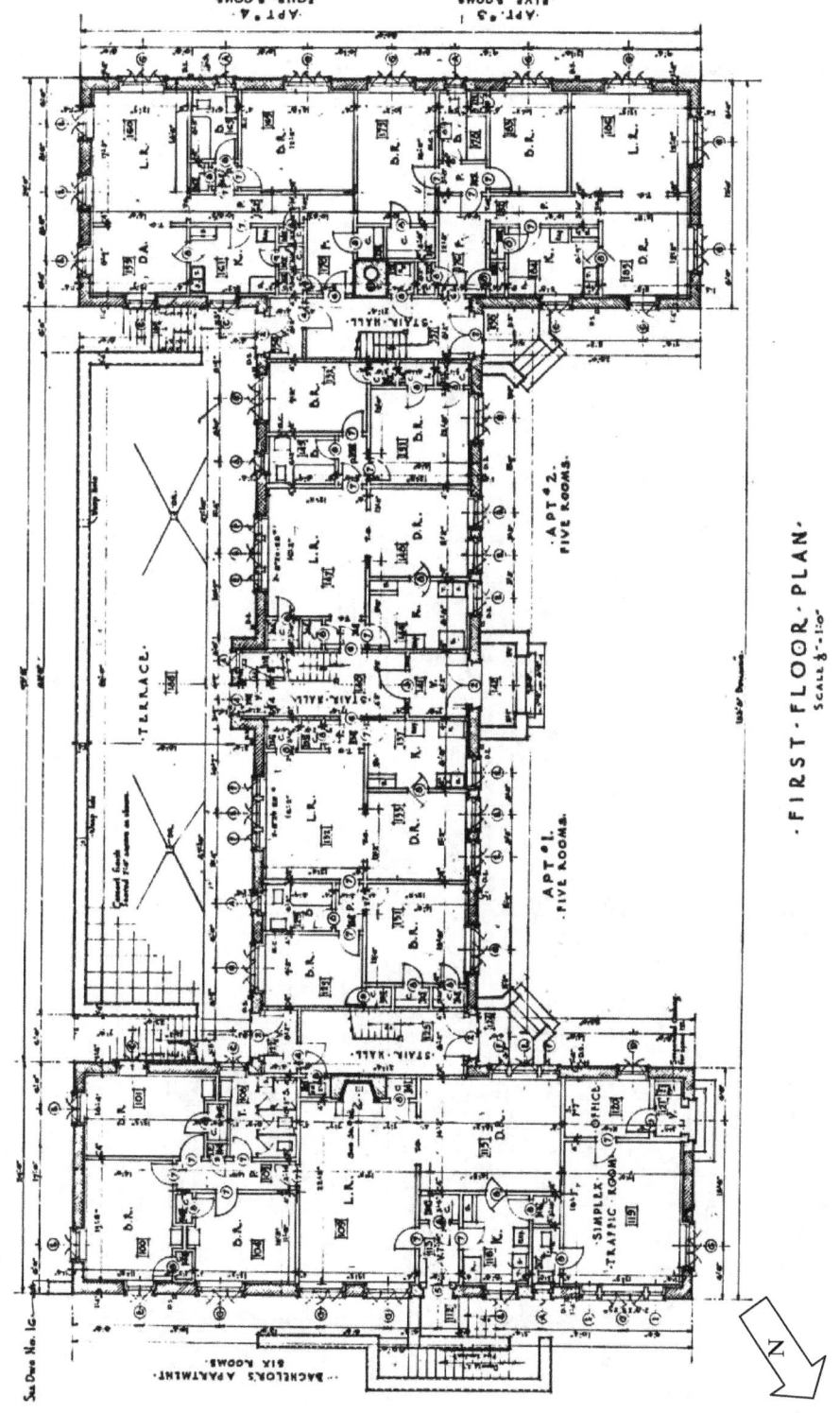

Figure 32. Apartment Building, Grosvenor Atterbury Architect, John Tompkins, First Floor Plan, May 26, 1933; (drawing number 2 of 37 sheets, this figure represents a portion of the original drawing reproduced at half-size, not to scale).

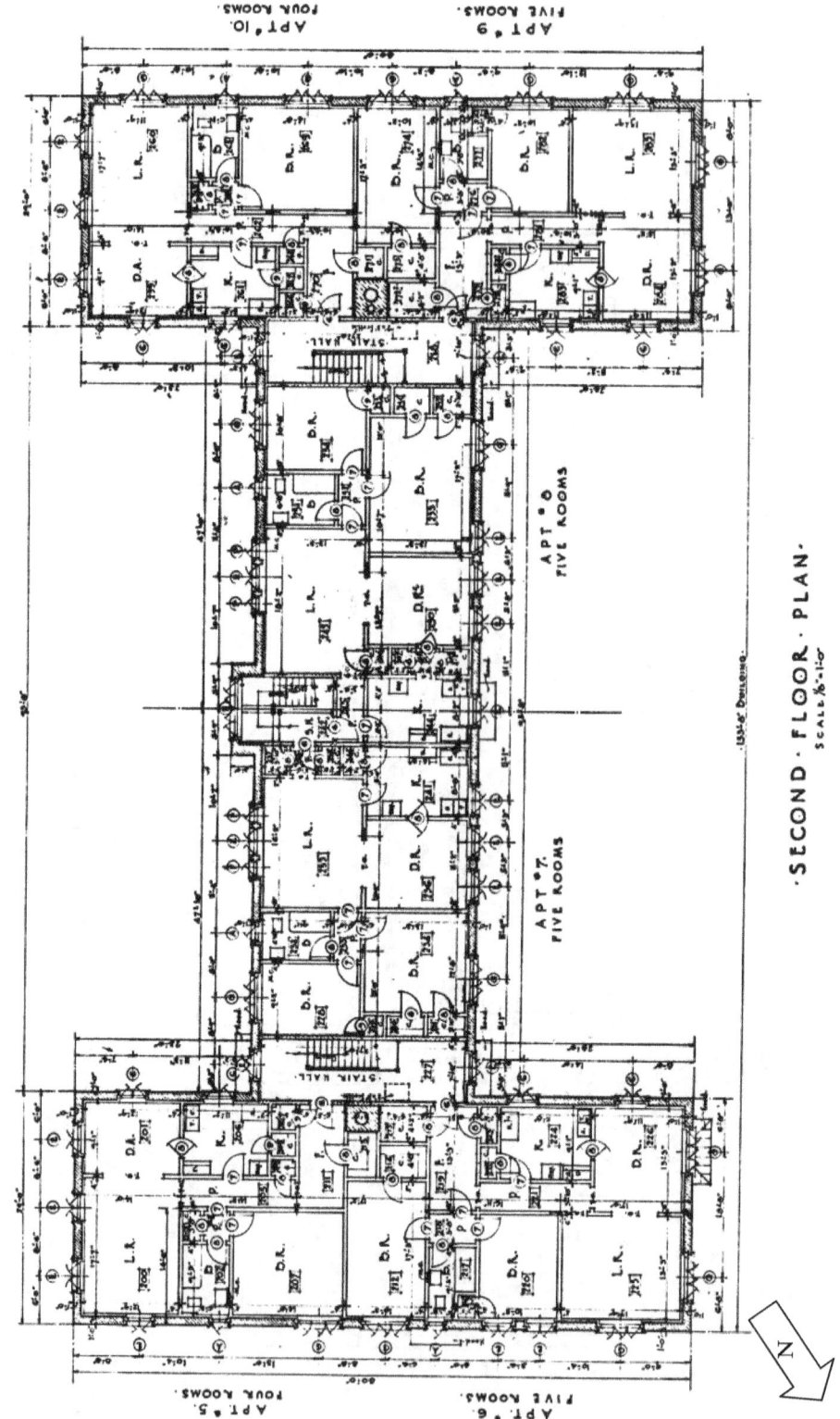

Figure 33. Apartment Building, Grosvenor Atterbury Architect, John Tompkins, Second Floor Plan, May 26, 1933; (this figure represents a portion of the original drawing reproduced at half-size, not to scale).

Power House

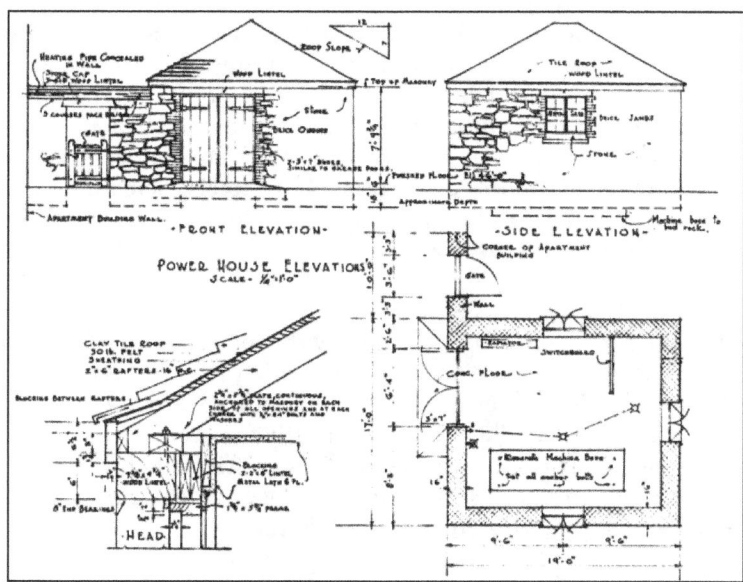

Figure 34. Power House, Naval Radio Station, Winter Harbor, ME. (drawing number 17 of 37 sheets, this figure represents a portion of the original drawing reproduced at half-size, not to scale).

The Power House was a masonry structure that supported the function of the Apartment Building and was built in concert with the main building. The architectural plans prepared by Atterbury's firm in 1933 included drawings of the Power House, as well as other ancillary buildings (Appendix A and fig. 34). Based on the progress reports and photographs, it was evident that the Power House was constructed at the same time as the Apartment Building (Appendix B). Indeed, Oliver Taylor's report dated December 28, 1933 noted that the Power House was complete except for the roof.[168] Later photographs indicated that the structure was completed when the Apartment Building was ready for occupancy.

At the basement story a masonry wall that connected the Apartment Building to the Power House abutted the east corner of the Northeast Pavilion. The wall was constructed with granite and brick that was laid in horizontal bands to match the exterior masonry of the Apartment Building. The top of the wall was constructed with five courses of brick and bluestone coping. The architectural drawings indicated that heating pipes between the two buildings were concealed within the top brick portion of the wall. A doorway in the wall led from the SE side of the Apartment Building to the NE side perimeter walkway. In keeping with the Apartment Building, the lintel of the doorway was constructed with pecky cypress. The drawings depicted a wooden gate installed in that doorway. The wall extended 10 feet from the SE elevation of the pavilion to the Power House and was integral with the SW elevation of the Power House.

---

[168] Taylor to Albright, Dec. 28, 1933; (copy courtesy of Rockefeller Archive Center).

The Power House measured 17 feet wide by 19 feet long. The exterior walls of the masonry building were constructed with granite and brick laid in the same manner as the Apartment Building. The SW elevation or front of the building had a large doorway that was framed with brick and had a pecky cypress lintel. A concrete ramp with a shallow incline was installed in front of the doorway. The doorway had a set of double doors that were constructed with splined vertical planks on a Z-braced frame. Like the garage doors, each of the Power House door leaves had three strap hinges and a Suffolk-type handle. The other three elevations were constructed with a single window opening centered on the respective elevation. The window openings were framed with brick jambs, pecky cypress lintels, and granite sills. All three of those window openings had two steel casement sashes with six lights each. The sashes were similar to the type-C windows in the Apartment Building, and as previously described, one original casement is extant on the SE elevation of the Power House (fig. 35).

The hipped roof of the Power House was framed with wooden 2-inch-by-6-inch rafters and ceiling joists. The roof was sheathed with boards, which were covered with a layer of 30-pound roofing felt. The roof surfaces were covered with terra-cotta clay tile, and the hips and ridge were covered with clay tiles made specifically for those applications. The cornice below the roof line was constructed with a plain wooden frieze that was 6 inches high. Like the exterior walls, the design and materials of the Power House roof were constructed to complement the roofs of the adjacent Apartment Building.

The interior of the Power House was one room that was roughly square. The floor was poured concrete and had a concrete pad for the Power House equipment. The interior of the masonry walls were apparently parged with plaster. The architectural drawings showed that the interiors of the windows and doorway were framed with dimensional lumber and covered with metal lath and plaster. The evidence of the extant window opening and sash indicated that the steel casement sashes had curved latching handles on the inside stiles and casement adjusting bars attached to the bottom rail (fig. 36). The ceiling of the room was framed with 2-inch-by-6-inch joists and was finished with metal lath and plaster. The interior of the Power House was utilitarian and the finish was probably similar to that of the original basement rooms in the Apartment Building.

The Power House was one of seven structures including the Apartment Building and the two radio towers that made up the original Schoodic Point Naval Radio Station complex. The architectural drawings by Grosvenor Atterbury's firm included the Apartment Building, Power House, Pump House, Intercept Building, and Radio Compass Station (Appendix A), and a map of U.S. Naval Radio Station dated June 30, 1935 depicted the arrangement of the structures (fig. 7).

Figure 35. Power House, SE elevation, window opening with brick jamb, granite sill, pecky cypress lintel, and steel casement sashes, 2008.

Figure 36. Power House, SE elevation, interior elements of window opening, 2008.

Alterations

Introduction

The Apartment Building was completed in December 1934 and commissioned by the U.S. Navy on February 28, 1935.[169] The U.S. Navy used the building until it was turned over to the National Park Service in 2002.[170] Comparison of the existing building and the original drawings, as well as research of historic photographs and an understanding of building alterations, showed that the Apartment Building has had few significant alterations since it was completed in 1934.

Records of building maintenance and rehabilitation projects were reviewed to help determine what alterations were made to the building. The records described routine maintenance and larger renovation projects. The most significant exterior alterations during the U.S. Navy tenure were completed in 1981 when the window sashes were replaced. Modifications to the interior spaces included changes to the basement rooms and the renovation of the apartment kitchens and bathrooms. These alterations as well as others were documented in the records and correspondence of the Navy and are presented in the following table. In addition to the information gleaned from documents, the following section includes alterations based on the current investigation of building materials.

U.S. Navy Occupancy

During the sixty-eight years the U.S. Navy occupied the Apartment Building, its primary use was as housing for the Naval Radio Station personnel and later the Naval Security Group personnel. The Northeast Pavilion did include the two-room suite for the Office and Simplex Traffic Room, but the needs of the operations soon outgrew that space and some operations were relocated to the basement of the building. The date of that change is not known, but it probably occurred in circa 1950 when Cold War activities at the Naval Radio Station intensified. Further alterations in the Northeast Pavilion joined those two operations rooms to the first-story apartment. In addition, the first-story apartment in the Northeast Pavilion was originally designated as the Bachelors' Apartment but at some point became the "Commanding Officer's Quarters," which for purposes of consistency will be referred to as the Commanding Officer's Apartment. The date of that change in use is also not known. Other alterations by the Navy did not significantly impact the layout of the first- and second-story apartments in the Apartment Building. Most of the electrical wiring has been upgraded and augmented by additional wall-mounted wiring, and the heating systems have been rehabilitated (see subsequent section "Current Physical Description"). There have been no significant alterations to the Apartment Building since it was transferred to the National Park Service.

---

[169] *A History of the U.S. Navy at Schoodic Peninsula*; p. 5.
[170] *Schoodic General Management Plan Amendment*; p. 2.

Brief Chronology 1935 through 2002

Date	Description and Comments	Source of Information
circa 1950	Bachelors' Apartment Living Room wooden fireplace surround is replaced with granite. This may have coincided with the change from the Bachelors' Apartment to the Commanding Officer's Apartment.	NR Registration Form, Continuation Sheet, Section 7, page 4; based on building history from Commander E.F. Williamson.
April 12, 1950	Alterations to the heating system including new thermostats in apartments and new temperature-control valve in Boiler Room.	Plans on file at Winter Harbor, Map Case C, drawer 2.
May 10, 1954	Alteration to Terrace: new quarry-tile terrace installed over a membrane and setting bed; new flashing below bluestone wall coping; new floor drains; new flashing under step at south doorway (D105) to Terrace; new wall flashing (SE elevation of building). The new terrace floor replaced concrete surface installed during construction.	Plans on file at Winter Harbor, Map Case C, drawer 2.
June 24, 1965	Interior alterations: new access hatch stairway to attic; revised wiring and new electrical fixtures (exterior and main hallway fixtures retained); plumbing and heating revisions (not specified).	Plans on file at Winter Harbor, Map Case C, drawer 2.
June 24, 1965	Bathroom renovations: new toilets; new tile around bathtub and shower enclosures; new recessed wall cabinets with lights.	Plans on file at Winter Harbor, Map Case C, drawer 2.
June 24, 1965	Kitchen renovations: remove all existing cabinets, counters, ranges, refrigerators, and floor coverings; prepare floor and install new resilient flooring, floor and wall cabinets, countertops, sinks, and range hoods; existing range and refrigerator were reinstalled; new accordion folding doors were installed in the pantry doorways.	Plans on file at Winter Harbor, Map Case C, drawer 2.
1976	Heating system repairs. The current baseboard fin-tube radiators that replaced the cast-iron radiators may have been installed at this time, but the exact date was not known.	Plans on file at Winter Harbor, Map Case C, drawer 2. See subsequent section "Current Physical Description."
1976	Terrace, flashing repairs: existing quarry tile, bedding, and gravel removed; existing water-proof membrane repaired and surface recovered; surface tested by flooding; new copper water stops installed at expansion joint and perimeter, to be soldered to existing copper flashing; bedding and quarry tile reinstalled.	Plans on file at Winter Harbor, Map Case C, drawer 2.

Date	Description and Comments	Source of Information
circa 1977	Alterations to the steps on either side of the Terrace included removing the bluestone steps and replacing them with concrete covered with metal treads. The brick risers were retained and appeared to have been repointed. The date of this work is not known but may have coincided with the other Terrace work in 1976 or possibly the work in 1979 subsequently cited. Had it occurred after 1988, it would have required review by the Maine SHPO, and no such review or approval was documented.	On-site observations and conclusions based on documentary evidence.
1978	Interior water line replaced.	Plans on file at Winter Harbor, Map Case C, drawer 2.
1979	Exterior masonry repointing; included replacing slabs at doors to Terrace; re-mortar under coping stones; two pier replacements	Plans on file at Winter Harbor, Map Case C, drawer 2.
circa 1980	Basement alterations: former Battery-Machine and Generator Room partitioned into two office rooms and a hallway (Rooms 002, 003, and 004); northernmost bay of eight-bay garage was partitioned off to serve as the ordnance armory (Room 006); former Storage Space at NE end of Main Block partitioned into two rooms that are currently the Telephone Room (Room 007) and the Laundry Room (Room 009); former Coal Storage Room partitioned for offices and storage (Rooms 016, 017, and 017a); a portion of the Boiler Room was also partitioned off (Room 014a).	Based on existing building conditions. This represents the existing configuration of the basement, but it was not known whether all alterations took place at the same time. See subsequent section "Current Physical Description."
March 1981	Window sash replacement: the rough openings were not altered, but all sashes were replaced; all steel casement sashes and the two fixed sashes (type I) were replaced with aluminum-clad sashes with removable muntin grills; snap-in muntin grills were designed to replicate the original number of sash lights; the new sashes did not include transom sashes, and therefore those windows that originally had transoms were replaced with taller sashes to fill the opening. For the groups of three sashes, the center sash in the replacement group was fixed (type G and type B) and the group of four casement sashes on the SE projecting bay (type H) was replaced with a group of three sashes with the center sash fixed.	Plans on file at Winter Harbor, Map Case C, drawer 2. On-site observations. See subsequent section "Current Physical Description."

Date	Description and Comments	Source of Information
September 5, 1983	Replace exterior doors SE elevation using insulated metal doors with tempered insulating safety glass. Doors measured 3 feet wide by 6 feet 8 inches high by 1¾ inches thick. The doors replaced the original double leaf doors leading from the NE and SW Hallways to the Terrace and also the door from the Center Hallway to the Terrace. The replacement doors from the NE and SW Hallways were constructed with sidelights.	Plans on file at Winter Harbor, Map Case C, drawer 2. See subsequent section "Current Physical Description."
circa 1985	Alterations to and expansion of Commanding Officer's Apartment including addition of doorway between Dining Room (CO-07) and former operations room (CO-10); small bathroom in Room CO-10 removed and kitchen enlarged; doorway from kitchen (CO-11) to vestibule (CO-01) closed off; minor kitchen renovation; laundry and bathroom added at NW end of apartment (CO-08 and CO-09); exterior doorway, NW elevation of Northeast Pavilion closed off.	Conclusions drawn from on-site observations of physical evidence and documentary evidence. See subsequent section "Current Physical Description."
April 2, 1984 and 1985	Fireplace repairs in Commanding Officer's Apartment. A chimney fire required that a portion of the chimney be rebuilt, and the original fireplace mantel that had been saved by Navy personnel was apparently reinstalled at that time.	Plans on file at Winter Harbor, Map Case C, drawer 2. NR Registration Form, which indicated that the chimney fire occurred in 1985.
May 12, 1988	Building 1 (Apartment Building) and Building 2 (Power House) at the Naval Security Activity Group, Winter Harbor, are determined eligible for listing on the National Register of Historic Places by the Maine State Historic Preservation Officer (SHPO).	Commander, D.J. Holen to Earle G. Shettleworth, Jr., Maine SHPO, May 25, 1988; ACAD archives.
May 25, 1988	Proposed renovations to Apartment Building include alterations to kitchens, bathrooms, exterior masonry, and roof repairs.	Commander, D.J. Holen to Earle G. Shettleworth, Jr., SHPO, May 25, 1988; ACAD archives.
January 3, 1989	Drawings of proposed exterior rehabilitation forwarded to Maine State Historic Preservation Officer.	Commander, D.J. Holen to Earle G. Shettleworth, Jr., SHPO, Jan. 3, 1989; ACAD archives.

Date	Description and Comments	Source of Information
1988 to 1989	Interior renovations to kitchens: new range hoods; new dishwashers; new cabinets; new countertops; new vinyl flooring and vinyl base trim; new ceramic backsplash; new bi-fold pantry doors; new trim elements; stoves and refrigerators reused.	Plans on file at Winter Harbor, Map Case C, drawer 2. See subsequent section "Current Physical Description."
1988 to 1989	Interior renovations to bathrooms: new vanity and vanity laminate top; new fiberglass tub surround; new ceramic base tiles; new wood chair rail around wall; patch Keene's Cement plaster walls to match existing; new gypsum wall board surfaces (where specified); cut and patch ceiling to provide for new exhaust ductwork.	Plans on file at Winter Harbor, Map Case C, drawer 2. See subsequent section "Current Physical Description."
October and November 1989	Exterior rehabilitation: seal cracks in foundation wall and ledge surface with mastic sealant; install new perimeter drainage and connect existing downspouts and drainpipes to new system; repoint exterior mortar joints; install new bond breaker tape between wood timbers and masonry; clean exterior masonry; install new water-repellent coating on exterior masonry; replace cracked, broken, and/or missing roof tiles (proposed use of tiles from Building 3 for repairs); replace lowest sheet of closed valley copper flashing; line existing gutters and downspouts.	Plans on file at Winter Harbor, Map Case C, drawer 2. Specifications as noted on Apartment Building drawings, Naval Facilities Engineering Command. See subsequent section "Current Physical Description."
August 10, 1992	Exterior repairs: copper gutter and down spout repairs.	Plans on file at Winter Harbor, Map Case C, drawer 2.
No date, circa 1995	New vinyl floor in Commanding Officer's Apartment: in kitchen remove two layers of existing flooring and install new flooring; in bathroom remove one layer of vinyl tile and install new flooring.	Plans on file at Winter Harbor, Map Case C, drawer 2.
August 7, 1996	Correspondence to Maine SHPO request approval of project to replace bluestone steps at three entrances on NW elevation of Apartment Building. Letter also requests approval of new roofing material on flat roof of Power House.	J. Miller, Environmental Coordinator, to James Hewatt for SHPO, August 7, 1996; ACAD archives.
August 13, 1996	Requests for rehabilitation of Apartment Building entrance steps and Power House roof approved by SHPO. The projects were evidently completed during the fall of 1996.	Earle G. Shettleworth, Jr. to J. Miller, August 13, 1996; ACAD archives.

Date	Description and Comments	Source of Information
August 14, 1996	SHPO approved request for the installation of new telephone lines to the Apartment Building and the Power House, which included boring conduit cores through the foundation of the Apartment Building. SHPO specified matte black or red-brown conduit.	Earle G. Shettleworth, Jr. to J. Miller, August 14, 1996; ACAD archives.
May 28, 1997	Request to replace the membrane and surface material of the Terrace at the Apartment Building was approved and considered to have no adverse effect on the condition that the Terrace is repaved with the "green slate" submitted as a sample with the proposal.	Earle G. Shettleworth, Jr. to J. Miller, May 28, 1997; ACAD archives.
September 8, 1998	SHPO correspondence in response for clarification of slate sample for Terrace rehabilitation. SHPO confirms the approval of the "green slate" as the best blend with the historic building. Upon approval, theterrace resurfacing project was presumably completed during the fall of 1998.	Earle G. Shettleworth, Jr. to Louis Plaud, Contract Surveillance Representative, September 8, 1998; ACAD archives.
May 23, 2001	Correspondence to Maine SHPO requesting concurrence on proposed replacement of damaged or missing roof tiles. Plan for replacement included: five new cap roof tiles; reinstall existing rake tiles that had lifted; install 46 feet of cap tiles; replace broken tiles; and install new tiles.	E.F. Williamson, Commander, to Earle G. Shettleworth, Jr., May 23, 2001; ACAD archives.
July 24, 2001	Correspondence to Maine SHPO enclosing report, prepared by Theriault/Landmann Associates, describing the condition of the Apartment Building and defining areas of critical repair. Phase II would consist of further assessment and development of plans and specifications for preservation.	E.F. Williamson to Earle G. Shettleworth, Jr., July 24, 2001; ACAD archives.
August 3, 2001	SHPO's response noted that the report was reviewed and recommendations posed no adverse effect on the building and were within the Secretary of the Interior's Standards.	Earle G. Shettleworth, Jr. to E.F. Williamson, August 3, 2001; ACAD archives.
December 20, 2001	Correspondence to Maine SHPO forwarding Phase II information and reports including "Limited Historical Restoration Plans," masonry restoration specifications; parapet wall guardrail replacement design and specifications; photographic documentation.	E.F. Williamson to Earle G. Shettleworth, Jr., December 20, 2001; ACAD archives.

Date	Description and Comments	Source of Information
February 7, 2002	SHPO is opposed to parapet railing finials and does not approve of diamond panels; requested simulation of new railing.	Earle G. Shettleworth, Jr. to E.F. Williamson, February 7, 2002; ACAD archives.
March 2002	SHPO approves color, texture, and size of roof tiles for Apartment Building roof repairs based on samples submitted by the Navy. Sample tiles were evidently from Building 3, as proposed in 1988 (letter dated March 12, 2001, but references a June 18, 2001 correspondence and was probably written in March 2002).	Earle G. Shettleworth, Jr. to E.F. Williamson, March 2002. Also see pervious citation dated May 23, 2001. ACAD archives.
June 12, 2002	SHPO made a conditional finding of no adverse effect for the parapet railing based on the simulation.	Earle G. Shettleworth, Jr. to E.F. Williamson, June 12, 2002; ACAD archives.
2002	The Terrace parapet wall was dismantled and rebuilt according to specifications.	
July 1, 2002	Naval Security Group Activity, Winter Harbor transferred to the National Park Service, including the Apartment Building.	*Schoodic General Management Plan Amendment*; p. 2

Landscape

Though not as well documented as building alterations, the changes to the landscape at the Apartment Building site were evident in historic photographs, maps, and by observation of the present conditions. Historic photographs and maps from 1935 depicted the planned landscape around the building with lawns, shrubs, and trees, as well as a more densely wooded site beyond the immediate setting. However, documentation and present conditions showed the evolution of the surrounding landscape.

The road to the Apartment Building approached from the northeast. Next to the NW elevation of the building was a circular driveway with trees and lawn in the center circle. At the bottom of the circular drive was the NW elevation courtyard, and the road continued to the west of the circle. There was also a driveway to the large service court adjacent to the SE elevation of the building. Both the circular driveway and the large SE service court appeared to follow the original layout of the site as documented by historic photographs and plans, and were not significantly altered. The driveway surfaces were most likely repaved with bituminous macadam that was similar to the historic paving material.

The most significant changes to the immediate landscape of the Apartment Building were apparently the removal of shrubs and trees. The historic photographs taken soon after the building was completed depicted the NW elevation and driveway circle with an abundance of shrubs and both mature and young trees that were planted according to the landscape plan (see previous section "Construction; Landscape"). The natural cycle of the flora and the increased use of the site have resulted in a significant decrease in the shrubs and trees around the building. More specifically, the impact on the NW elevation can be observed by comparison of photographs taken in 1935 and in circa 1990 (figs. 37 and 38). Due to the age of the trees, more have been removed since the circa-1990 photograph, making that elevation even more sparsely planted.

The overall appearance of the site was certainly impacted by the construction of additional buildings near the Apartment Building. The construction of Buildings No. 8 and No. 10 encroached on the surrounding landscape and also altered the picturesque view from the Apartment Building out over Schoodic Harbor. Another change to the site was the installation of a tennis court north of the driveway. These changes had taken place by 1944 and represent just the beginning of the expansion of the Navy facility on Big Moose Island. The addition of these structures as well as others over the period of the Navy occupancy has altered the original appearance of the site.

Additionally the historic plans indicated that a flagstaff was installed in the driveway circle, but at some point the flagstaff was moved to the NE side of the building. A photograph of the NE elevation from circa 1970 depicts the flagstaff in the latter location with a cement walkway leading up to the flagstaff. Based on that photograph and the existing elements, the cement walkway apparently led from the SE driveway up to the flagpole and had a set of cement steps about halfway up the path. Other changes included the addition of stockade fencing near the north corner of the Northeast Pavilion and the addition of two memorial anchors to the lawn NE of the building. Historic photographs suggested that the fence was added after circa 1970 and was probably added in sections. These additional changes did not significantly impact the site but do change the historic appearance of the site.

Figure 37. Apartment Building, NW elevation, depicting shrubs and trees in front courtyard and driveway circle, June 1935.

Figure 38. Apartment Building, NW elevation, depicting landscape in front courtyard and a portion of the driveway circle, circa 1990.

CURRENT PHYSICAL DESCRIPTION

Figure 39. Apartment Building, NW elevation, 2008.

Introduction

The elements of the Apartment Building (Bldg 1) have not significantly changed since the original construction. The most significant exterior alteration was the replacement of the steel window sashes. Other exterior and interior alterations were previously described and were relatively minor. The exterior and interior elements currently appear very similar to how the building was originally intended and retain a high degree of historic integrity. There have been no significant alterations to the structural system, and the structure of the building will not be discussed in this section. Please refer to a previous discussion found in section "Original Appearance, Structural Elements." The following sections will describe the current exterior and interior elements in the context of the changes to the building. This section will augment the previous sections on "Original Appearance" and "Alterations."

Exterior Elements

Design

The overall design of the Apartment Building has not been significantly altered since the original construction (fig. 39). The building retains the exterior elements that were used to execute the French Eclectic design envisioned by Grosvenor Atterbury. However, the replacement of the window sashes does affect the overall appearance of the building. As previously described, the new window sashes do not have true divided lights but are constructed with snap-in muntin grills. The muntins of the original sashes provided a clearly defined grid of glazed lights that was part of the exterior pattern of materials and character defining; whereas the muntins of the new windows are generally not discernible from the exterior and the sashes often appear as a single pane of glass (figs. 43 – 46). Thus that aspect of the design does not appear as it did historically. Otherwise the current exterior design is very similar to the original appearance.

Foundation

The masonry foundations of the Apartment Building have been retained. The records indicated that minor repairs were made over the years including some patching of cracks and installation of waterproof membrane. In addition some changes were made to allow for upgraded utilities. Recent inspections of the building did not find any deficiencies in the foundation, which presently appears to be in good condition.

Walls

The description of the exterior masonry and half-timber walls in the section on "Original Appearance" applies to the current description of the Apartment Building. The changes to the exterior appearance have been caused by the wear, efflorescence, and repairs to the exterior elements. The masonry walls have been repointed numerous times, and in some cases the mortar has not been a good match to the texture and color of the original mortar. This has left some areas of masonry with a mottled appearance, but otherwise the masonry appears to be in good condition. A 2001 inspection by Theriault/Landmann Associates, an architectural firm hired by the Navy to produce a condition assessment and preservation specifications, noted that with few exceptions, the masonry veneer was in excellent condition and required no additional repairs.[171] There are some areas of efflorescence and minor spalling of bricks, but these problems do not indicate significant masonry failure. The issues

---

[171] Theriault/Landmann Associates. Rockefeller Building, Building #1 NSGA, Winter Harbor, Maine, Limited Building Assessment (Theriault/Landmann Associates, July 2001) p. 5.

with the exterior masonry walls appear to be isolated and can be addressed according to the preservation specifications prepared by Theriault/Landmann Associates.[172]

The wooden elements of the exterior walls also retain the original elements (fig. 47). The pecky cypress half-timbering exhibits some areas of deterioration but overall appears to be in good condition. In some cases the carved brackets have decayed and are not representative of the original design (figs. 47a and 48). Throughout the half-timbering the wooden pegs have fallen out and although this condition changes the appearance of the timbering, it does not appear to pose an imminent threat to the building. Most of these conditions were described by Theriault/Landmann Associates and should be remedied according to their recommendations. The masonry and half-timbered exterior walls do retain a significant amount of original material and have a high degree of historic integrity.

Decorative wooden shields have been mounted on the masonry walls of the building near the three NW elevation entrance doorways (D102, D103, and D104). The shields list the apartment numbers that are accessible through the respective doorways. It is not known when the shields were added, but they were evident in the circa-1990 photographs (fig. 38).

Entrance Stoops and Terrace

The design of the three NW elevation entrance stoops has not been altered. The stoops appear to retain the original knee walls and most of the original masonry materials (fig. 49). The bluestone stoop steps were replaced with similar bluestone and are representative of the original appearance. All three of these entrances exhibit signs of masonry failure: there is some efflorescence and mortar deterioration, as well as vegetation growth. During on-site investigation, standing water was noted on all three entrance stoops.

On the Northeast Pavilion the masonry wall supporting the NE entrance stoop exhibits efflorescence, mortar failure, and signs of shifting of the granite stones. These conditions were more pronounced on the SE side of the wall where previous mortar repairs have failed, but cracking was noted on all sides of the masonry wall (fig. 50). These concerns were noted by Theriault/Landmann Associates,[173] and the problems can be addressed according to the specifications written by them. The entrance stoops are important features of the Apartment Building and should be repaired, restored, and retained.

The plan of the Terrace on the SE elevation of the Apartment Building has not been changed since the original construction. Park documents indicated that the deck of the SE Terrace has been resurfaced and the parapet wall has been repaired. Copper base flashing and counter flashing is installed between the deck and the walls on all sides of the Terrace, including along the parapet wall. Currently the deck is covered with a "green slate" that was determined to be an appropriate material by the Maine SHPO (fig. 51). During the current investigation water damage was noted along the joints that run the width of the Terrace on either side of the projecting center bay. The repairs to the Terrace maintained the overall historic appearance and future repairs should be done with in kind materials.

---

[172] Theriault/Landmann Associates. Rockefeller Building, Building #1 NSGA, Winter Harbor, Maine, Preservation Specifications (Theriault/Landmann Associates, Oct. 2001)

[173] Theriault/Landmann Associates. Limited Building Assessment; p. 6.

The staircases on either side of the Terrace have been repaired but not significantly altered (fig. 52). The steps are currently covered with concrete treads covered with metal runners that replaced the original bluestone treads. The current risers are brick, as were the original. Steel pipe handrails are installed on both sides of each staircase. The handrails have ball finials at the ends and are painted black. Theriault/Landmann Associates do suggest that the bluestone treads be restored to the Terrace staircases, which would restore an important feature of the staircases.

An important issue addressed by Theriault/Landmann Associates was the condition of the Terrace parapet wall, which has been rehabilitated since their 2001 report. The rehabilitation of the parapet wall reused the original granite and brick set in new mortar, with new copper flashing. The wall retains the historic appearance and is no longer in danger of catastrophic failure. A new railing was installed along the top of the parapet wall. The railing follows a design similar to the extant handrails on the Terrace staircases and was approved by the Maine SHPO. The Terrace was an important feature of Atterbury's design for the Apartment Building, and the rehabilitation of some elements does not detract from the historic integrity of the Terrace.

Doorways

The original locations of the doorways at the Apartment Building have been retained, except for the NW doorway on the Northeast Pavilion (D101), which was closed off (figs. 40 and 41). The materials that originally framed the doorways, including the brick jambs and pecky cypress lintels, have also been retained. Most of the first-story doorways currently have replacement door leaves, but the basement doorways have retained original doors and some original hardware.

At the basement story, D001 has the original surround, and the plank door is original. The door handle was changed to a brass knob with a rectangular backplate containing a deadbolt lock. The door is hinged on three butt hinges, and the decorative strap hinges remain intact.

The garage doorways (D002 through D009) under the Terrace parapet wall have a similar appearance to the original doorways (figs. 14, 26, and 44). They are framed with brick piers and pecky cypress lintels and have double door leaves. The repairs to the parapet wall above the garage openings included some repair and replacement of the lintels, as well as replacement of the flashing over the lintels. Some repairs have also been made to the brick piers. The doors appear to be original and are constructed with vertical planks on braced frames. Each door has two glazed lights and original hardware, although some of the escutcheons around the door locks are missing. There are some cracks in the concrete ramps leading to the doorways with some vegetation growing between those cracks. Overall, the garage doorways represent the original appearance and are in good condition.

The two garage doorways on the SE elevation of the Northeast Pavilion (D010 and D011) also retain their original appearance. Other than some minor cracks in the concrete ramps, there do not appear to have been any significant changes to those two doorways or the associated elements.

The design of the NE basement doorway (D012) grouped it with the adjacent window opening (W007). The doorway was constructed with brick jambs, but on the SE side of the doorway the brick jamb ends at the window-opening level and changes to a cypress timber that forms the mullion between the doorway and window opening. The original doorway lintel is intact and extends over the window openings. The original plank door and hardware have been kept on this doorway, and an exterior aluminum storm door is hung on the SE jamb.

On the first story of the Apartment Building all of the doorways had some alterations. As previously described, D101 has been closed off. The original brick jambs and cypress lintel are intact and the doorway has been infilled with textured plywood that has the appearance of a vertical plank door. Decorative hardware has been attached to the plywood to give the further effect of a door. The doorway does retain the metal hood supported by decorative metal brackets and also retains the bluestone steps and threshold.

The three NW façade entrance doorways (D102, D103, and D104) currently have original elements including the entrance stoops, bluestone thresholds, brick reveals, and cypress lintels. The entrance doorway hoods appear to retain the original elements. The only modifications to the stoops appear to have been the rehabilitation of the bluestone steps, which were replaced in kind. All three doorways have replacement double doors. Each doorway has two metal-clad door leaves that have one large double-glazed pane over two vertical panels. The replacement doors are not as tall as the original doors, and the head of the doorway between the existing doors and the original lintel is filled in with wood trim. The doors are hinged with three brushed-steel butt hinges and have steel doorknobs.

The three first-story exterior doorways from the Terrace on the SE elevation (D105, D106, and D107) also have replacement doors. On that elevation the original brick jambs and cypress lintels are intact, as are the doorway hoods over the doorways at either end of the SE Terrace (D105 and D107). The records indicate that the thresholds were replaced with new concrete slabs in 1973 and the doors were replaced in September 1983. The doors in all three doorways were replaced with insulated metal doors that have nine simulated lights over a cross-buck panel. Both D105 and D107 were originally constructed with double door leaves, but since these were replaced with a single door, the two doorways have sidelights installed to fill the width of the former double doorway. The sidelights were also constructed with insulated metal and have three simulated-lights over a single panel. The replacement doors are hung with steel butt hinges and have decorative handles that attempted to match the original Suffolk-style handles.

The doorway on the NE elevation (D108) has an aluminum storm door mounted on the door jamb but is otherwise unaltered and represents a good example of the original doorway elements. The brick jambs, pecky cypress lintel, plank door, and both decorative and functional hardware are all well preserved. An example of the decorative hardware that was very similar to the hardware used at the Apartment Building was found in a 1940 P. and F. Corbin catalogue and was probably available from the same manufacturer in 1934 (fig. 53). Examples of this reproduction hardware are still extant on the basement doors, some interior doors (fig. 53a), and D108, but it is best preserved on D108 (fig. 53b).

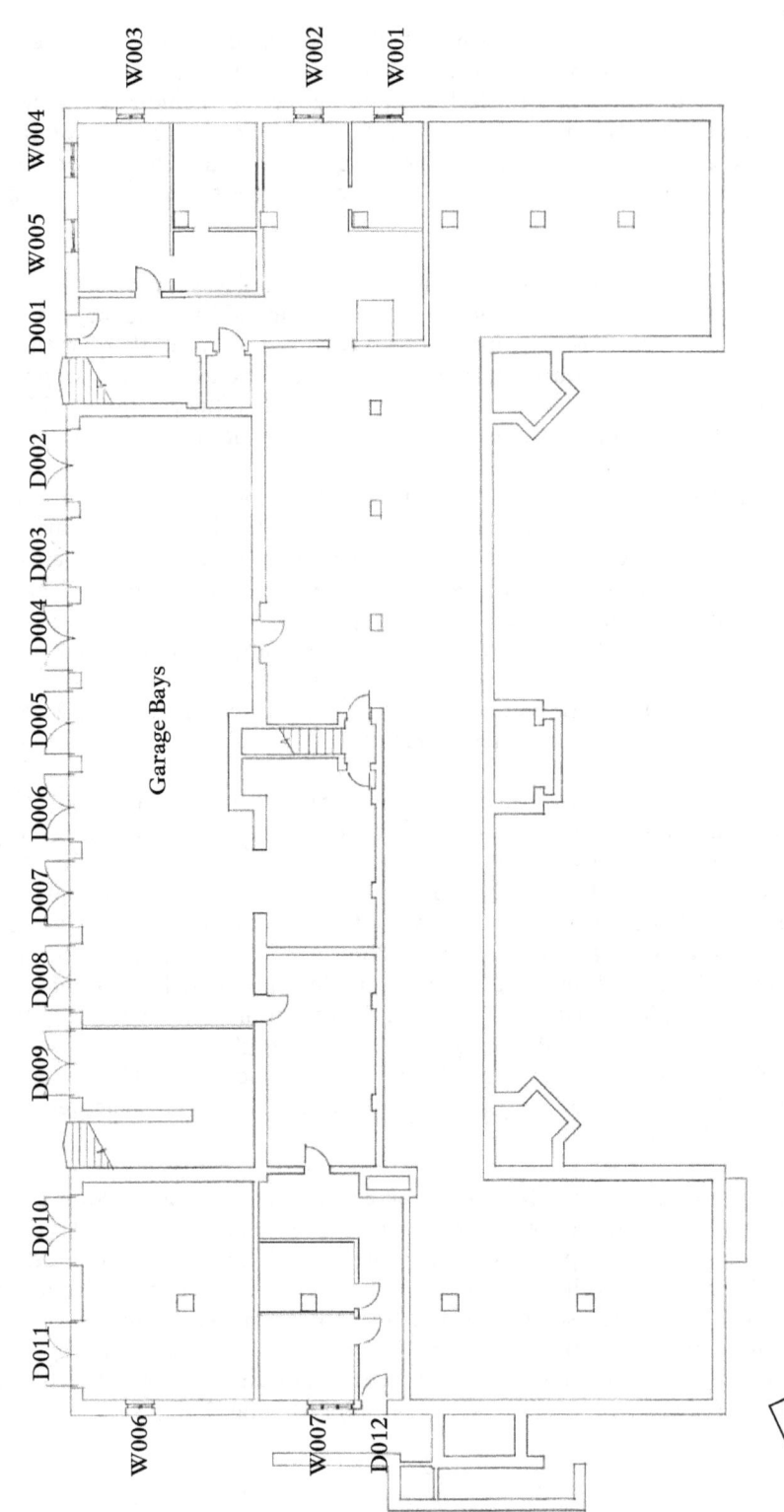

Figure 40. Apartment Building, basement-story floor plan with window opening and doorway numbers assigned during the current project (not to scale).

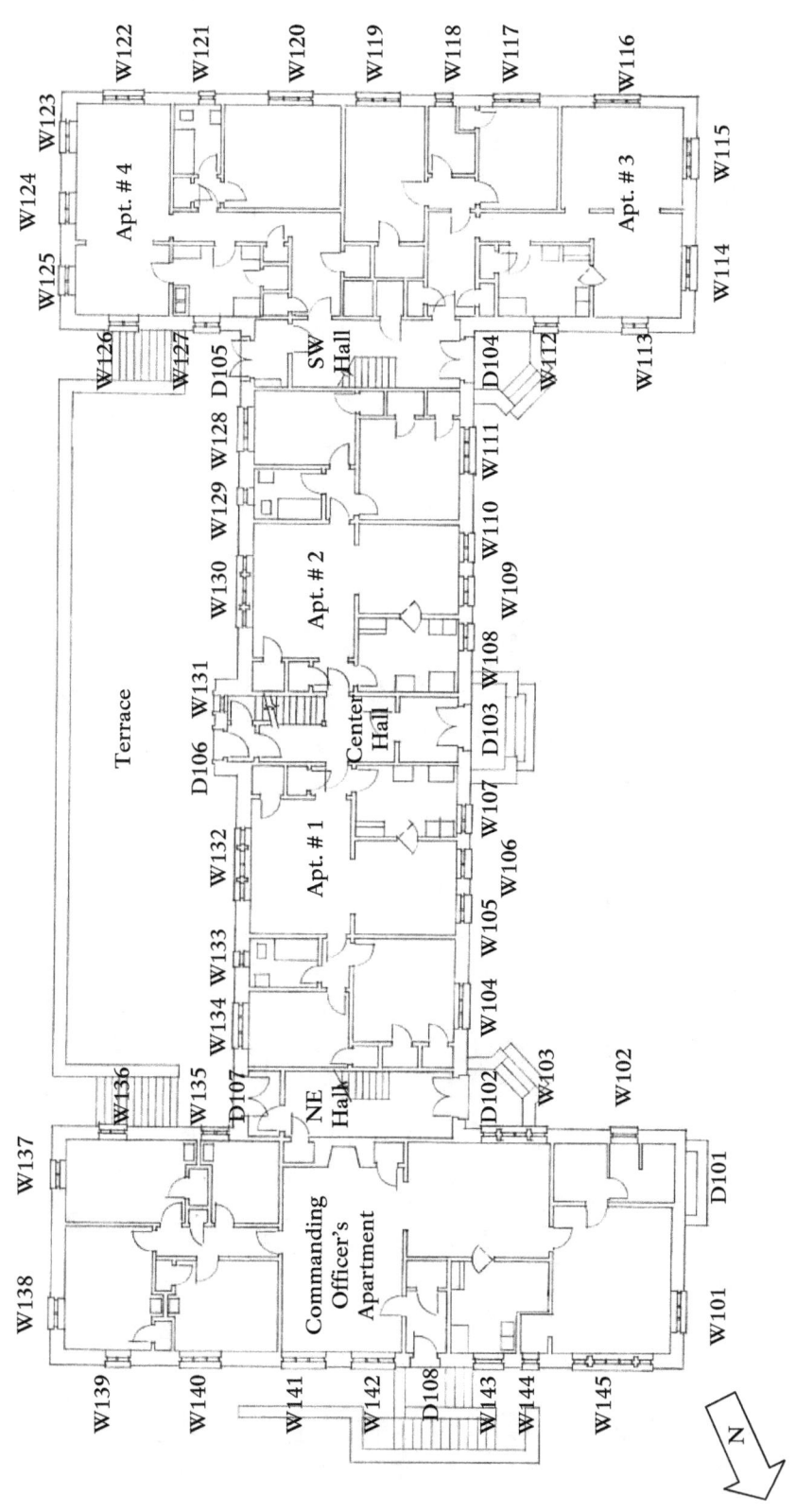

Figure 41. Apartment Building, first-story floor plan with exterior window opening and doorway numbers assigned during the current project (not to scale).

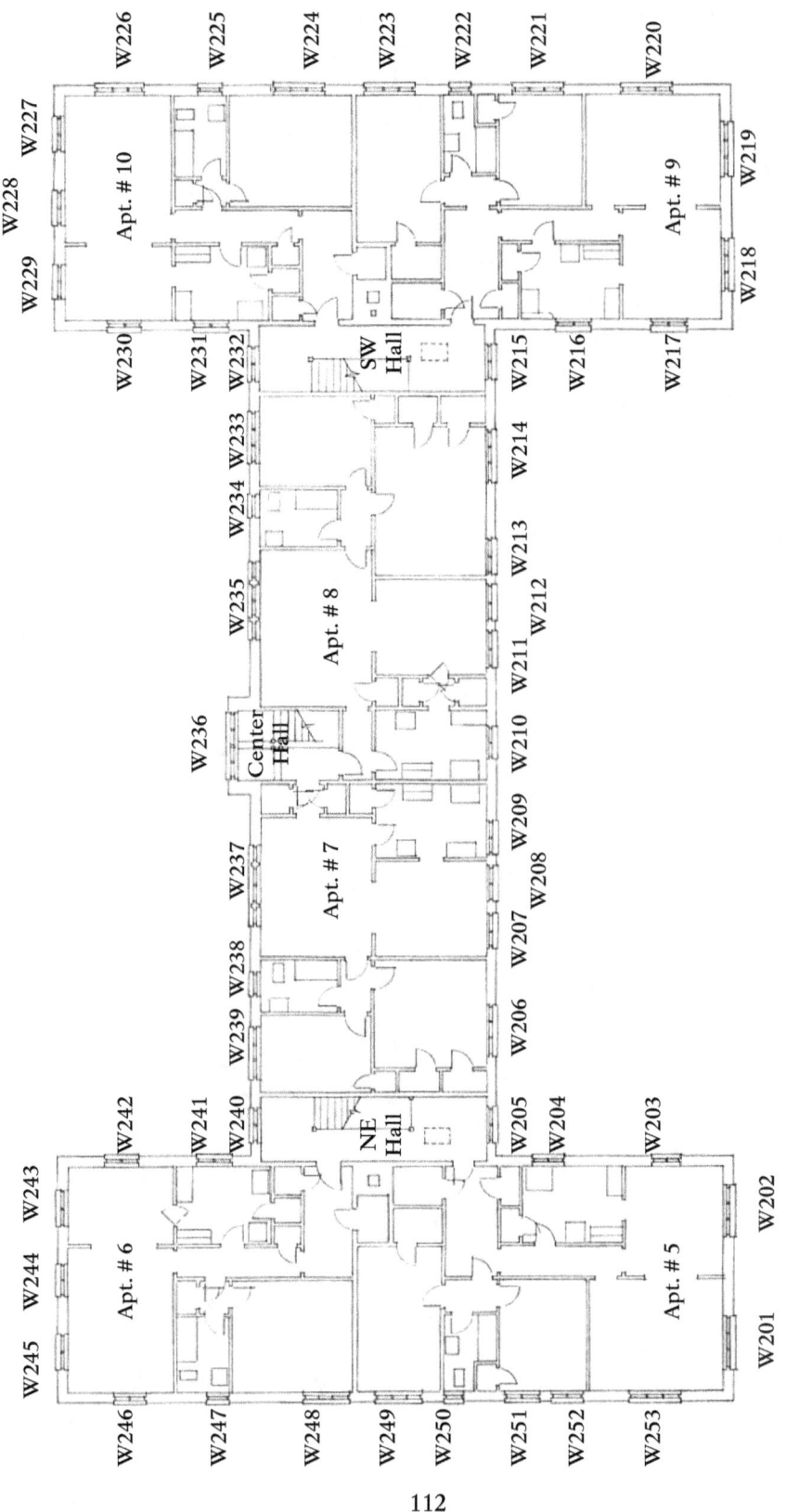

Figure 42. Apartment Building, second-story floor plan with window opening numbers assigned during the current project (not to scale).

112

Window Openings

The original locations of the window openings and the original window opening surrounds were retained when the window sashes were replaced in 1981. The rough openings were not altered and the schedule for the new window sashes followed the same type designations that were assigned in the 1933 plans (see previous section "Original Appearance; Window Openings"). The exterior elements of all the replacement sashes are aluminum clad with a dark brown finish (fig. 54). The exterior jamb and head elements between the sashes and the window surrounds are aluminum clad. The mullions separating the sashes in the double and triple sash window openings are also aluminum clad. The following window schedule describes the various window types. The subsequent tables record the window openings by numbers assigned during the current project (figs. 40, 41, and 42) and document the current configuration.

Window Schedule

Type	Size	Window Type Description
A	1'8" x 3'1"	One aluminum-clad casement sash with a snap-in muntin grill simulating six lights. First-story type-A windows are framed with brick sides, granite lintels, and granite sills with a wooden upper sill. Second- and attic-story type-A windows are surrounded with pecky cypress and have wood sills.
B	5'0" x 3'1"	Three aluminum-clad sashes. The two end sashes are casements and the center sash is fixed. All the sashes have snap-in muntin grills simulating six lights in each sash, totaling eighteen lights. The type-B window is surrounded with pecky cypress half timbers and has a wood sill.
C	3'4" x 3'1"	Two aluminum-clad casement sashes with snap-in muntin grills simulating six lights in each sash, totaling twelve lights. Basement-story type-C windows are framed with brick sides, pecky cypress lintels flashed with copper, and granite sills with wood upper sills. Upper-story type-C windows are enframed with pecky cypress half timbers and wood sills.
D	3'4" x 4'0"	Two aluminum-clad casement sashes with snap-in muntin grills simulating eight lights in each sash, totaling sixteen lights. Type-D windows are typically framed with brick sides, pecky cypress lintels flashed with copper, and granite sills with wood upper sills.
E	3'4" x 5'0"	Two aluminum-clad casement sashes with snap-in muntin grills simulating ten lights in each sash, totaling twenty lights. Type-E windows are typically surrounded with pecky cypress half timbers and have a wood sill.
F	1'8" x 5'0"	One aluminum-clad casement sash with a snap-in muntin grill simulating ten lights. Type-F windows are typically surrounded with pecky cypress half timbers and have a wood sill.

Window Schedule continued

Type	Size	Window Type Description
G	5'0" x 5'0"	Three aluminum-clad sashes. The two end sashes are casements and the center sash is fixed. All the sashes have snap-in muntin grills simulating ten lights in each sash, totaling thirty lights. Type-G windows are typically surrounded with pecky cypress half timbers and have a wood sill.
H	6'7" x 3'1"	Three aluminum-clad sashes. The two end sashes are casements and the center sash is fixed. All the sashes have snap-in muntin grills simulating six lights in each sash, totaling eighteen lights. The type-H window is surrounded with pecky cypress half timbers and has a wood sill.
I	1'6" x 1'6"	Single-light fixed aluminum-clad sashes with pecky cypress half timber surrounds and wood sills.
J	3'4" x 2'2"	Single dormer sashes hinged at the bottom of the opening and tilting inside. The sashes are surrounded with aluminum-clad trim.

Basement-Story Exterior Window Opening Elements

Window Opening Number	Window Location, Type, and Description
W001	Location: Southwest Pavilion, SW elevation, Boiler Room 014. Type: The opening originally held a type-C window and is currently filled with metal louvers that are finished with a dark brown color.
W002	Location: Southwest Pavilion, SW elevation, Boiler Room 014. Type: C with two casement sashes and twelve simulated lights.
W003	Location: Southwest Pavilion, SW elevation, Room 016. Type: C with two casement sashes and twelve simulated lights.
W004	Location: Southwest Pavilion, SE elevation, Room 016. Type: D with two casement sashes and sixteen simulated lights.
W005	Location: Southwest Pavilion, SE elevation, Room 016. Type: D with two casement sashes and sixteen simulated lights.
W006	Location: Northeast Pavilion, NE elevation, Room 001. Type: C with two casement sashes and twelve simulated lights.
W007	Location: Northeast Pavilion, NE elevation, Room 002. Type: B with three metal-clad replacement sashes and eighteen simulated lights. The window opening is framed with brick on the SE side and a pecky cypress mullion on the NW side that separates the window from the adjacent doorway (D012). It has a pecky cypress lintel that extends over the adjacent doorway and is flashed with copper.

First-Story Exterior Window Opening Elements

Window Opening Number	Window Location, Type, and Description
W101	Location: Northeast Pavilion, NW elevation, Room CO-10 Type: G window with three aluminum-clad sashes and thirty simulated lights.
W102	Location: Northeast Pavilion, SW elevation, Room CO-09. Type: D window with two casement sashes and sixteen simulated lights. It is framed by pecky cypress half timbers and a wood sill.
W103	Location: Northeast Pavilion, SW elevation, Room CO-07. Type: E window flanked on both sides by type-F windows to form a three-window group (F–E–F). The window types are separated by pecky cypress mullions, and the group is surrounded by pecky cypress half timbers.
W104	Location: Main Block, NW elevation, Room 104. Type: G window with three sashes and thirty simulated lights.
W105	Location: Main Block, NW elevation, Room 103. Type: E with two casement sashes and twenty simulated lights. On the exterior, this window is visually grouped with W106 and W107 to form a band of windows within one of the NW elevation cross gables.
W106	Location: Main Block, NW elevation, Room 103. Type: E with two casement sashes and twenty simulated lights.
W107	Location: Main Block, NW elevation, Room 102. Type: E with two casement sashes and twenty simulated lights.
W108	Location: Main Block, NW elevation, Room 102. Type: E with two casement sashes and twenty simulated lights. On the exterior this window opening is visually grouped with W109 and W110 to form a band of windows within one of the NW elevation cross gables.
W109	Location: Main Block, NW elevation, Room 203. Type: E with two casement sashes and twenty simulated lights.
W110	Location: Main Block, NW elevation, Room 203. Type: E with two casement sashes and twenty simulated lights.
W111	Location: Main Block, NW elevation, Room 204. Type: G window with three sashes and thirty simulated lights.
W112	Location: Southwest Pavilion, NE elevation, Room 302. Type: C with two casement sashes and sixteen simulated lights.
W113	Location: Southwest Pavilion, NE elevation, Room 303. Type: C with two casement sashes and sixteen simulated lights.
W114	Location: Southwest Pavilion, NW elevation, Room 303. Type: G window with three sashes and thirty simulated lights.
W115	Location: Southwest Pavilion, NW elevation, Room 304. Type: G window with three sashes and thirty simulated lights.

First-Story Exterior Window Opening Elements continued

Window Opening Number	Window Location, Type, and Description
W116	Location: Southwest Pavilion, SW elevation, Room 304. Type: G window with three sashes and thirty simulated lights.
W117	Location: Southwest Pavilion, SW elevation, Room 305. Type: G window with three sashes and thirty simulated lights.
W118	Location: Southwest Pavilion, SW elevation, Room 306. Type: A with a single casement and six simulated lights.
W119	Location: Southwest Pavilion, SW elevation, Room 307. Type: G window with three sashes and thirty simulated lights.
W120	Location: Southwest Pavilion, SW elevation, Room 406. Type: G window with three sashes and thirty simulated lights.
W121	Location: Southwest Pavilion, SW elevation, Room 405. Type: A with a single casement and six simulated lights.
W122	Location: Southwest Pavilion, SW elevation, Room 404. Type: G window with three sashes and thirty simulated lights.
W123	Location: Southwest Pavilion, SE elevation, Room 404. Type: E with two casement sashes and twenty simulated lights.
W124	Location: Southwest Pavilion, SE elevation, Room 404. Type: E with two casement sashes and twenty simulated lights.
W125	Location: Southwest Pavilion, SE elevation, Room 403. Type: E with two casement sashes and twenty simulated lights.
W126	Location: Southwest Pavilion, NE elevation, Room 403. Type: C with two casement sashes and twelve simulated lights.
W127	Location: Southwest Pavilion, NE elevation, Room 402. Type: C with two casement sashes and twelve simulated lights.
W128	Location: Main Block, SE elevation, Room 205. Type: G window with three sashes and thirty simulated lights.
W129	Location: Main Block, SE elevation, Room 206. Type: A with a single casement and six simulated lights.
W130	Location: Main Block, SE elevation, Room 207. Type: E window flanked on both sides by type-F windows to form a three-window group (F–E–F). The window types are separated by pecky cypress mullions and surrounded by half timbers.
W131	Location: Main Block, SE elevation, Center Hallway, basement staircase landing. Type: A with a single casement and six simulated lights.
W132	Location: Main Block, SE elevation, Room 107. Type: E window flanked on both sides by type-F windows to form a three-window group (F–E–F). The window types are separated by pecky cypress mullions and surrounded by half timbers.
W133	Location: Main Block, SE elevation, Room 106. Type: A with a single casement and six simulated lights.
W134	Location: Main Block, SE elevation, Room 105. Type: G window with three sashes and thirty simulated lights.

First-Story Exterior Window Opening Elements continued

Window Opening Number	Window Location, Type, and Description
W135	Location: Northeast Pavilion, SW elevation, Room CO-06. Type: C with two casement sashes and twelve simulated lights.
W136	Location: Northeast Pavilion, SW elevation, Room CO-05. Type: C with two casement sashes and twelve simulated lights.
W137	Location: Northeast Pavilion, SE elevation, Room CO-05. Type: E with two casement sashes and twenty simulated lights.
W138	Location: Northeast Pavilion, SE elevation, Room CO-04. Type: E with two casement sashes and twenty simulated lights.
W139	Location: Northeast Pavilion, NE elevation, Room CO-04. Type: E with two casement sashes and twenty simulated lights.
W140	Location: Northeast Pavilion, NE elevation, Room CO-03. Type: G window with three sashes and thirty simulated lights.
W141	Location: Northeast Pavilion, NE elevation, Room CO-02. Type: G window with three sashes and thirty simulated lights.
W142	Location: Northeast Pavilion, NE elevation, Room CO-02. Type: G window with three sashes and thirty simulated lights.
W143	Location: Northeast Pavilion, NE elevation, Room CO-11. Type: E with two casement sashes and twenty simulated lights.
W144	Location: Northeast Pavilion, NE elevation, Room CO-10a. Type: A with a single casement and six simulated lights.
W145	Location: Northeast Pavilion, NE elevation, Room CO-10. Type: G window flanked on both sides by type-I windows.

Second-Story Exterior Window Opening Elements

Window Opening Number	Window Location, Type, and Description
W201	Location: Northeast Pavilion, NW elevation, Room 504. Type: G window with three sashes and thirty simulated lights.
W202	Location: Northeast Pavilion, NW elevation, Room 503. Type: G window with three sashes and thirty simulated lights.
W203	Location: Northeast Pavilion, SW elevation, Room 503. Type: C with two casement sashes and twelve simulated lights.
W204	Location: Northeast Pavilion, SW elevation, Room 502. Type: C with two casement sashes and twelve simulated lights.
W205	Location: Main Block, NW elevation, NE Hallway. Type: E with two casement sashes and twenty simulated lights.
W206	Location: Main Block, NW elevation, Room 704. Type: G window with three sashes and thirty simulated lights.
W207	Location: Main Block, NW elevation, Room 703. Type: E with two casement sashes and twenty simulated lights. On the exterior this window opening is visually grouped with W208 and W209 to form a band of windows within one of the NW elevation cross gables.

Second-Story Exterior Window Opening Elements continued

W208	Location: Main Block, NW elevation, Room 703. Type: E with two casement sashes and twenty simulated lights.
W209	Location: Main Block, NW elevation, Room 702. Type: E with two casement sashes and twenty simulated lights.
W210	Location: Main Block, NW elevation, Room 802. Type: E with two casement sashes and twenty simulated lights.
W211	Location: Main Block, NW elevation, Room 803. Type: E with two casement sashes and twenty simulated lights. On the exterior this window opening is visually grouped with W212 and W213 to form a band of windows within one of the NW elevation cross gables.
W212	Location: Main Block, NW elevation, Room 803. Type: E with two casement sashes and twenty simulated lights.
W213	Location: Main Block, NW elevation, Room 804. Type: E with two casement sashes and twenty simulated lights.
W214	Location: Main Block, NW elevation, Room 804. Type: G window with three sashes and thirty simulated lights.
W215	Location: Main Block, NW elevation, SW Hallway. Type: E with two casement sashes and twenty simulated lights.
W216	Location: Southwest Pavilion, NE elevation, Room 902. Type: C with two casement sashes and twelve simulated lights.
W217	Location: Southwest Pavilion, NE elevation, Room 902. Type: C with two casement sashes and twelve simulated lights.
W218	Location: Southwest Pavilion, NW elevation, Room 903. Type: G window with three sashes and thirty simulated lights.
W219	Location: Southwest Pavilion, NW elevation, Room 904. Type: G window with three sashes and thirty simulated lights.
W220	Location: Southwest Pavilion, SW elevation, Room 904. Type: G window with three sashes and thirty simulated lights.
W221	Location: Southwest Pavilion, SW elevation, Room 905. Type: G window with three sashes and thirty simulated lights.
W222	Location: Southwest Pavilion, SW elevation, Room 906. Type: A with a single casement and half-timber surrounds.
W223	Location: Southwest Pavilion, SW elevation, Room 907. Type: G window with three sashes and thirty simulated lights.
W224	Location: Southwest Pavilion, SW elevation, Room 1006. Type: G window with three sashes and thirty simulated lights.
W225	Location: Southwest Pavilion, SW elevation, Room 1005. Type: A with a single casement and half-timber surrounds.
W226	Location: Southwest Pavilion, SW elevation, Room 1004. Type: G window with three sashes and thirty simulated lights.
W227	Location: Southwest Pavilion, SE elevation, Room 1004. Type: E with two casement sashes and twenty simulated lights.
W228	Location: Southwest Pavilion, SE elevation, Room 1004. Type: E with two casement sashes and twenty simulated lights.

Second-Story Exterior Window Opening Elements continued

Window Opening Number	Window Location, Type, and Description
W229	Location: Southwest Pavilion, SE elevation, Room 1003. Type: E with two casement sashes and twenty simulated lights.
W230	Location: Southwest Pavilion, NE elevation, Room 1003. Type: C with two casement sashes and twelve simulated lights.
W231	Location: Southwest Pavilion, NE elevation, Room 1002. Type: C with two casement sashes and twelve simulated lights.
W232	Location: Main Block, SE elevation, SW Hallway. Type: E with two casement sashes and twenty simulated lights.
W233	Location: Main Block, SE elevation, Room 805. Type: G window with three sashes and thirty simulated lights.
W234	Location: Main Block, SE elevation, Room 806. Type: A with a single casement and half timber surrounds.
W235	Location: Main Block, SE elevation, Room 807. Type: E window flanked on both sides by type F windows to form a three-window group (F–E–F). The window types are separated by pecky cypress mullions and surrounded by half timbers.
W236	Location: Main Block, SE elevation, Center Hallway, staircase landing. Type: H with three aluminum-clad sashes. The fixed center sash is wider than the side casement sashes. The 1981 plans indicated that the replacement sashes would replicate the original window, which had four sashes. However, the current window has three sashes.
W237	Location: Main Block, SE elevation, Room 707. Type: E window flanked on both sides by type-F windows to form a three-window group (F–E–F). The window types are separated by pecky cypress mullions and surrounded by half timbers.
W238	Location: Main Block, SE elevation, Room 706. Type: A with a single casement and half-timber surrounds.
W239	Location: Main Block, SE elevation, Room 705. Type: G window with three sashes and thirty simulated lights.
W240	Location: Main Block, SE elevation, NE Hallway. Type: E with two casement sashes and twenty simulated lights.
W241	Location: Northeast Pavilion, SW elevation, Room 602. Type: C with two casement sashes and twelve simulated lights.
W242	Location: Northeast Pavilion, SW elevation, Room 603. Type: C with two casement sashes and twelve simulated lights.
W243	Location: Northeast Pavilion, SE elevation, Room 603. Type: E with two casement sashes and twenty simulated lights.
W244	Location: Northeast Pavilion, SE elevation, Room 604. Type: E with two casement sashes and twenty simulated lights.
W245	Location: Northeast Pavilion, SE elevation, Room 604. Type: E with two casement sashes and twenty simulated lights.
W246	Location: Northeast Pavilion, NE elevation, Room 604. Type: E with two casement sashes and twenty simulated lights.

Second-Story Exterior Window Opening Elements continued

Window Opening Number	Window Location, Type, and Description
W247	Location: Northeast Pavilion, NE elevation, Room 605. Type: A with a single casement and half-timber surrounds.
W248	Location: Northeast Pavilion, NE elevation, Room 606. Type: G window with three sashes and thirty simulated lights.
W249	Location: Northeast Pavilion, NE elevation, Room 507. Type: G window with three sashes and thirty simulated lights.
W250	Location: Northeast Pavilion, NE elevation, Room 506. Type: A with a single casement and half-timber surrounds.
W251	Location: Northeast Pavilion, NE elevation, Room 505. Type: E with two casement sashes and twenty simulated lights.
W252	Location: Northeast Pavilion, NE elevation, Room 505. Type: E with two casement sashes and twenty simulated lights.
W253	Location: Northeast Pavilion, NE elevation, Room 504. Type: G window with three sashes and thirty simulated lights.

Attic-Story Exterior Window Opening Elements

Window Opening Number	Window Location, Type, and Description
W301	Location: Main Block, NW elevation, attic cross gable. Type: A with a single casement and half-timber surrounds.
W302	Location: Main Block, NW elevation, attic cross gable. Type: A with a single casement and half-timber surrounds.
W303	Location: Southwest Pavilion, SW elevation, attic dormer. Type: J with a single tilt-in sash hinged at the bottom.
W304	Location: Southwest Pavilion, SW elevation, attic dormer. Type: J with a single tilt-in sash hinged at the bottom.
W305	Location: Main Block, SE elevation, attic cross gable. Type: A, which was replaced by metal louvers for the buildings ventilation system. The window opening retains the half-timber surrounds.
W306	Location: Main Block, SE elevation, attic cross gable. Type: A with a single casement and half-timber surrounds.
W307	Location: Northeast Pavilion, NE elevation, attic dormer. Type: J with a single tilt-in sash hinged at the bottom.
W308	Location: Northeast Pavilion, NE elevation, attic dormer. Type: J with a single tilt-in sash hinged at the bottom.

Overall, the window openings appear to be in good condition. The original window openings have been retained, and original window surrounds appear to be intact. The 2001 inspection by Theriault/Landmann Associates noted that some of the windowsills required repair and that the sealants around the windows were deteriorated.[174] In addition, during the current on-site investigation some horizontal cracks were noted in the half-timbering around the windows that should be monitored in the future. Most of these conditions were described by Theriault/Landmann Associates and should be remedied according to their recommendations.[175]

As previously noted, the replacement windows do not have true divided lights and are therefore are not in keeping with the original design. However, they do appear to function adequately. Some of the sashes are missing the snap-in muntin grills and interior screens. Some water infiltration around certain window sashes was observed during the recent site visits. These conditions should be monitored and corrected if necessary.

Roofs and Related Elements

The overall design and configuration of the roofs of the Apartment Building have not been altered since the original construction. The building retains both the historic clay roofing tiles and the original "nailcrete" sheathing panels. The terra-cotta tiles include special tiles for the ridges, ends of ridges, hips, tops of hips, ends of hips, and rakes of cross gables. Like the roof tiles, the special tiles were installed with the upper courses overlapping the lower courses. In cross section the ridge tiles were molded at an angle to cover the ridge and had a lip on the overlapping edge. The hip tiles were molded in a similar manner but did not have a lip at the overlapping edge. At the junction of the ridge and hip, saddle-shaped tiles were installed. The tile at the end of the hip had a closed end. The cross gables were constructed with clay tiles that were molded at right angles to wrap around the edge of the rake, and the tile at the end of the ridge was closed at the roof peak.

Currently the clay tile roof appears to be in overall good condition. The current investigation did note some missing, broken, and loose roof tiles that should be repaired/replaced in kind. Some areas of the tile roof have taken on a green patina from moss growth, which is most evident on the NW elevation. By comparison, the SE elevation has little moss growth and illustrates the original color and texture of the roof. The records indicated that repairs were made to the roof tiles and flashing during various rehabilitation projects. The repairs were apparently made with similar clay tile materials and did not alter the overall appearance of the roofs. Indeed, crates of terra-cotta tiles stamped with "Ludowici-Celadon Co, Chicago, Imperial tile" were apparently left over from the original construction and are stored in the basement of the Apartment Building. The tiles include flat roof tiles and special application tiles, which provide a record of the historic clay tiles.

---

[174] Theriault/Landmann Associates. Rockefeller Building, Building #1 NSGA, Winter Harbor, Maine, Limited Building Assessment (Theriault/Landmann Associates, July 2001) p. 6.

[175] Theriault/Landmann Associates. Rockefeller Building, Building #1 NSGA, Winter Harbor, Maine, Preservation Specifications (Theriault/Landmann Associates, Oct. 2001).

The ventilation pipes project through the roof and are located directly above the second-story bathrooms. The clay tile roofing is cut around the pipes, and the pipes retain the historic copper boots and flashing.

The copper gutters are installed along edges of the roofs and connect to copper downspouts and underground drainage. The documents indicated that the gutters and downspouts have been repaired, but they retain the original appearance. The current gutters and downspouts appear to be conducting the water away from the foundation effectively.

The two masonry chimneys do not appear to have been significantly altered (fig. 55). Both chimneys retain the original masonry materials of granite stone and brick, and the terra-cotta chimney pots are intact. The exterior masonry repointing projects most likely included some work on the chimney stacks. Currently the mortar and masonry appear to be in good condition.

Utilities and Fixtures

Two of the original exterior light fixtures have been retained. These are located on the SE elevation at the basement level: one by D001 on the Southwest Pavilion and one by D010 on the Northeast Pavilion (fig. 56). Both fixtures retain the brass brackets and lanterns depicted in the historic photographs (fig. 21). The fixture by D106 originally had the same type of lamp, but it has been changed to a six-sided brass lamp. The does not replicate the historic lamp, but it is compatible and the original bracket was retained.

The overhead light fixtures above the façade doorways (D102, D103, and D104) are currently brass lanterns with six rounded panels, a domed top with brass finial, and a brass backplate. Though there was no documentation for the original lanterns, these fixtures appear to be replacements. Similar light fixtures are installed over the SE first-story doorways that have the same type of doorway hood (D105 and D107). The fixture over D108 is different from the others (fig. 57). It is a copper lantern with a dome-shaped copper top and a ring at the base. Four posts attach to the top and bottom and enclose a cylindrical glass globe. The fixture hangs from a copper-pipe bracket that extends from the exterior wall and has a backplate. The fixture appears to be older than the other doorway lanterns and could possibly be original to the building. The recessed fixture set in the soffit of the metal hood over D101 is in an original location and may retain original elements.

Landscape

The road still approaches the building from the NE and the circular driveway on the NW elevation currently has a paved parking area at the top of the circle. The lower driveway and the large SE parking lot have not been significantly changed. The existing bituminous macadam surfaces have a similar appearance to the historic paving.

The existing landscape features include walkways covered with bituminous paving that extend around all sides of the building and approach each of the façade doorways. On the NE elevation the walkway joins the staircase that leads from the first-story grade SE to the basement ground level. At the basement ground level the walkway continues and is bordered part way by a knee-high retaining wall. The NE elevation staircase and the retaining wall appear to retain original elements including the granite wall with bluestone coping, the bluestone treads, and the brick risers. An iron-pipe hand railing is installed on the SW side of the staircase. With the exception of the walkway along the SW elevation, the existing walkways appear to follow the 1934 landscape plan (fig. 19).

The 1943 historic site plans depict a tennis court that was situated across the driveway, due north of the NW elevation of the Apartment Building. The existing tennis court is in the same location and is currently enclosed with chain-link fence.

Additional existing landscape features include the stockade fence that was erected at the north corner of the Northeast Pavilion, enclosing a small yard. The fence was not evident in circa-1970 photographs, but a portion of the fence was built by circa 1990. The fence has been extended along the NW side of the pavilion since the circa-1990 photograph (fig. 38) was taken. There is currently a lamp post near the north corner of the Northeast Pavilion and a lamp post next to the NE elevation walkway at the basement ground level. A flagpole with the cement walkway and the memorial anchors are presently situated on the lawn NE of the building (fig. 45).

Figure 43. Apartment Building, NW elevation of Main Block and Southwest Pavilion including NE courtyard elevation of pavilion, 2008.

Figure 44. Apartment Building, SE elevation depicting garage bay doorways at basement story, 2008.

Figure 45. Apartment Building, NE elevation with Power House on the left, 2008.

Figure 46. Apartment Building, SW elevation, 2008.

Figure 47. Apartment Building, SE elevation, cross gable and projecting center bay, 2008.

Figure 47a. Apartment Building, SE elevation, deteriorated cross-gable bracket, 2008.

Figure 48. Apartment Building, SE elevation, well preserved cross-gable brackets supporting second-story window opening bay, 2008.

Figure 49. Apartment Building, NW elevation entry stoop to D102, 2008.

Figure 50. Apartment Building, Northeast Pavilion, SE wall of NE entrance stoop to D108, 2008.

Figure 51. Apartment Building, SE elevation, terrace, 2008.

Figure 52. Apartment Building, SE elevation, terrace staircase, 2008.

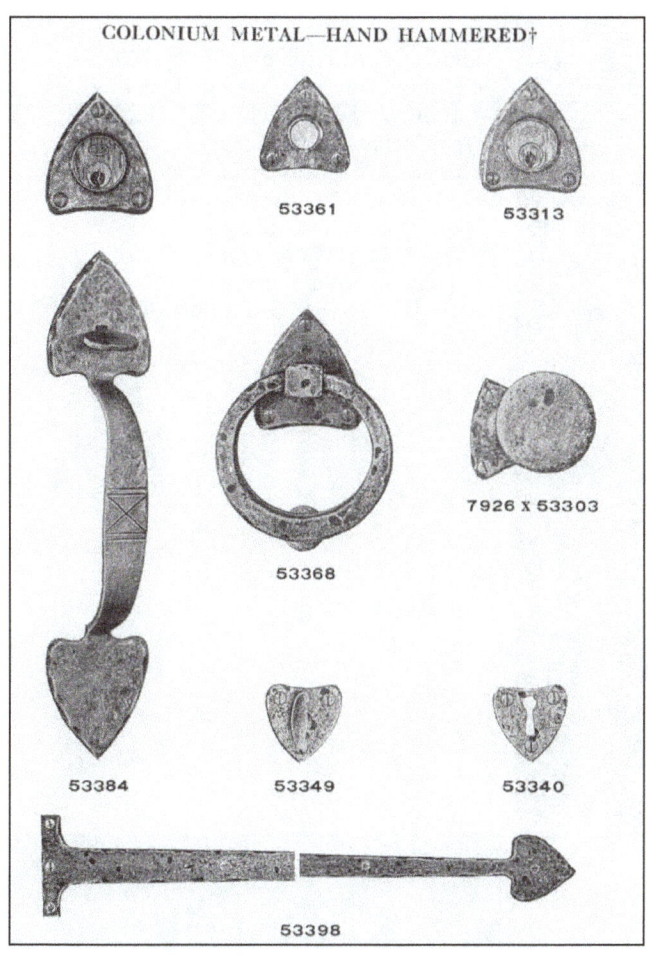

Figure 53. Reproduction door hardware from 1940 P. & F. Corbin catalog.

Figure 53a. Extant Suffolk-style latch and escutcheon on interior door to NE Hallway vestibule. Note the similarities to the hardware in the catalog illustration.

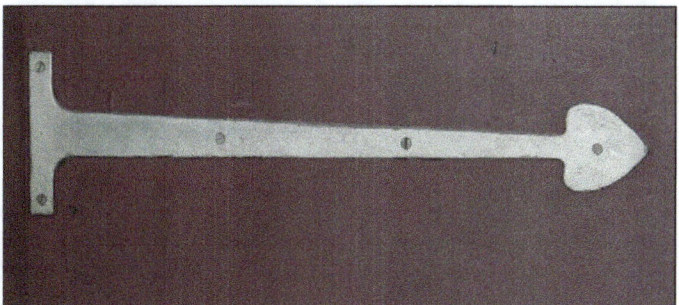

Figure 53b. Extant reproduction strap hinge on Northeast Pavilion entrance door, D108. Note the similarities to the hardware in the catalog illustration.

Figure 54. Apartment Building, SW elevation, window openings depicting exterior elements of different window types including:
Basement, W002 (type C);
First Story, W120 (type G), W121 (type A, masonry surround);
Second Story, W224 (type G), W225 (type A, wood surround);
Attic, W304 (type J in dormer), 2008.

Figure 55. Apartment Building, SW chimney, 2008.

Figure 56. Apartment Building, SE elevation, exterior light fixture on Northeast Pavilion, 2008.

Figure 57. Apartment Building, NE elevation, exterior light fixture above D108, 2008.

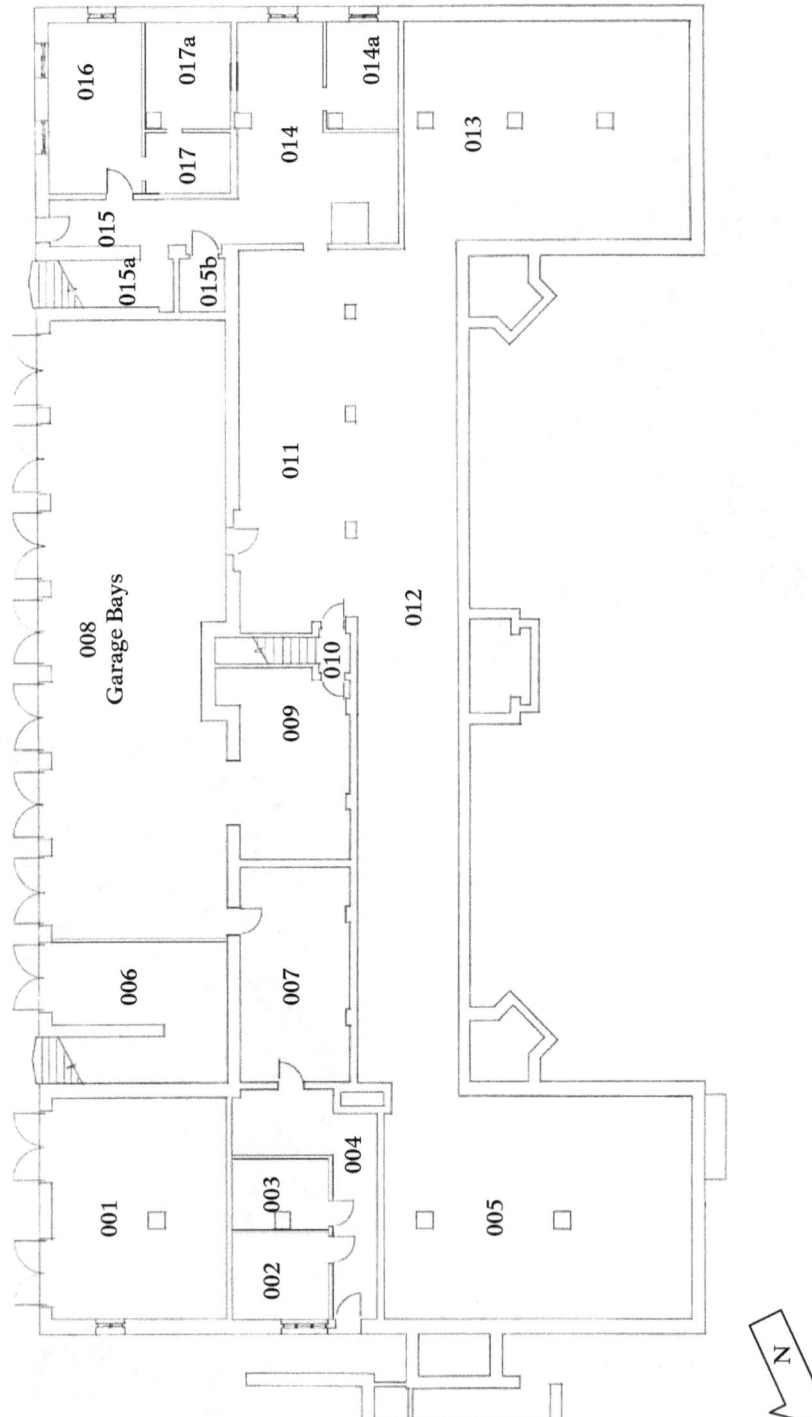

Figure 58. Apartment Building, basement-story floor plan with room numbers assigned during the current project, (not to scale).

132

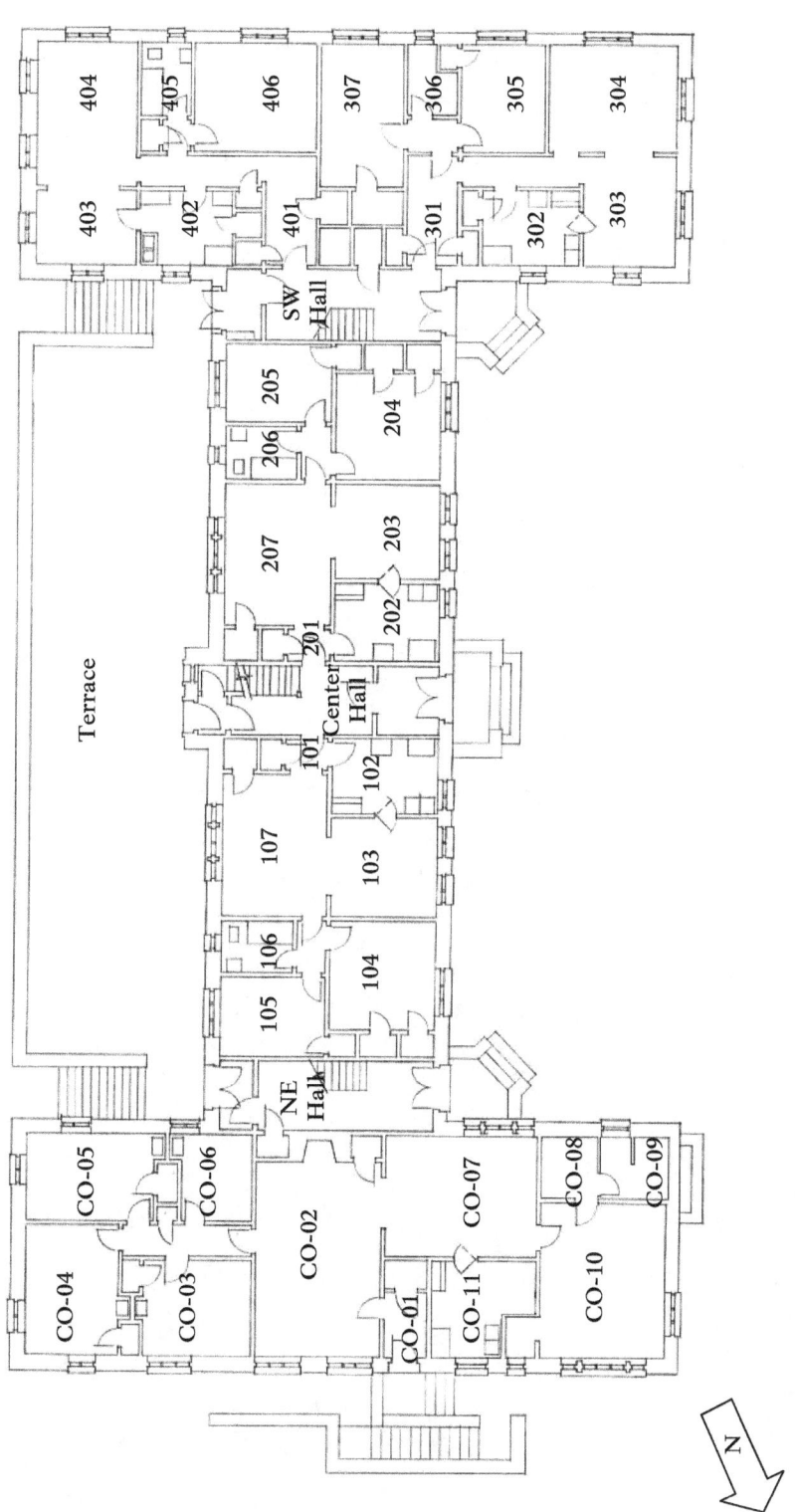

Figure 59. Apartment Building, first-story floor plan with room numbers assigned by apartment number during the current project (not to scale).

133

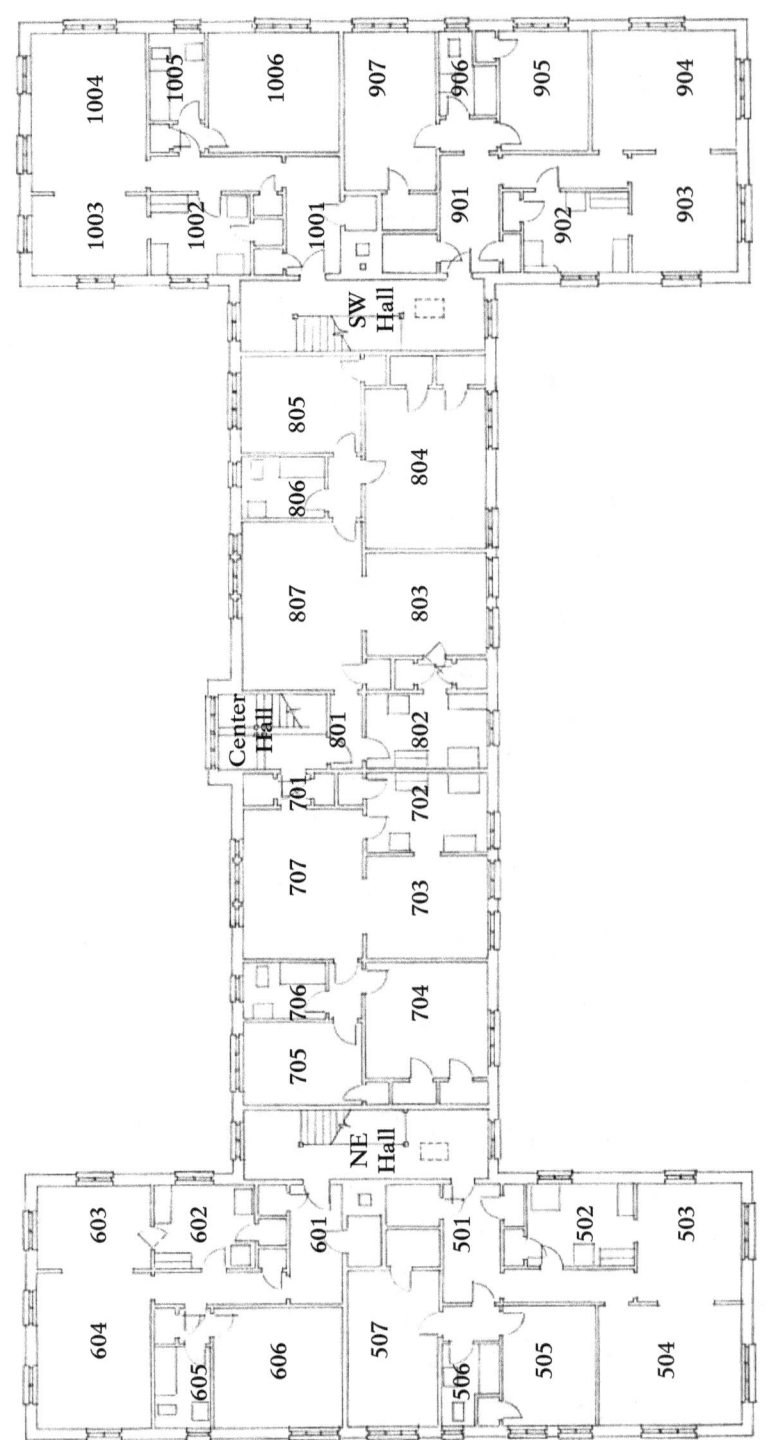

Figure 60. Apartment Building, second-story floor plan with room numbers assigned by apartment number during current project (not to scale).

Interior Elements

Basement Story

Portions of the basement story of the Apartment Building were altered over the years to accommodate the changes in use of the space. However, the overall function of the basement rooms has remained utilitarian, serving the needs of the Apartment Building (fig. 58). The current basement plan includes offices, a laundry room, utility rooms, storage rooms, garage bays, and open areas.

Northeast Pavilion

Room 001

The two garage bays at the SE end of the Northeast Pavilion continue to function as garage and storage spaces. The concrete slab floor is intact and the outer walls of the space have not been significantly altered. A stud partition separating the two garage bays was constructed in the middle of the space, and cabinets were installed on NE side of the partition. Both bays have fluorescent light fixtures hanging from the ceiling. A concrete-block wall at the NW end of the garage bays separate the space from the adjacent basement rooms (Rooms 002, 003, and 004).

Room 002

The former Battery-Machine and Generator Room was partitioned into three spaces, including two offices and a hallway. In the east corner of the former room, Room 002 was most recently used as an office and has an exterior wall. The room is accessed on the SE wall of the hallway (Room 004) through a doorway with a hollow-core door surrounded with plain wood trim. The doorway is located near the west corner of the room. The concrete floor is covered with wall-to-wall carpet; the walls are paneled; and the room has a drop ceiling with two fluorescent light fixtures. The outer wall retains the original window opening with three replacement sashes (W007) and associated trim.

Room 003

The second room situated on the SE side of the hallway is Room 003. It is also accessed through a doorway with a hollow-core door and plain trim. The floors of the room are vinyl tile over concrete; the walls are gypsum board with a painted finish; and the ceiling is a drop ceiling with two fluorescent light fixtures. The room has no exterior walls.

Room 004

The hallway (Room 004) on this side of the basement is accessed through the NE elevation exterior doorway (D012). Room 004 provides access to the two offices and the telephone room (Room 007). The concrete floor is covered with vinyl tile; the walls of the partitioned rooms are covered with gypsum board; the original concrete walls retain the parged surface; and the ceiling is open to the concrete slab that forms the subfloor for the first story and has two fluorescent light fixtures. The doorway at the SW of the hallway that leads to Room 007 retains the two-panel metal-clad door and the historic trim elements.

Room 005

In Room 005 at the NW end of the Northeast Pavilion, the basement remains an unfinished crawl space with an earth floor and the exterior masonry foundation walls. The concrete support piers are evident at the center of the space, and the concrete slab subfloor for the first story forms the ceiling of the crawl space.

Main Block

Room 006

The northernmost bay (Room 006) of the garage bays constructed under the Terrace was partitioned off as an ordnance storage area. Upon entering the room through the exterior garage doorway (D009), there is a small anteroom that is partitioned from the rest of the space. A doorway with a solid wood door in a metal frame leads from that room into the main room. The partition walls are covered with gypsum board and the original walls are concrete. The ceiling is open to the concrete subfloor and has fluorescent lighting. On the NE wall of the room is a doorway to a storage closet under the exterior stairway. The walls around the closet doorway are in-filled with brick, and the doorway has a steel door and trim.

Room 007

Room 007 was formerly part of the larger storage area at the northeast end of the Main Block basement. The room was partitioned off to serve as a telephone and communication systems room and currently serves that purpose. At the doorway from the connecting hallway (Room 004) there is a step up into the room. The floor retains the original concrete slab, and the original walls are concrete and concrete block. The partition wall at the SW end of the room is covered with gypsum board and has a wood baseboard. A doorway in the SE wall has a steel door with steel trim and opens into the garage bays. The ceiling is open to the concrete subfloor and has fluorescent light fixtures.

Room 008

The garage bays (room 008) are situated on the southeast side of the basement. Since the end bay was partitioned, there are currently seven bays in this space. Each bay has a separate doorway with double-leaf doors that appear to be original. On the NW wall there is a doorway to Room 007 and a rough opening was cut into the concrete wall for access to Room 009. Also on that wall the original doorway to the storage area (Room 011) is extant. The garage floor is covered with poured concrete, and the walls are concrete. The concrete-covered beams supporting the Terrace above the garage are evident at the ceiling. Fluorescent light fixtures are attached to the underside of three of the beams. A fuel oil storage tank has been installed in the southernmost bay of the garage.

Room 009

Room 009 occupies the former storage space NE of the basement staircase and is currently used as a laundry facility. A stud partition wall covered with gypsum board separates this room from Room 007, and the other walls retain the original concrete materials. The doorway to the garage bays is unfinished. Near the west corner of the room a step leads up to the doorway to the landing at the bottom of the basement staircase (Room 010).

Room 010

Room 010 is a small landing at the base of the basement staircase, which has access to the Center Hallway on the first story. Doorways on both sides of the landing lead to the adjacent Laundry Room (Room 009) and Storage Room (Room 011). Both doorways have steel-clad doors with steel trim.

The basement staircase retains the steel structure and concrete treads. Portions of the concrete walls in the stairwell are covered with sheet vinyl trimmed with wood, and other areas have a composite wall covering with metal trim. All of the wall coverings appear to be later alterations. The landing near the top of the staircase has a window opening with a single casement sash and the doorway from the stairwell to the Center Hallway rear vestibule retains the historic door and elements.

Room 011

Room 011 is an unfinished storage space. Partitions were built between the concrete piers on the NW side of the space, and a doorway to the adjacent basement area (Room 012) was installed between to of the piers. The doorway has two five-panel wooden doors. A second doorway near the west corner of the room provides access to the SW end of the basement.

Room 012

This basement area at the NW side of the Main Block is an open storage space that extends to the NE crawl space and has access to the SW end of the basement. A portion of the basement floor in this section is concrete, and the portion along the NW foundation wall was excavated down to earth and bedrock. Sections of the unfinished portion along the NW wall are covered with wood shelving.

Southwest Pavilion

Room 013

The area at the NW end of the Southwest Pavilion basement remains unfinished. The floor is excavated down to earth and bedrock; the walls were open to the foundation; and the ceiling was concrete slab that was the subfloor of the first story. The concrete piers at the center of the room support the concrete-covered beam and the upper-story structure. This area of the basement does not appear to have been significantly altered since the original construction.

Room 014

The former Boiler Room was portioned into two rooms (Room 014 and 014a). A wood stud partition covered with fire-rated gypsum board encloses a rectangular room (Room 014a) that houses the current boiler, which is still vented through the original chimney. This room has one window opening that has metal louvers for ventilation. The rest of the former Boiler Room (Room 014) has otherwise had minimal alterations. The original chimney is intact on the NE wall of the room. The doorway at the NE end of the room leads to the adjacent storage spaces and was part of the original construction. It is currently equipped with a steel-clad door. The space is open to the basement hallway (Room 015) at the east corner of the room.

Room 015

Room 015 is the hallway that leads from the SE basement doorway (D001) to Room 014. The hallway also has access to the basement storage closets (Rooms 015a and 015b) and offices (Rooms 016, 017, and 017a). The floor of the hallway is concrete. The first section of the hallway has wood paneled walls and a drop ceiling. A small partition with a doorway separates the SE end of the hallway from the NW end. The NW end of the hallway has unfinished concrete walls, and the ceiling is open to the concrete slab subfloor of the first story. The exterior doorway (D001) has not been significantly altered. The doorway to Room 016 has a hollow-core wood door with a brass-coated locking doorknob and three brass butt hinges. The doorway is trimmed with a plain surround. The doorway to the closet under the Terrace staircase (Room 015a) has a board-and-batten door with strap hinges. The doorway to Room 015b retains the historic two-panel door and brass hardware. Room 015b was originally the Pump Room and is currently used as storage.

Room 016

Room 016 is an office that was built in a portion of the former Coal Storage Room. It is a rectangular room with a concrete floor, wood paneled walls, and a drop ceiling with four fluorescent light fixtures. There is a doorway to the hallway (Room 015) and a doorway to Room 017. Both doorways have hollow-core doors and are trimmed with plain boards. The room retains two window openings on the SE elevation each with two casement sashes (type D) and a window opening on the SW elevation with two casement sashes (type C). The window openings are also trimmed with plain boards.

Room 017

Room 017 is a small rectangular storage room within the former Coal Storage Room. It has partition walls separating it from the office and the adjacent storage (Room 017a). The partition walls are covered with gypsum board, and the room has a drop ceiling with one fluorescent light fixture. The adjacent room (Room 017a) is an unfinished storage space.

First-Story Elements

The room layout of the Apartment Building has not been significantly altered since the original construction (fig. 59). The first story retains the two apartments in the Main Block and the two apartments in the Southwest Pavilion. The former operations rooms and three bedroom Bachelors'/Commanding Officer's Apartment were combined to form a four-bedroom apartment that occupies the entire first story of the Northeast Pavilion. Since the changes were minimal, the first-story layout continues to reflect the Atterbury plan and retains a high degree of historic integrity.

The interior elements of the Apartment Building have been left intact with minimal alterations. Most of the alterations and renovations were documented in architectural drawings. Similar materials were used in all the apartments, giving the apartments a consistent appearance. The original interior elements were constructed with high-quality materials that are well preserved in the extant apartment units and hallways.

The following descriptions of the apartments and hallways document the current elements. Since most of the original plan and many of the original interior elements remain intact, the following sections will not reiterate the details that were included in the section on "Original Appearance." Overall the first-story interior plan and elements appear to be in good condition and retain a high degree of historic integrity.

First-Story Northeast Pavilion

Commanding Officer's Apartment

The original plan for the first story of the Northeast Pavilion included an eight-room apartment designated as the Bachelors' Apartment and a two-room operations area. Later alterations included the addition of a doorway between the apartment and operations room (CO-10), which created a four-bedroom apartment. The former Office (CO-08) and vestibule of the operations suite (CO-09) were also altered and a laundry room and bathroom were added in that corner of the Northeast Pavilion. Those changes included the construction of partition walls, closing off the exterior doorway (D101), and some other minor changes. In addition to these changes, the kitchen plan was altered. The partition wall between the kitchen and the small bathroom was moved to make more space in the kitchen, which made the bathroom smaller. The bathroom was probably eliminated at that time and now is a closet (CO-10a). Also a doorway the led directly from the vestibule (CO-01) to the kitchen was closed off. Otherwise, the overall room plan in the Commanding Officer's Apartment has not been significantly altered.

The original flooring in most of the rooms remains intact. The vestibule (CO-01) retains the terrazzo flooring, and the other rooms retain the tongue-and-groove wood flooring. In the Living Room (CO-02) and Dining Room (CO-07) the wood floor is currently covered with wall-to-wall carpet. There is vinyl floor covering in both bathrooms (CO-06 and CO-09), the laundry room (CO-08), and the Kitchen (CO-11). The former bathroom (CO-10a) retains the original ceramic tile. The current flooring throughout the apartment appears to be in good condition.

Generally the historic wall materials appear to be retained. The rough-textured plaster is extant in Rooms CO-01, CO-02, CO-07, and the hallway to the bedrooms. Most other rooms have smooth plaster walls. The Kitchen (CO-11) walls were renovated with ceramic tile covering the lower half of one wall and installed as the counter backsplash. A pass-through from the Kitchen to the Dining Room (CO-07) was cut into the SW partition wall of the Kitchen. The partition walls in CO-08 and CO-09 are constructed with gypsum board and skim-coated with plaster.

Many of the historic ceilings in the apartment have not been significantly altered. Drop ceilings have been installed in the Kitchen and the new bathroom (CO-09). The ceiling in CO-06 has been more refinished with a textured plaster material. Some minor cracking was noted in some of the older ceiling materials; otherwise the ceiling materials appear to be intact.

The interior of the entry doorway (D108) has the historic surround that has been preserved with the other doorway elements. Likewise, interior doorways throughout the apartment preserve the historic materials, including the hardware. The doorways are typically constructed with plain board surrounds with quarter-round trim, and the doorways have the original two-panel wood doors. The swinging door between CO-07 and CO-11 has been removed and replaced with an accordion door. The doorway connecting CO-07 and CO-10 was constructed with a surround and door that match the historic materials. The door to CO-10a was also replaced with a bi-fold door. The doorways in the newer partitions in CO-09 were constructed with plain trim and hollow-core doors.

Throughout the apartment the replacement windows were trimmed with pine boards and quarter-round molding to replicate the historic trim. Plain board trim was also installed on the window mullions separating the casements and on the 10-inch mullions that separate the sashes in the four-sash window opening (W103). The new sashes have wooden snap-in muntin grills, and the operable sashes have interior screens. The window surrounds were stained dark brown and varnished to match other interior trim. The window openings retain the original interior windowsills including the marble windowsills in the original bathrooms (CO-06 and CO-10a). The interior plaster jambs are intact and the apron trim below the windowsill was also retained.

Most of the baseboard and doorway trim in the apartment appears to retain the historic materials. The vestibule has terrazzo base trim, including a piece on the NW wall that was filled in when the former doorway to the Kitchen was removed. The wooden baseboard in the rest of the apartment is plain board with quarter-round caps. The same type of trim was installed around the original doorways and was used on the doorway between CO-07 and CO-10. Vinyl base trim was installed in CO-09, and ceramic base trim is present in CO-06.

The Living Room fireplace was apparently restored in 1985 and currently retains the original surround and mantelpiece. The hearth is currently covered with terra-cotta-colored ceramic tiles, and the fireplace has a brass insert with glass doors.

When the Bachelors' Apartment was first constructed, each of the three bedrooms had its own sink. However, the sinks were removed from CO-03 and CO-04, and the area where the sinks were located is currently used for shelving. In CO-03 plain board trim was installed around that area, but in CO-04 no trim was added. CO-05 retains the sink area, which has a replacement sink.

The Kitchen (CO-11) cabinets were replaced with plywood cabinets that have plain doors, and the countertops are Formica. In comparison with the other kitchens in the Apartment Building, the cabinet and counter materials in CO-11 appear to date from an earlier renovation and may not have been updated when the other kitchens were rehabilitated in the 1990s. The pass-through to CO-07 is trimmed with plain boards and has a wooden shelf.

The bathrooms (CO-06 and CO-09) are currently equipped with modern equipment and cabinets. CO-06 was originally designed with two toilet stalls and a shower stall, which were later replaced. That bathroom currently has a single toilet and combination tub/shower.

The utilities throughout the apartment were updated during various periods of renovation. In addition to the original electrical switches and wall sockets, wall-mounted conduit that serves new sockets and switches has been added in most rooms. The light fixtures in most rooms have been updated. However, the vestibule retains a historic ceiling-mounted fixture that may be original to the building and appears to be the only extant historic interior light fixture. The ceiling lights in the bedrooms and hallways are currently flush-mounted circular fixtures with translucent white globes. The center-mounted ceiling lights in both the Dining Room and Living Room are currently Mission-style hanging fixtures. Fluorescent light fixtures are installed in the bathrooms and the kitchen. In addition to the electrical upgrades, the radiators were replaced with fin-tube baseboard radiators in all of the rooms. The baseboard heating units are generally installed along the outside walls in each room.

First-Story Main Block

Northeast (NE) Hallway

The interior plan and architectural elements of the NE Hallway have not been significantly altered since the original construction. At the NW end of the hallway D102 remains as the primary access. The exterior doorway has replacement doors but the interior retains the historic surrounds. As previously described, there is an added filler strip at the head of the doorway to accommodate the short replacement doors. The doorway to the vestibule retains the original door and hardware (fig. 53a), as well as the door trim. The doorway to the utility closet has not been altered, and the elements of the closet have not been significantly altered (fig. 62). There are radiators in the back vestibule and at the NW end of the hallway. Both radiators are installed along the SW wall and are protected with metal covers, which appear to be historic. The ceiling light fixture near D102 is a brass lantern and is a replacement fixture. With the exception of the exterior doorway (D107), the vestibule at the SE end of the hallway has not been changed. The replacement doorway has sidelights with a single panel below three lights, and the doorway is trimmed with plain boards.

The staircase to the second story ascends along the SW wall of the hallway and has not been altered. The steel stringers, riser, base trim, and molding are still intact, and the terrazzo treads supported by steel have been retained. The steel balustrade and wooden handrail are also well preserved. The elements of the NE Hallway appear to be in good condition and the space preserves the original materials of the Apartment Building.

Center Hallway

The Center Hallway has not been notably altered and, as with the NE Hallway, many original elements are preserved. In plan the Center Hallway has a large NW vestibule, a central staircase hallway, and a small SE vestibule with access to the basement staircase. A replacement brass lantern-style light fixture hangs from the ceiling in each section of the hallway. The terrazzo floors and the skim-coated plaster walls and ceilings appear to be original.

The interior trim of D103 retains the plain surround with quarter-round molding. The same trim is retained around the doorway from the vestibule to the main hallway and around the doorway to the SE vestibule. The doorway separating the NW vestibule from the staircase hallway preserves the original elements that were illustrated in the 1933 architectural drawings (Appendix A, drawing number 13 of 37 sheets, fig. 61). Likewise, the doorway from the staircase hallway to the SE vestibule retains the original elements. The doorways to Apartment No. 1 and Apartment No. 2 retain the molded-steel surround and the two-panel doors that are typical of the apartment entry doorways. The doorknob on the apartment entry doors were replaced with the current brass locking knobs with a brass backplate. A steel surround is also installed in the doorway leading from the SE vestibule to the basement staircase. The SE exterior doorway (D106) is trimmed with plain boards.

Both the basement staircase and the staircase to the second story preserve the original elements. From the first story the staircase ascends along the SW wall to the intermediate landing and then to the second story. All of the elements of that staircase are intact and are representative of the original staircase illustrated in Atterbury's drawings.

Apartment No. 1

Apartment No. 1 is currently used as the office for the laundry service. The interior elements in Apartment No. 1 were typical for all the apartments in the Apartment Building. The plan of the apartment has not been altered since the original construction. The renovations to the Kitchen and bathroom not withstanding, most of the original materials have also been retained. The wood floors, plaster walls, and skim-coated plaster ceilings appear to be intact, and the baseboard trim and doorway surrounds have been preserved. Typical of all the apartments, the Kitchen (Room 102) was renovated in the 1990s and the swinging door leading to the Dining Room was removed. The floor is currently covered with 12-inch-square vinyl tile, and vinyl base trim is installed around the room. The new wood cabinets have single-panel wood doors and plain wood drawer fronts. The counters are covered with Formica with a low back, and ceramic tile is installed as the backsplash above the counters. The bathroom fixtures and medicine cabinet have been changed, but the floor, walls, and ceiling were not altered. In addition the porcelain tub appears to be original. The tub area was enclosed by a partition that was constructed between the tub and toilet. The walls of the tub enclosure have been covered with a fiberglass liner. The changes to Apartment No. 1 are typical of the rest of the building, and the interior elements are generally in good condition.

The historic doorway elements are well preserved throughout Apartment No. 1. The replacement windows have wooden snap-in muntin grills, and pine trim matched to the historic trim including the wide mullions of the four-sash window opening (W132, fig. 63). Other interior window elements retain the original materials including the interior plaster jambs, wood sills, sill aprons and associated trim (fig. 64).

As with other apartments, the utilities have been upgraded. The changes include new circular ceiling light fixtures in Rooms 103, 104, 105, and 107 and a globe-shaped fixture in the bedroom hallway. A fluorescent light fixture is installed in the Kitchen, and the bathroom medicine cabinet has a fluorescent light. Surface-mounted electrical conduit, sockets, and switches have been added to the rooms. The electrical upgrades include a circuit breaker box that has been installed in the foyer closet. New baseboard radiators are installed along the outer walls in each room.

The apartment appears to retain a significant amount of original materials in good condition and has a high degree of historic integrity.

Apartment No. 2

Apartment No. 2 is a two-bedroom apartment that mirrors the layout of Apartment No. 1. The renovations to the apartment were similar to those in Apartment No. 1 and included new windows, kitchen cabinets, counters, and appliances and new fixtures in the bathroom. The heating, electrical, and lighting have been upgraded too, including a circuit breaker box that is installed in the Foyer closet. The interior window trim was changed when the new sashes were installed, but the interior window jambs, windowsills, and associated trim are intact. Otherwise the rooms in the apartment retain the original elements and are in good condition.

Southwest (SW) Hallway

Like the other hallways in the Main Block, the SW Hallway was not significantly altered (figs. 65 and 66). The plan follows the original layout consisting of a main hallway with a staircase on the NE wall and access to the first-story apartments in the Southwest Pavilion, and the back vestibule with an exterior doorway to the Terrace. The hallway floors, walls, ceiling, and staircase appear to retain original elements and are generally in good condition. A new brass lantern light fixture is installed in the ceiling near D104.

Though the NW doorway (D104) has new doors the interior retains the original surround. The doorways to Apartment No. 3 and Apartment No. 4 retain the molded-steel surrounds and original two-panel doors, which have replacement brass knobs and plates. The doorway to the back vestibule has not been changed and preserves an example of the original materials. The doorway to the Terrace (D105) has a replacement door with sidelights and has plain board trim. The utility closet doorway and the interior elements of the closet have not been noticeably altered.

First-Story Southwest Pavilion

Apartment No. 3

Apartment No. 3 is a two-bedroom apartment at the NW end of the Southwest Pavilion. The renovations to Apartment No. 3 are similar to the other first-story apartments. The Kitchen cabinets, counters, and appliances were renovated with similar materials as Apartment No. 1. The door to the Kitchen closet was replaced with a folding door, but the doorway surround was left intact. The bathroom renovations included a new toilet, sink and vanity, shower fixtures, and a tub/shower liner. The replacement medicine cabinet above the sink has a fluorescent light fixture. Other alterations to the apartment included upgrading the electrical service, and installing baseboard radiators. The ceiling light fixtures have been changed to flush-mounted fixtures with circular globes in Rooms 301, 303, 304, 305, and 307. Ceiling fixtures with round globes were installed in the hallway to the Dining Room and the hallway to the bedrooms. A ceiling-mounted fluorescent light fixture is centered in the Kitchen ceiling. The electrical upgrades include a circuit breaker box that is installed in the northwest foyer closet. The interior window trim was replaced when the new sashes were installed, but the original interior plaster jambs, windowsills, and sill aprons were retained. The new sashes have wooden snap-in muntin grills and the operable sashes have interior screens. Otherwise the rooms of the apartment retain the original elements.

Apartment No. 4

The room plan of Apartment No. 4 has not been altered since the original construction. Both the Kitchen and the bathroom were renovated with similar materials as the other first-story apartments. Apartment No. 4 was more recently renovated to serve as an office and has wall-to-wall carpet over the wood floors throughout the apartment with the exception of the Kitchen, bathroom, and closets. The electrical upgrades included new circular ceiling fixtures in Rooms 401, 403, and the hallway, as well as new surface-mounted conduit, sockets, and switches. The ceiling light fixtures in both Rooms 404 and 406 were replaced with lighted ceiling fans. The electrical upgrades include a circuit breaker box that has been installed in the SE Foyer closet. Baseboard radiators were generally installed along the outer walls in each room. The rooms of Apartment No. 4 retain the historic wall and ceiling materials, as well as the baseboard trim, doorway trim, and windowsills. With the exception of the interior jambs, windowsills, and sill aprons, the interior window trim was altered when the sashes were replaced. The new sashes have wooden snap-in muntin grills, and the operable sashes have interior screens. The interior elements in Apartment No. 4 are in good condition and preserve some of the original materials of the Apartment Building.

Second-Story Elements

The room plan of the second-story apartments at the Apartment Building has not been altered since the original construction (fig. 60). Staircases in the NE Hallway, Center Hallway, and SW Hallway continue to serve as the access to the second-story apartments. The one-bedroom apartment and two-bedroom apartment in the Southwest Pavilion follow the same layout as the first-story rooms, and the apartments in the Northeast Pavilion mirror those in the Southwest Pavilion. There are also two apartments in the second story of the Main Block that followed a similar design as the first story Main Block apartments with slight variations. The original plan is well preserved in the extant apartments.

As with the first story, the interior elements of the second-story apartments have been left intact with minimal alterations. The most significant alterations were the window openings and the kitchen renovations, which were both documented in architectural drawings. The extant original interior elements are well preserved and retain a high degree of historic integrity.

The following descriptions of the apartments and hallways document the current elements. Since the original second-story plan and many of the original interior elements remain intact, the following sections will not reiterate the details that were included in the section on "Original Appearance." Overall the second-story interior plan and elements appear to be in good condition and retain a high degree of historic integrity.

Second-Story Northeast Pavilion

Apartment No. 5

Apartment No. 5 is a two-bedroom apartment that is accessed from the second story of the NE Hallway of the Main Block. Apartment No. 5 has been rehabilitated in the same manner as the other apartments. The Kitchen (Room 502) renovations included vinyl tile flooring, wood cabinets with single-panel doors, ceramic tile backsplashes, a fluorescent light fixture, and new appliances. The Kitchen closet has louvered bi-fold doors, and the swinging door in the doorway to Room 503 was removed. The bathroom (Room 506) has a new toilet, sink and vanity, shower fixtures and liner, and medicine cabinet with a light. The electrical system was upgraded with a circuit breaker box in the foyer closet, new circular overhead lights in the rooms, and surface-mounted conduit, sockets, and switches. It is evident from the two types of surface-mounted conduit that the electrical system has been upgraded at least twice. The rooms are currently heated by fin-tube baseboard radiators that are generally installed along the outside walls. There was evidence of water damage in some of the rooms due to problems with the heating system.

The alterations to the window openings in Apartment No. 5 are typical of the building. All sashes and surrounding trim were replaced, and the original interior plaster jambs, windowsills, and sill aprons were retained. The new sashes have wooden snap-in muntin grills, and the operable sashes have interior screens. The interior surfaces of the sashes are wood and the new trim around the sashes is wood, all of which was stained and varnished to match the historic trim. Throughout the apartment original wood floors, doorway surrounds, two-panel wooden doors, wooden baseboards, plaster wall surfaces, and ceiling surfaces are intact and representative of the historic appearance of the apartment. Apartment No. 5 is in overall good condition and has a high degree of historic integrity

Apartment No. 6

The alterations to Apartment No. 6 are typical for the building, and the apartment retains the original one-bedroom plan and a significant amount of original elements. The wood floors in most of the rooms are intact with some water damage due to heating problems. The ceramic tile floor in the bathroom (Room 605) has also been kept. The Kitchen (Room 602) has a vinyl tile floor that was installed during the most recent renovations. The plaster walls and ceilings have not been significantly altered and have the rough-textured finish in Rooms 601, 603, and 604 and the smooth finish in Rooms 602, 605, and 606. The doorways have the historic surrounds, and most original doors were retained with the hardware, including the chrome-plated hardware in Rooms 602, and 605. Apartment No. 6 is one of two apartments in which the doorway between the Kitchen and the Dining Room has an extant swinging door. Overall the apartment has a considerable number of historic elements that are well preserved and has a high degree of historic integrity.

The renovations to Apartment No. 6 included changes to the Kitchen (Room 602), bathroom (Room 605), and the installation of new window sashes and associated trim. All of those alterations were performed with the same materials that were used in other apartments and were previously described. The Kitchen closet doorway has a replacement bi-fold door. The improvements to the utilities were also typical for the building and included new baseboard radiators, surface-mounted electrical conduit, sockets, switches, and new ceiling light fixtures.

Second-Story Main Block

Northeast (NE) Hallway

The second story of the NE Hallway is essentially unchanged since the original appearance. The window openings at both ends of the hallway currently have replacement sashes that have a wood finish on the interior, snap-in wooden muntin grills, and interior screens. The interior window trim was replaced with pine trim finished to match the historic elements and the original interior plaster jambs and windowsill elements are extant. The ceiling light fixtures are brass lanterns that match the first story of the hallway. Fire-protection alarms and lights, as well as extinguishers have been installed in the hallway. Otherwise the NE Hallway retains a significant amount of original material and has a high degree of historic integrity.

Center Hallway

The Center Hallway retains the original staircase that ascends along the SW wall of the hallway to the intermediate double landing. From the landing the staircase continues to the second-story apartments. The steel staircase appears to retain the original elements with few alterations. The window opening at the double landing has three replacement sashes and replacement trim. The two end sashes are casements and the center sash is fixed. The original interior plaster jambs, windowsill, and sill apron are extant in the window opening.

The second story of the Center Hallway is essentially a large landing that is open to the stairwell, which is protected by the staircase balustrade. The terrazzo floor is intact, and the walls and ceiling appear to retain the original materials. Some peeling paint was noted on the ceiling. The doorways to the apartments have the original steel surrounds and two-panel doors with replacement brass locking knobs and brass plates. The absence of alterations in the Center Hallway gives the area a high degree of historic integrity.

Apartment No. 7

As previously described, Apartment No. 7 has the same plan as Apartment No. 1 with slight changes due to the location of the apartment doorway. In general the interior elements of the apartment are representative of the original materials and the renovations are similar to those in other apartments. The changes to the bathroom (Room 706) are typical and include replacement of the toilet, sink, vanity, and medicine cabinet. A partition wall was added in Room 706 between the tub and toilet, creating the tub enclosure which has shower fixtures and is covered with a fiberglass liner. The Kitchen (Room 702) has replacement wood cabinets, Formica counters, ceramic backsplashes, and vinyl tile flooring. The Kitchen closet doorway has historic trim with a replacement bi-fold door. The doorway from the Kitchen to the Dining Room retains the swinging door. Extensive water damage was noted in the Kitchen (Room 702) but it appears to be primarily cosmetic damage. Like the other apartments, Apartment No. 7 retains original elements in good condition.

The electrical utilities were upgraded with surface-mounted conduit, sockets, and switches, as well as replacement ceiling light fixtures and a circuit breaker box in the SE foyer closet. The heating was changed to baseboard radiators that are generally installed along the outside walls. A chase for plumbing was constructed in the east corner of Room 707.

Apartment No. 8

Apartment No. 8 has not been significantly altered. The room layout follows a similar plan as Apartment No. 2 on the first story, but the apartment is larger due to the floor area over the first story of the Center Hallway, as previously described. The elements that make the apartment unique are intact including the additional Kitchen closets and the larger room size. Also extant are the wood floors, plaster walls, plaster ceilings, wood baseboards, doorway surrounds, and certain window opening elements including the plaster jambs, wood windowsills, and sill aprons.

The Kitchen (Room 802) was renovated with the same materials and elements used in the other apartments. The closets in the passage between the Kitchen and the Dining Room (Room 803) retain the original doorways and associated elements including the chrome-plated hardware, which is representative of the original hardware used in the kitchens of the Apartment Building.

Other alterations to Apartment No. 8 were typical and included window sash and trim replacement, upgraded electrical service, and replacing the radiators with baseboard units. Alterations to the bathroom included enclosing the tub area, adding shower fixtures and lining the shower walls, a new toilet, a new sink and vanity, and a new medicine cabinet with a light over the mirror. A plumbing chase was constructed on the NE wall of Room 805.

Apartment No. 8 preserves the plan and original elements in good condition and retains a high degree of historic integrity.

Southwest (SW) Hallway

The second story of the SW Hallway has not been notably altered. The floor, wall, and ceiling surfaces retain original materials. The staircase also retains all of the original elements. Fire-protection alarms, lighting, and extinguishers have been mounted on the walls, and some sections of the walls surfaces are deteriorated and peeling. The ceiling light fixtures are brass lanterns that match the other replacement hallway fixtures. The window sashes and trim were altered, but the windowsills, sill aprons, and interior plaster jambs were retained. The doorways to Apartment No. 9 and Apartment No. 10 have the original molded-steel surrounds, and the two-panel wood doors have replacement brass locking knobs with brass plates.

Second-Story Southwest Pavilion

Apartment No. 9

The plan of Apartment No. 9 has not been altered. It generally follows the two-bedroom apartment plan of Apartment No. 3 on the first story with the previously noted difference in the Foyer (Room 901) closet. With the exception of the Kitchen and bathroom, the rooms in the apartment appear to have original elements with few alterations (fig. 67). As with the other apartments, the electrical service was upgraded with surface-mounted conduit, switches, and sockets, as well as new ceiling light fixtures. The heating was changed to baseboard radiators. The Kitchen (Room 902) has been renovated with replacement wood cabinets, Formica countertops, ceramic backsplashes, vinyl tile floors, and new appliances (fig. 68). The doorway to the Kitchen closet has a bi-fold door and retains the historic surround. The bathroom (Room 906) has been renovated with a new toilet, sink and vanity, shower fixtures and liner, and medicine cabinet with light. However, it retains the original ceramic tile floor, porcelain tub, plaster walls with faux tile, and plaster ceiling with ceiling vent.

The window openings in Apartment No. 9 have replacement sashes and interior trim. The sashes have wooden interiors and wooden snap-in muntin grills. The trim around the sashes was constructed to match the historic trim and the original windowsills, sill apron, and interior plaster jambs are intact, including the marble windowsill in Room 906. The operable sashes have interior screens.

The interior elements of Apartment No. 9 are in good condition and the original plan is intact. Due to the preservation of the elements and plan, the apartment retains a high degree of historic integrity.

Apartment No. 10

Apartment No. 10 is a one-bedroom with the same plan as Apartment No. 4 on the first story. The plan of the apartment has not been altered since the original construction and is representative of the original appearance. Currently the Kitchen (Room 1002) has vinyl tile floors, replacement wood cabinets, Formica countertops, ceramic tile backsplashes, a fluorescent ceiling light fixture, new appliances, and a bi-fold door in the closet doorway. The swinging door was removed from the doorway from the Kitchen to Room 1003. Renovations to the bathroom (Room 1005) included replacement sink and vanity, toilet, and medicine cabinet with an overhead light. The porcelain tub appears to be original, and a shower and fiberglass shower liner were added to the tub. The tub area is enclosed by a partition between the tub and toilet that is an alteration.

The apartment electrical service includes a circuit breaker box in the foyer closet, original switch and socket locations, as well as additional wall-mounted conduit, sockets, and switches. The ceiling light fixtures in most rooms are currently surface-mounted lights with circular white globes that are typical of the Apartment Building. The rooms are heated with fin-tube baseboard radiators that are generally installed along the outside walls.

Apartment No. 10 retains original elements including wood flooring, plaster walls, plaster ceilings, wood baseboards, wood doorway surrounds, and doors. The window openings have replacement sashes that are the same throughout the Apartment Building. The window openings retain the original interior plaster jambs, windowsills, and sill aprons (fig. 64). The interior elements of Apartment No. 10 are in good condition, and the apartment has a high degree of historic integrity.

Attic Story

Access to the attic story is through the drop staircases in both the NE and SW Hallways. The attic layout has not been altered and remains open above all sections of the Apartment Building. The wood plank catwalk that extends down the middle of each building section and to the window openings appears to be from the original construction. The attic remains unfinished and open to the steel framing, roof sheathing, wood framing of the cross-gable ends, and the brick chimneys (figs. 69 and 70). The only additions to the attic appear to be ductwork for the ventilation system and changes to the plumbing and electrical utilities.

The window openings in the cross gables have replacement aluminum-clad casement sashes with wooden interior finish and wooden snap-in grills. The SE elevation SW gable window opening has metal louvers for the current ventilation system in place of the sash. There is no interior trim on the cross-gable window openings (fig. 69). The dormer window openings were also rehabilitated with replacement sashes but are otherwise unchanged. The attic story preserves some important original elements, especially the steel framing members and the "nailcrete" roof sheathing (fig. 70), and has a high degree of historic integrity.

Figure 61. Apartment Building, Center Hallway NW vestibule interior doorway, 2008.

Figure 62. Apartment Building, NE Hallway utility closet, 2008.

Figure 63. Apartment Building typical interior of window opening with four sashes (W237), 2008.

Figure 64. Apartment Building typical interior of window openings with two sashes (W227) and three sashes (W226), 2008.

Figure 65. Apartment Building, SW Hallway looking NW at staircase and interior of D104, 2008.

Figure 66. Apartment Building, SW Hallway looking SE at staircase, utility closet doorway, and doorway to Apartment No. 4, 2008.

Figure 67. Apartment Building typical apartment interior elements, Apartment No. 9 looking NE from Living Room to Dining Room, 2008.

Figure 68. Apartment Building typical apartment kitchen elements, Apartment No. 9, Room 902, 2008.

Figure 69. Apartment Building, attic story, typical framing of roof and cross gable, 2008.

Figure 70. Apartment Building typical steel framing of hipped roof and "nailcrete" sheathing panels, 2008.

Figure 71. Power House adjacent to the Apartment Building,
SW and SE elevations looking north, 2008.

Power House

The Power House was enlarged in 1943[176] with the addition of a masonry structure to the NE elevation of the original structure. The addition was constructed with masonry walls of granite stone and horizontal bands of brick that copied the construction of the original Power House. The hipped roof of the addition was higher than the original building but again used the same type of materials, including terra-cotta roof tiles to match the original structure. The roof line of the original structure was extended to the NE to tie into the hipped roof of the addition. The window openings in the addition to the Power House were also constructed to match the original structure. However, the sashes were removed and replaced with louvers. Another less prominent brick structure was added to the NW elevation of the Power House at a later date. That addition has brick walls and a low-pitched shed roof. The additions to the Power House were constructed with compatible materials and do not detract from the overall appearance of the original Power House.

The documentary materials and extant evidence suggested that the small masonry structure that is at the SW end of the existing structure is the original portion of the Power House. That portion of the Power House measures approximately 17 feet by 19 feet and retains the historic double garage doors on the SW elevation, and an original window opening and casement sashes on the SE elevation. Though the Power House was added to twice since its construction in 1933, the original section retains original elements and has a high degree of historic integrity.

---

[176] Deborah Thompson, Ph.D., "National Register of Historic Places Continuation Sheet," for "The Power House, Building 2; Naval Security Group Activity, Winter Harbor, ME," July 2001, section 7, p. 1.

CHARACTER-DEFINING FEATURES AND GENERAL RECOMMENDATIONS

INTRODUCTION

A historic structure may be significant for its architectural features and/or its association with historic events and persons. The Apartment Building is recognized by the Maine SHPO as eligible for the National Register under all of those criteria (see the previous section "Introduction, National Register"). The character-defining features (CDFs) of a structure are those visual features and elements that define the structure and contribute to its historic integrity. To retain the historic integrity of the structure it is important to retain and preserve those CDFs.

The proposed treatment of the Apartment Building is rehabilitation with reuse as offices, conference rooms, visitor contact, exhibit space and housing.[177] The rehabilitation of a structure includes the retention of CDFs. *The Secretary of the Interior's Standards for Rehabilitation* address this in the definition of "rehabilitation," which is "the act or process of making possible a compatible use for a property through repair, alterations, and additions while preserving those portions or features which convey its historical, cultural, or architectural values."[178] The Secretary of the Interior further addresses rehabilitation in the following standards:

1. A property will be used as it was historically, or be given a new use that requires minimal change to its distinctive materials, features, spaces, and spatial relationships.

2. The historic character of a property will be retained and preserved. The removal of distinctive materials or alteration of features, spaces, and spatial relationships that characterize a property will be avoided.

3. Each property will be recognized as a physical record of its time, place, and use. Changes that create a false sense of historical development, such as adding conjectural features or elements from other historic properties, will not be undertaken.

4. Changes to a property that have acquired historic significance in their own right will be retained and preserved.

5. Distinctive materials, features, finishes, and construction techniques or examples of craftsmanship that characterize a property will be preserved.

6. Deteriorated historic features will be repaired rather than replaced. Where the severity of deterioration requires replacement of a distinctive feature, the new feature will match the old in design, color, texture, and, where possible, materials. Replacement of missing features will be substantiated by documentary and physical evidence.

---

[177] *Schoodic General Management Plan Amendment.* (Department of the Interior, NPS, April 2006).
[178] NPS website URL – http://www.cr.nps.gov/hps/tps/stanguide/rehab/rehab_index.htm.

7. Chemical or physical treatments, if appropriate, will be undertaken using the gentlest means possible. Treatments that cause damage to historic materials will not be used.

8. Archeological resources will be protected and preserved in place. If such resources must be disturbed, mitigation measures will be undertaken.

9. New additions, exterior alterations, or related new construction will not destroy historic materials, features, and spatial relationships that characterize the property. The new work shall be differentiated from the old and will be compatible with the historic materials, features, size, scale and proportion, and massing to protect the integrity of the property and its environment.

10. New additions and adjacent or related new construction will be undertaken in such a manner that, if removed in the future, the essential form and integrity of the historic property and its environment would be unimpaired.[179]

The following sections will identify the character-defining features and make general recommendations for the rehabilitation and reuse of the Apartment Building and the Power House. The CDFs and general recommendations for landscapes are meant to provide general guidance and should be reviewed by a Historical Landscape Architect.

The rehabilitation of the Apartment Building should conform to the appropriate fire, safety, and accessibility codes for historic buildings that are open for public use. This may include the installation of fire-suppression systems, which should be installed in a manner that does the least amount of damage to the historic building materials (see subsequent section "General Recommendations").

---

[179] NPS website URL – http://www.cr.nps.gov/hps/tps/stanguide/rehab/rehab_standards.htm

CHARACTER-DEFINING FEATURES

Apartment Building Exterior Elements

Design and Context

- The French Eclectic design of the Apartment Building by Grosvenor Atterbury, which followed the similar design employed for the gate lodges at Brown Mountain and Jordan Pond on Mount Desert Island.

- The original design of the Apartment Building for the U.S. Naval Radio Station, Winter Harbor, Maine, to accommodate two different uses (housing and operations).

- Site and location, and their related association with John D. Rockefeller, Jr., within the context of his facilitating the U.S. Naval Radio Station move from Otter Cliffs to Winter Harbor, the resulting development of the U.S. Naval Radio Station on Big Moose Island, and the extension of Ocean Drive on Mount Desert Island.

- The overall massing of the Apartment Building with the H plan formed by the Main Block, connecting hyphens, and the flanking pavilions, including the NW elevation courtyard and the SE Terrace that are defined by the flanking wings.

Walls

- Exterior masonry walls with granite and brick set in mortar and laid in alternating bands.

- Half-timbered portions of the exterior walls using pecky cypress timbers and the cypress wooden brackets supporting the projecting cross gables and window openings on the NW and SE elevations.

- The red brick panels between the half timbers that are laid in varying patterns including chevrons, zigzags, and basket-weave.

- The wooden cornice elements at the junction of the exterior walls and the overhang of the roof.

Entrance Stoops and Terrace

- The original elements of the entrance stoops including the NW elevation façade entrance stoops (D102, D103, and D104) and the NE elevation entrance stoop (D108) and adjacent stairway. The extant elements include the original designs with knee walls and terraced steps, and the masonry materials including granite and bluestone.

- The extant plan of the SE Terrace and extant historic materials including the granite and brick and bluestone coping of the parapet wall.

- The extant original location of the staircases flanking the Terrace.

Doorways

- The doorway locations in relation to the overall design and the function of the interior spaces.

- The extant original doorway materials including the brick jambs, pecky cypress lintels, and bluestone thresholds. D001, D012, and D108 also retain character-defining original door elements including the vertical board doors and decorative hardware.

- The design and extant materials of the hoods that were installed over the first-story doorways (D101, D102, D103, D104, D105, D107, and D108).

- The ten garage doorways on the SE elevation, especially the doorway locations and extant original materials including the brick piers, pecky cypress lintels, and vertical-plank double doors with strap hinges, Suffolk latch handles, heart-shaped escutcheons, and keeper bars.

Window Openings

- The overall design, proportions, and locations of the exterior window openings. This includes the mix of window opening sizes and styles that are extant at the Apartment Building.

- The exterior window opening materials including the surrounds, lintels, and windowsills that reflect the architectural style of the Apartment Building.

Roof and Related Elements

- The overall massing and design of the Apartment Building roofs that reflect that French Eclectic design and architectural style, including the steeply pitched hipped roofs, the cross gables, and the flat roofs over the hyphens.

- The terra-cotta roof tiles including the flat roof tiles and the different types of tile used for ridge, hip, and rake applications.

- The "nailcrete" panels used to sheath the roofs of the Apartment Building.

- The masonry chimneys at both ends of the Main Block, including the granite and brick chimney stacks and the terra-cotta chimney pots.

- The copper gutters installed along the edges of all the roofs and copper downspouts leading to the underground drainage system.

Utilities and Fixtures

- The surviving original exterior lights and brackets on the SE elevation near D001 and on the Northeast Pavilion near D010, and the bracket for the exterior light near D106.

Landscape

- The overall design and layout of the original driveways, service lot, and walkways, as well as the tennis court NE of the building that was added during the historic period.

- The historic planting around the building, especially the trees in the NW elevation courtyard and driveway circle.

Power House Exterior Elements

Design and Context

- The original construction of the Power House as part of the U.S. Naval Radio Station, Winter Harbor, Maine, and as a support structure for the Apartment Building.

- The design of the original section of the Power House by Grosvenor Atterbury to complement the design of the Apartment Building. Also the design and construction of the masonry wall connecting the Power House to the Apartment Building.

Walls

- Exterior masonry walls with granite and brick set in mortar and laid in alternating bands to match the exterior walls of the Apartment Building, especially in the original portion of the Power House but also in the addition that copies the same patterns of masonry walls.

Doorways

- The extant original doorway materials on the SW elevation doorway including the brick jambs, pecky cypress lintels, concrete ramp, and garage door leaves constructed with vertical-plank double doors, strap hinges, and Suffolk latch handles.

- The extant original doorway and doorway elements in the wall connecting the Power House and Apartment Building, including the pecky cypress lintel.

Window Openings

- The extant original window opening on the SE elevation of the Power House and all of the associated elements, especially the steel casement sash that is the only extant example of the original sashes for both the Power House and the Apartment Building.

Roof and Related Elements

- The hipped roof design of the Power House that complements the roof design of the Apartment Building.

- The terra-cotta roof tiles that match the roofing on the Apartment Building, including the flat roof tiles and the different types of tile used for ridge and hip applications.

Apartment Building Structural Elements

- The structural masonry elements including the reinforced concrete foundation, the concrete piers in the basement, the exterior masonry walls, the concrete block walls behind the half-timbering on the second story, the interior concrete walls on both sides of each of the main hallways, and the concrete slab subfloors for the first and second stories.

- The steel framing including steel beams covered with concrete, steel Lally columns, steel framing above doorways and window openings, and the steel ceiling joists on the second story.

- The steel roof framing including plates, rafters, purlins, ridges, posts, and collar ties.

Apartment Building Interior Elements

Plan

- The overall layout of the apartments and hallways in the Main Block, Northeast Pavilion, and Southwest Pavilion.

- The room plans of the two-bedroom apartments in the Main Block, and the one-bedroom and two-bedroom apartments in the pavilions.

- The open plan of the attic.

Floors

- Wood floors constructed with tongue-and-groove boards in the rooms of the apartments throughout the Apartment Building.

- Terrazzo flooring in the main hallways.

- Ceramic tile flooring in the bathrooms.

Walls

- The rough-textured plaster walls that were generally installed in hallways, living rooms, and dining rooms in the apartments, and the smooth plaster walls that were generally installed in the bedrooms and bathrooms.

- The lower portion of the plaster walls in the bathrooms and utility closets made with "Keene's Cement" and scored to resemble 6-inch square tile.

- Interior wall trim elements including wooden baseboards in the apartments, and terrazzo base trim in the main hallways and CO-01.

- Interior concrete walls constructed on both sides of the main hallways.

Ceilings

- The high ceilings on the first story and second story of the Apartment Building.

- Smooth and textured plaster-like skim coat over the concrete slabs on the first-story ceilings and finish plaster on the second-story ceilings.

Doorways

- The location of the interior doorways reflecting the original plan of the Apartment Building and the layout of the apartments.

- The elements of the interior doorways in the three main hallways, including the interior Center Hallway doorway with original surround, door, hardware, and sidelights.

- The interior doorway materials including the molded-steel surrounds of the apartment entrance doorways, the wood surrounds, the wood thresholds, the marble thresholds to the bathrooms, and the two-panel interior doors with original hardware.

Window Openings

- The location and configuration of the window openings within the apartments.

- The different sizes and types of window openings in relation to the function of the interior spaces.

- The extant original interior window opening elements including plaster jambs, molded wooden windowsills, and molded wooden sill aprons, as well as the marble windowsills in the bathrooms.

Staircases and Related Elements

- The elements of the steel staircases in the three main hallways including the steel stringers, steel risers, terrazzo treads, steel newel posts, and steel balustrade.

GENERAL RECOMMENDATIONS APARTMENT BUILDING AND POWER HOUSE

Introduction

The Schoodic GMPA proposes the rehabilitation and reuse of the Apartment Building in conjunction with the Schoodic Education and Research Center (SERC) activities at the site. The rehabilitation and reuse may require modifications for ADA accessibility; upgrading utilities; installing fire-protection systems; and reconfiguring interior spaces for offices, conference rooms, visitor contact, exhibit space, and/or housing.[180] The rehabilitation of the building should be done in a manner that does not diminish the historic integrity of the structure. It is recommended that any reuse of the building that would require the creation of larger meeting rooms be planned with awareness to the historic elements of the building. The feasibility of any alterations to the exterior or interior should be studied and any alterations should be planned with minimal impact to the CDFs. The Schoodic GMPA recommends reusing the Power House in its historic capacity as a utility. The building is integral to the Apartment Building and should be part of the rehabilitation. The following general recommendations are meant to guide the rehabilitation of the Apartment Building and the Power House.

Exterior Elements

Design and Context

- The French Eclectic design and overall plan of the Apartment Building and the Power House are important CDFs. The rehabilitation of the buildings should not alter the original design, massing, or orientation; should retain extant historic elements; and should strive to preserve the CDFs. The installation of ADA-compliant ramps and entrances, as well as emergency exits, should be done in a manner that does not adversely impact these CDFs (see subsequent section "Accessibility").

---

[180] *Schoodic GMPA*, p. 40.

- The rehabilitation of the Apartment Building should consider the important contextual associations of the building and site with certain people. Those include Grosvenor Atterbury Architect and John D. Rockefeller, Jr. as key figures in the development of the site and the design and construction. The rehabilitation and reuse of the Apartment Building should include an exhibit or published materials that describe the importance of these associations.

- Likewise the significance of the Apartment Building as part of the U.S. Naval Radio Station, Winter Harbor, should be incorporated into any exhibit space and visitor contact station.

Walls

- The exterior masonry and half-timber wall elements should be preserved during the rehabilitation of the Apartment Building. Any rehabilitation projects should retain the extant configuration and patterns of the masonry and half-timbered walls. The installation of fire-protection systems, such as alarms and exterior emergency lights, should be done in a manner that has minimal impact on the exterior wall elements. The deficiencies and deterioration of the exterior wall elements should be rehabilitated in accordance with the specifications for masonry and wood restoration prepared by Theriault/Landmann Associates.[181]

- Likewise, the exterior masonry walls of the Power House and the associated wood trim elements should be preserved. The rehabilitation of the exterior wall elements should be performed according to the preservation specifications prepared by Theriault/Landmann Associates.

Entrance Stoops and Terrace

- The design and materials of the entrance stoops on the NW and NE elevations are important features of the exterior of the Apartment Building and should be preserved. The rehabilitation of the stoops should follow the specifications for masonry restoration prepared by Theriault/Landmann Associates.[182] The construction of an ADA-compliant ramp and entrance should be planned with attention to the preservation of the original elements of the entrance stoops. The feasibility of alternate locations for ADA-compliant access should be carefully studied with consideration for minimal impact on the Apartment Buildings CDFs (see subsequent section "Accessibility").

---

[181] Theriault/Landmann Associates. Rockefeller Building, Building #1 NSGA, Winter Harbor, Maine, Preservation Specifications (Theriault/Landmann Associates, Oct. 2001).

[182] Theriault/Landmann Associates. Preservation Specifications.

- The rehabilitation and reuse of the Terrace should preserve the design, plan, and extant historic materials that are CDFs. Since the original Terrace deck materials are not extant, the repair of the deck should be done with a material similar to the existing slate, which was approved by the Maine SHPO.

- The rehabilitation and reuse of the Apartment Building should preserve the location and design of the staircases flanking the Terrace. As observed by Theriault/Landmann Associates, the current deterioration of the brick risers and concrete treads should be addressed. The stair treads were originally constructed with bluestone and should be restored with the same material following the specifications by Theriault/Landmann Associates. If an ADA-compliant chairlift is installed along one of the staircases, the installation should be done with minimal impact on the building materials.

Doorways

- The doorway locations and extant original doorway elements should be preserved during the rehabilitation of the Apartment Building and the Power House. The brick surrounds, pecky cypress lintels, bluestone thresholds, and doorway hoods should be retained as part of any rehabilitation projects. The existing exterior doors in D101, D102, D103, D104, D105, D106, and D107 are not historic. If feasible, the doors should be restored with doors that more closely match the historic doors, which were illustrated in original architectural drawings and historic photographs. The exterior doors in D001, D012, and D108 are original elements and should be retained and preserved. Any projects that would affect these doorways should be planned to have minimal impact on the extant original elements.

- Rehabilitation and reuse projects that include alterations to the garage bays should retain the extant garage doorway locations and surrounds, as well as representative examples of the garage doors and door elements.

Window Openings

- The rehabilitation of the Apartment Building should retain the existing locations, design, proportions, and extant original elements of the exterior window openings. If feasible, repair and replacement of the window sashes should be done with sashes that more accurately match the original divided-light steel sashes. Since replacing all the sashes with true divided-light sashes would be cost prohibitive, this could be accomplished with energy-efficient sashes with simulated divided lights that are more defined than the existing muntin grills. It may also be possible to rehabilitate the existing sashes to better match the original divided-light sashes by installing different muntin grills and/or some type of applied grill on the exterior of the sashes.

- The extant original window opening with the steel casement sashes on the SE elevation of the Power House should be retained and preserved during the rehabilitation of the Power House and the Apartment Building as it is the only surviving original example from either structure.

Roof and Related Elements

- The roofs and roof materials of the Apartment Building and the Power House should be preserved during the rehabilitation of the building. Repairs to the roof materials should be performed with in-kind materials, especially the replacement of broken or missing terra-cotta roof tiles. In addition, the "nailcrete" sheathing panels should be kept intact and not altered during the rehabilitation of the building.

- The repair and rehabilitation of the chimneys should preserve the extant original masonry elements. If repairs require the replacement of original elements, the replacement should be done with in-kind materials. Rehabilitation and repairs to deteriorated mortar should be performed according to the specifications prepared by Theriault/Landmann Associates.

Utilities and Fixtures

- The exterior lights and brackets on the SE elevation near D001 and on the Northeast Pavilion near D010 as well as the bracket for the exterior light near D106 are original elements and should be preserved and retained.

Landscape

- The overall design and layout of the original driveways, service lot (SE parking lot), and walkways are mostly intact and should be maintained in their current configuration. In addition the extant tennis court should be left in its current location. If feasible, the parking area that was added to the top/northwest side of the circular driveway should be removed so that portion of the driveway will more closely represent the historic appearance. The Conceptual Site Plan included in the Schoodic GMPA appears to achieve that goal by redesigning the parking lot and adding a buffer of trees between the upper lot and the circular driveway. However, that plan did eliminate the tennis court, which is not recommended. If the redesign of the parking area is not feasible, alternatives should be carefully considered with attention to the historic landscape and landscape features.

- Natural change in the trees and plants around the building has taken place since the construction of the building. The existing trees in the NW elevation courtyard are mature birches, and the rest of the site is primarily lawn and mature evergreens. With the guidance of a Historical Landscape Architect a plan should be developed that would replace some of the trees that were removed from the courtyard and the driveway circle. The plan should address replacement of existing trees as they die and are removed. The plan should take into consideration the historic planting plan and historic plant materials for the landscape around the building.

Structural Elements

- The structural elements of the Apartment Building including the reinforced concrete and steel framing, are representative of the construction techniques employed by Atterbury and should be preserved. Any rehabilitation projects that will affect these elements should be planned to have minimal impact on the original building materials.

Interior Elements

Plan

- The rehabilitation of the Apartment Building should preserve the overall layout of the building and examples of the two-bedroom apartments in the Main Block, and the one-bedroom and two-bedroom apartments in the pavilions. The reuse of the building may require the addition of ADA-compliant access, meeting rooms, and facilities. It is recommended that several options be reviewed and that the pros and cons of any alterations be considered when determining the feasibility of rehabilitating the Apartment Building. Any rehabilitation of the apartments should strive to preserve as much of the extant plan as feasible. The following options may be helpful for planning the reuse of the building:
    - ➢ The plan and layout of the basement rooms has been altered and does not retain the same level of integrity as the first- and second-story plans. If plans for the reuse of the building include the creation of larger meeting rooms, consideration should be given to converting some of the basement space for that purpose. Specifically the garage bays on the SE side of the basement that are currently used for storage offer an open space that might be adapted as a large meeting space. Additionally this location on the ground story would allow ADA access from the SE elevation of the building. An ADA-compliant entrance would have to be constructed within one of the garage doorways, and some of the garage doorways would need to be retrofitted with window sashes. These alterations could be done with compatible materials to have minimal impact on the exterior elements.

- ➢ The original configuration of the first-story apartment in the Northeast Pavilion (Commanding Officer's Apartment) has been altered by the addition of the two operations rooms to the original apartment layout and the changes to the Kitchen and bathrooms. However, a majority of the rooms that make up the apartment do retain their original plan. If the reuse of the Apartment Building does include the installation of ADA-accessible facilities and the creation of larger meeting rooms on the first story, consideration should be given to using this apartment for those purposes. The NW entrance to the Northeast Pavilion (D101) could be altered for an accessible entrance. In addition the previous alterations and existing larger rooms would make this a good option for ADA-compliant rooms. Conversely, the Commanding Officer's Apartment is the only one of its kind in the building, a majority of the rooms that make up the apartment do retain their original plan, and the apartment retains unique features such as the vestibule (CO-01) and the fireplace and mantelpiece in Room CO-02. Therefore, further alteration would affect the historic integrity of that apartment.

- ➢ Though it has not been extensively altered, the first story of the Southwest Pavilion may also be considered for an ADA-accessible location for the building. The entrance doorway (D104) could accommodate a ramp that approached along the NE elevation of the Southwest Pavilion (see subsequent section "Accessibility"). The SW Hallway could accommodate ADA access, and the SE doorway (D105) could be altered for access to the Terrace. The creation of accessible rooms and facilities on the first story would require alteration to Apartments No. 3 and No. 4, but examples of those types of apartments could be retained on the second story, which has the same layout as the first story. The impact of creating ADA-compliant rooms on the first story of the Southwest Pavilion would be the alteration of the entrance stoop at D104 and the alteration of the first-story apartments that remain relatively unchanged since the historic appearance.

- The open plan of the attic should be preserved during the rehabilitation of the Apartment Building and should only be used for services and utilities. Compliance with local fire codes and the installation of additional utilities should be planned to have minimal impact on the open plan of the attic.

- The extant plan of the Power House should be retained during the rehabilitation of the building. Depending upon the intended use of this building, it may be feasible to install a visitor contact station in the Power House. The wide doorway on the SW elevation could be rehabilitated to be ADA compliant, and the interior of the building could have an open plan that would allow access.

Floors

- The previous CDFs section indentified original flooring throughout the Apartment Building that should be retained during the rehabilitation and reuse of the building. The installation of additional utilities and fire-suppression systems should be planned with minimal alteration of the existing flooring. Existing chases and closet spaces should be used to conceal additional conduit and pipes for new systems. When feasible, damaged flooring should be repaired with in-kind materials that match the extant flooring material, size, and color.

Walls

- The extant original wall elements, including wall trim identified as CDFs should be preserved when feasible. The installation of fire-suppression systems, alarms, and additional utilities should be planned to have minimal impact on the extant wall materials. Fire-suppression systems should be surface mounted and not be installed inside wall partitions. When feasible, existing chases and closet space should be used to conceal additional conduit and pipes for new systems. Damaged wall elements should be repaired with in-kind materials that match the material, texture, and color of the extant materials.

- If feasible, the alteration of walls to comply with ADA accessibility should be minimized. When possible, rehabilitation projects should reuse extant wall and trim elements, and new elements should match in kind the extant original materials.

- The removal of wall elements and related features to create larger meeting spaces should be thoughtfully planned in order to preserve as much of the extant wall materials as possible. The larger meeting and conference rooms would preferably be located in the garage bays.

Ceilings

- The ceiling height and materials on the first and second stories should be preserved during the rehabilitation of the Apartment Building. The installation of fire-suppression systems, alarms, and additional utilities should be planned to have minimal impact on the extant ceiling materials. Openings for the installation of additional utilities and fire-suppression systems should be thoughtfully located and their impacts minimized. Fire-suppression systems should be surface-mounted. When feasible, existing chases and closet space and existing holes in these spaces should be used to conceal additional conduit and pipes for new systems. Damaged ceiling elements should be repaired with in-kind materials that match the material, texture, and color of the extant materials.

Doorways

- When feasible, the rehabilitation and reuse of the Apartment Building should preserve the locations and extant original elements of the interior doorways. The installation of ADA-compliant interior doorways will require the alteration of existing doorways to meet code requirements. If it is necessary to alter existing doorways for ADA access, the extant doorway elements should be reused when feasible. Repair and replacement of doorway elements should be performed with in-kind materials.

Window Openings

- The location and type of the window openings, as well as the extant original interior elements identified as CDFs should be preserved and retained. Rehabilitation of the window openings and the repair or replacement of any window sashes should be accomplished with minimal impact on the extant window surrounds, sills, and associated elements. Repair and replacement of interior window opening elements should be performed with in-kind materials.

Staircases and Related Elements

- The elements of the steel staircases in the three main hallways should be retained and preserved during the rehabilitation of the Apartment Building. The elements of the staircases are currently intact and should not be altered. The installation of fire-suppression systems should eliminate the need for fire-separation walls at the stairwells. This should be confirmed during the review of fire regulations and local codes.

Accessibility

Compliance with ADA accessibility requirements is planned as part of the rehabilitation and reuse of the Apartment Building. Since the building has been determined eligible for the National Register of Historic Places, by ADA definition, it qualifies as an historic building. It is recommended that the requirements for an ADA-compliant building be reviewed and a feasibility study for several alternatives for accessible areas to the building undertaken.[183] The following recommendations should help guide the placement of ADA-accessible facilities at the Apartment Building.

- The building should have at least one accessible route from an ADA-compliant parking space or spaces. The accessible route should include an access ramp and ADA-compliant entrance doorway. The requirements for an ADA-compliant access route should be reviewed and alternate routes to the building should be considered.

- One option for such a route would be on the SE elevation of the building at the basement story. As previously described, conversion of a section of the garage bays to meeting space would provide an opportunity for an ADA-compliant access point. One of the garage doorways could be altered as an ADA-compliant doorway, and a ramp could be provided from the nearby parking area.

- In addition to the latter, or as an alternative, an access route could be planned for the first story of the Northeast Pavilion. This space might be considered for larger meeting space as well as exhibit space and could be altered to accommodate ADA accessibility. An access ramp could be constructed from an ADA parking space to D101 on the NW elevation of the pavilion. That doorway is currently closed off and could be opened and made ADA compliant. This doorway has the added advantage of being closer to grade level than any of the other first-story doorways. Thus the required ramp could be shorter and less obtrusive. The interior floor plan and doorways could also be altered to conform to ADA requirements. The pros and cons previously discussed should be taken into consideration. If the construction of an ADA-compliant entrance requires alterations to the interior doorways, when feasible the doorways and doorway elements should be constructed to replicate the appearance of the historic elements. Likewise alterations to interior floor, wall, and/or ceiling elements should be constructed with materials that match the historic elements when feasible.

- As an alternative, creating an ADA-compliant entrance and accessible rooms in the Southwest Pavilion should also be considered. The entrance stoop leading to D104 would have to be reconstructed to accommodate a ramp. One possible location for the ramp would be along the NE elevation of the Southwest Pavilion. This approach would require removing one of the knee walls of the entrance stoop and the alteration of D104 as an accessible entrance. At the SE end of the hallway, D105 would require alteration to conform to ADA requirements. However, since both D104 and D105 were previously altered, the impact on the doorways is minimal. If feasible the installation of accessible doorways should be done to more closely match the historic

---

[183] http://www.access-board.gov/adaag/about/index.htm

appearance of the doorways. At its narrowest point the SW Hallway is over 4 feet wide and should be able to accommodate ADA access in its current configuration. The doorway to the vestibule at the SE end of the hallway is over 3 feet wide, which is above the ADA-required minimum of 32 inches. As previously described alterations to Apartments No. 3 and No. 4 would be required for accessible rooms and facilities, including accessible restrooms.

- As part of the ADA-compliant accessible route, ADA parking spaces should be created in the SE elevation parking area and near the NW elevation courtyard. The existing walkways should be maintained to provide stable surfaces from the parking lot to the accessible ramps and the building.

- Compliance with ADA regulations requires the installation of an accessible restroom. The construction of any restrooms should be accomplished with the least amount of alterations to historic elements as possible. The existing bathroom on the first story of the Northeast Pavilion (CO-06) could be reconfigured into a unisex accessible restroom. It appears to be large enough to accommodate accessible utilities with minimal alterations. The existing toilets and sinks will need to be replaced with accessible utilities that are placed in the proper locations to allow access. It may be necessary to widen certain doorways and hallways to meet the ADA requirements. If the construction of ADA-compliant restrooms requires alterations to the doorways, the doorways and doorway elements should be constructed to replicate the appearance of the historic elements. An ADA-compliant restroom could also be constructed on the basement story as part of the conversion of the existing garage bays.

- The ADA-accessible area should include exhibit space and interpretive materials. Interpretive panels that describe the history of the site and building should be installed in the accessible space.

BIBLIOGRAPHY

PRIMARY SOURCES

Primary source materials compiled by Lee Terzis from records at the Rockefeller Archive Center, Sleepy Hollow, New York, were used in researching the "Historical Background and Context" of the Apartment Building. Additional correspondence from the Rockefeller Archive Center also provided information pertinent to the report.

Primary source materials from the Acadia NP Archives, Bar Harbor, included records of the U.S. N.S.G.A., Winter Harbor, Progress Report Photographs (Appendix B), project reports, and newspaper clippings. The primary documents at Acadia NP, Winter Harbor, included architectural drawings stored in Map Case C, Drawer 5, folders 1, 2 and 5 and Map Case C, Drawer 2, Folder 4. Maps of the U.S. Naval Radio Station, Winter Harbor, Maine, are stored in the Map Case A, Drawer 2, folder 4. In addition, the following primary documents were used in the preparation of the HSR.

Atterbury, Grosvenor. "Notes on the Architectural and Other Esthetic Problems Involved in the Development of Our Great National Parks," August and September 1929 (Technical Information Center, Denver Service Center, NPS).

Bar Harbor Times, April 12, 1933 (copy ACAD Archives).

The Bangor Daily News, August 3, 1933 (copy ACAD Archives).

Grossman, Leo. "Final Construction Report—1935, Acadia National Park, Frazer's Creek—Big Moose Island, Hancock County, Maine, Project No. 2A4." National Park Service; February 17, 1936 (Technical Information Center, Denver Service Center).

P. and F. Corbin Division Catalog, American Hardware Corp., Successor. New Britain, CT, November 1, 1940 (Historic Architecture Program Library, Lowell, MA).

Sherman, Richard, NPS Engineer, and George Gordon, NPS Assistant Landscape Architect, "Statement of Cost, Buildings, Equipment, Service Facilities, etc., Schoodic Naval Radio Station," April 1, 1935 (Acadia NP Archives).

Terzis, Lee. "Rockefeller Family Archives, John D. Rockefeller, Jr. correspondence—Naval Radio Station, Schoodic Peninsula, Acadia National Park." Primary documents from the Rockefeller Archive Center, Sleepy Hollow, NY (Acadia NP Archives).

SECONDARY SOURCES

Cultural Resources Survey, Naval Security Group Activity, Winter Harbor, ME. United States Department of the Navy, Naval Facilities Engineering Command, Northern Division. The Cultural Resources Group, Louis Berger and Associates, Inc., September 1999 (copy ACAD Archives).

Dorr, George B. *Acadia National Park: Its Origin and Background, Book I.* Bangor, ME: Burr Printing Company, 1942.

Dorr, George B. *Acadia National Park: Its Growth and Development, Book II.* Bangor, ME: Burr Printing Company, 1948.

Ernst, Joseph W. *Worthwhile Places: Correspondence of John D. Rockefeller, Jr. and Horace M. Albright.* New York: Fordham University Press for Rockefeller Archives Center, 1991.

Fosdick, Raymond B. *John D. Rockefeller, Jr.: A Portrait.* New York: Harper and Brothers, Publishers, 1956.

Foulds, H.E., and Lauren G. Meier. *Cultural Landscape Report for Blackwoods and Seawall Campgrounds, Acadia National Park.* Boston, MA: U.S. DOI, NPS, Olmsted Center for Landscape Preservation, September 1996

General Management Plan, Acadia National Park, Maine. Washington, DC: U.S. Department of the Interior, National Park Service, October 1992.

Goodwin, R. Christopher and Associates. *Navy Cold War Communication Context: Resources Associated with the Navy's Communication Program, 1946 – 1989.* Frederick, MD: R. Christopher Goodwin and Associates, Inc., December 1997.

Harris, Cyril M. *Dictionary of Architecture and Construction; Fourth Edition.* New York: The McGraw-Hill Companies, Inc., 2005.

A History of the U.S. Navy at Schoodic Peninsula. U.S. Navy, 2001 (copy ACAD Archives).

Rieley, William D. and Roxanne S. Brouse. *Historic Resource Study for the Carriage Road System, Acadia National Park, Mount Desert Island, Maine.* Charlottesville, VA: Rieley and Associates, Landscape Architects, May 1989.

McAlester, Virginia and Lee. *A Field Guide to American Houses.* New York: Alfred A. Knopf Publishing, 1984.

MacKay, Robert B., Anthony K. Baker, and Carol A. Traynor. *Long Island Country Houses and Their Architects, 1860 – 1940.* New York: W.W. Norton and Company, 1997.

Moore, Charles. *The Life and Times of Charles Follen McKim.* Boston and New York; Houghton Mifflin Company, 1929.

Schoodic General Management Plan Amendment, Acadia National Park, Maine (Washington, DC: U.S. Department of the Interior, National Park Service, April 2006).

Thompson, Deborah, Ph.D. National Register of Historic Places Registration Form: Apartment Building; Building 1. Naval Security Group, Winter Harbor, Maine, September 2001.

Weeks, Kay D. and Anne E. Grimmer. *The Secretary of the Interior's Standards for the Treatment of Historic Properties, with Guidelines for Preserving, Rehabilitating, Restoring and Reconstructing Historic Buildings.* Washington, DC: U.S. Department of the Interior, National Park Service, 1995.

Wentworth, Brandon. *The Fabulous Radio NBD, Otter Cliffs, Acadia National Park.* Southwest Harbor, ME: Beech Hill Publishing Co., 1984 (copy ACAD Archives).

APPENDICES

APPENDICES

APPENDIX A

**Apartment Building Architectural Drawings, 1933
by Grosvenor Atterbury Architect and
Navy Department, Bureau of Yards and Docks**[184]

---

[184] Apartment Building Drawings 1 through 37 by Grosvenor Atterbury Architect and the Navy Department, Bureau of Yards and Docks, May and June 1933. (ACAD Archives, Winter Harbor, ME).

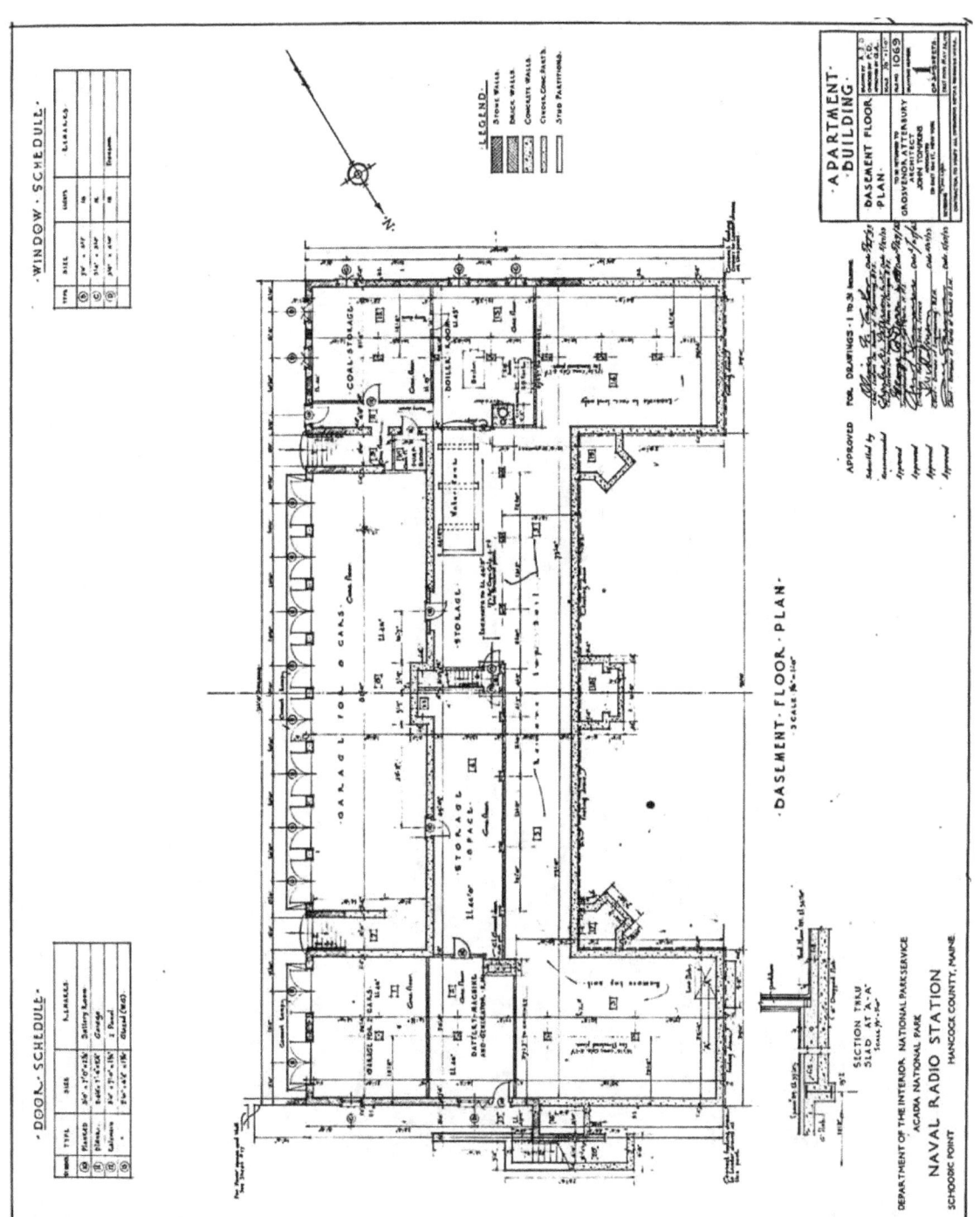

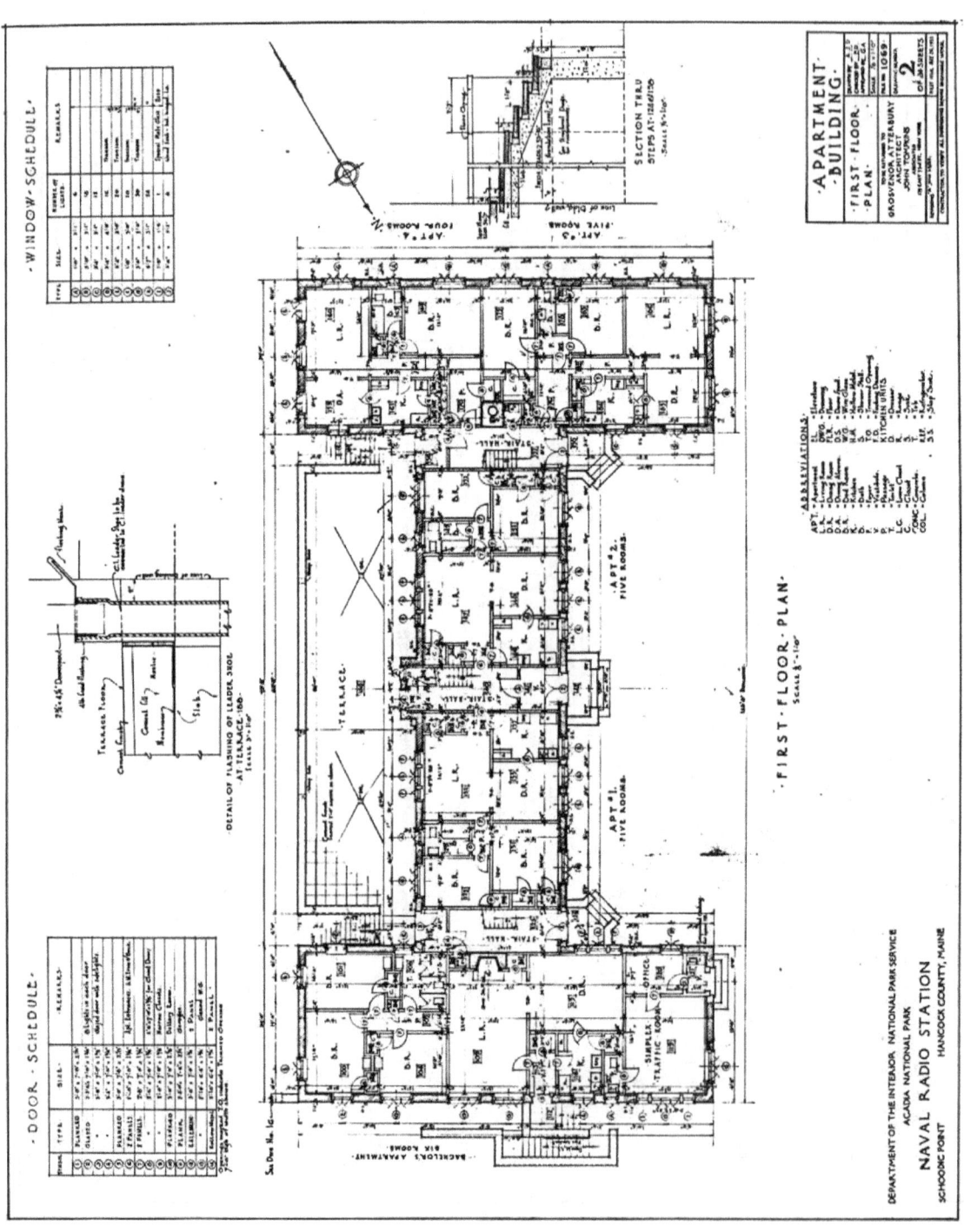

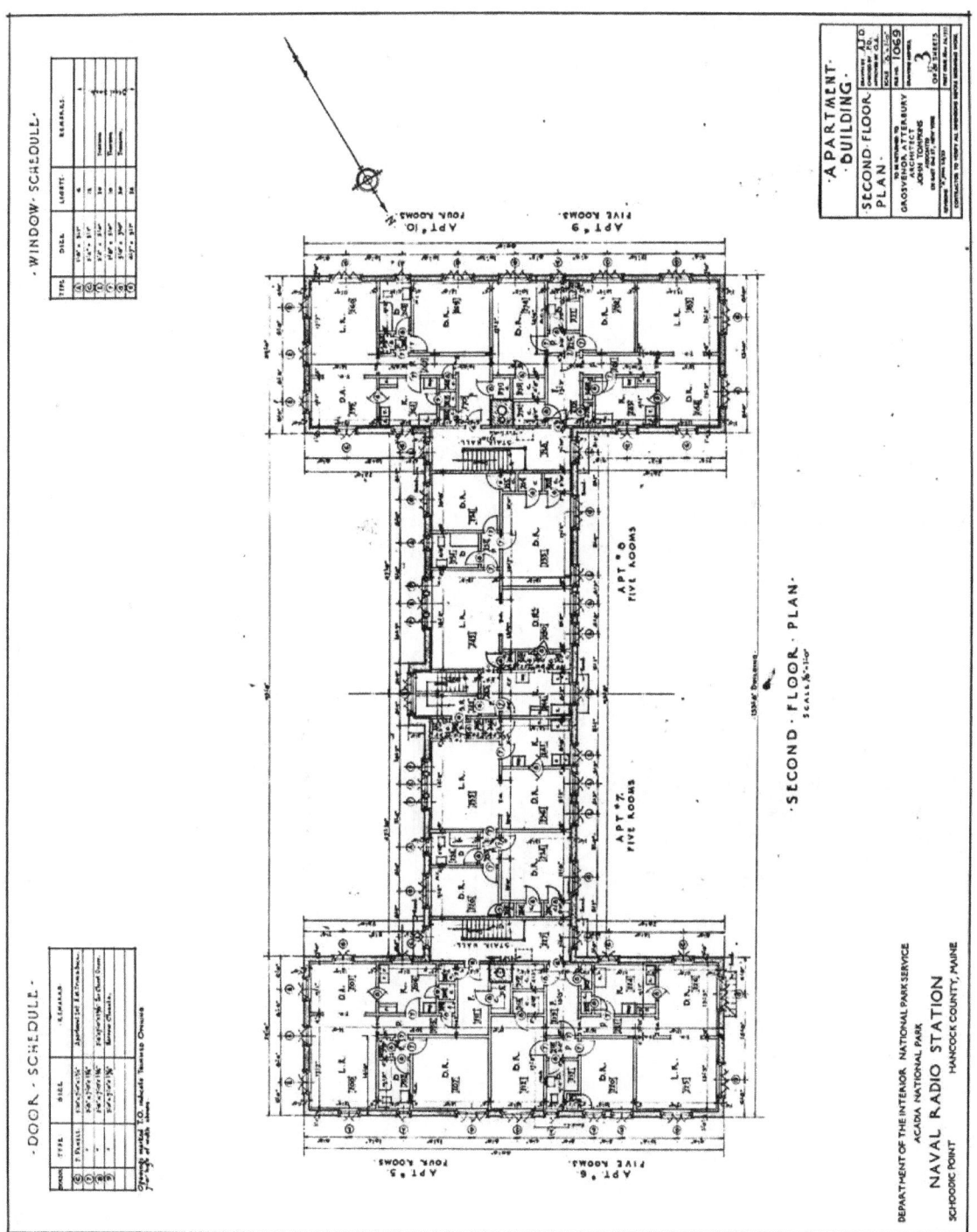

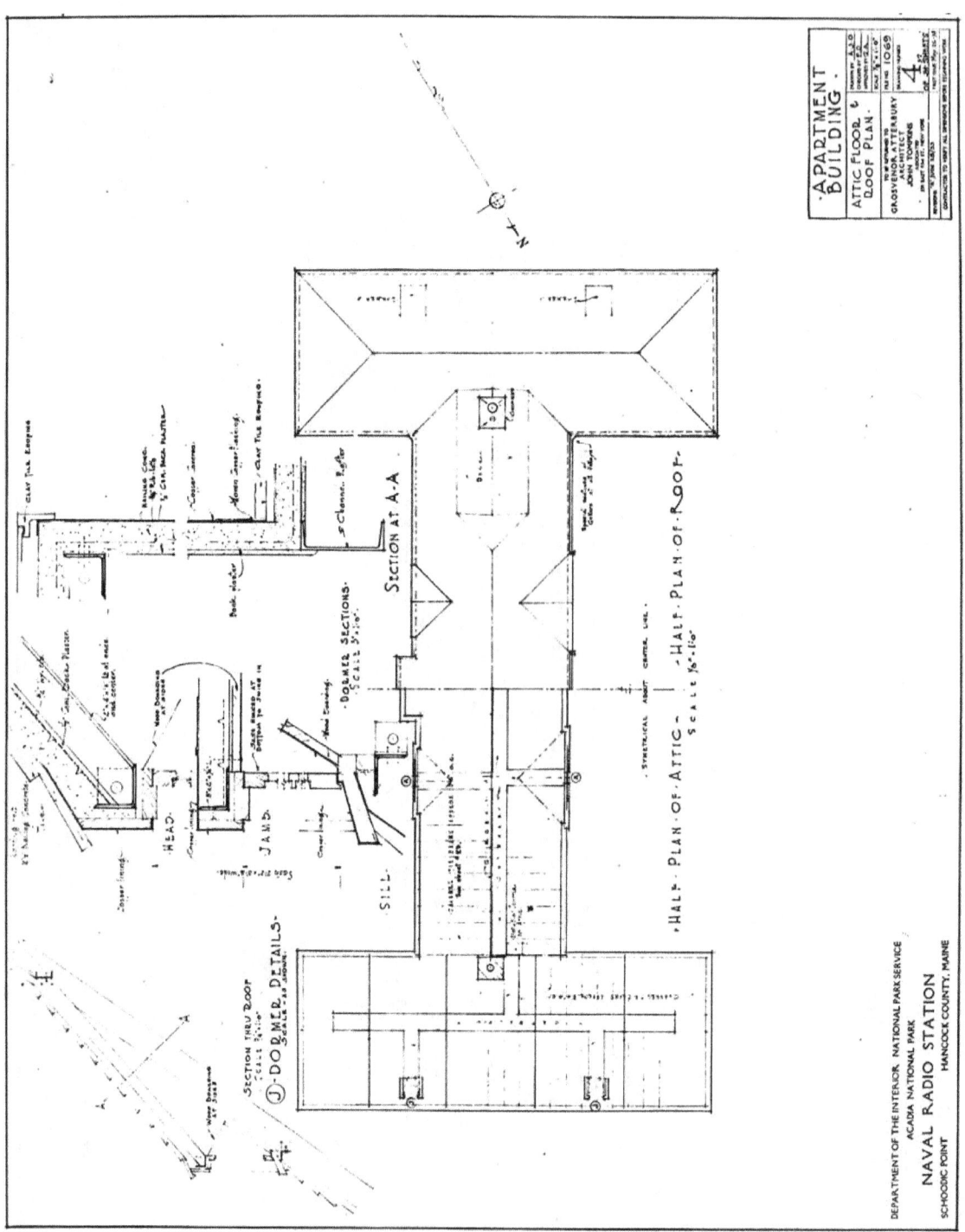

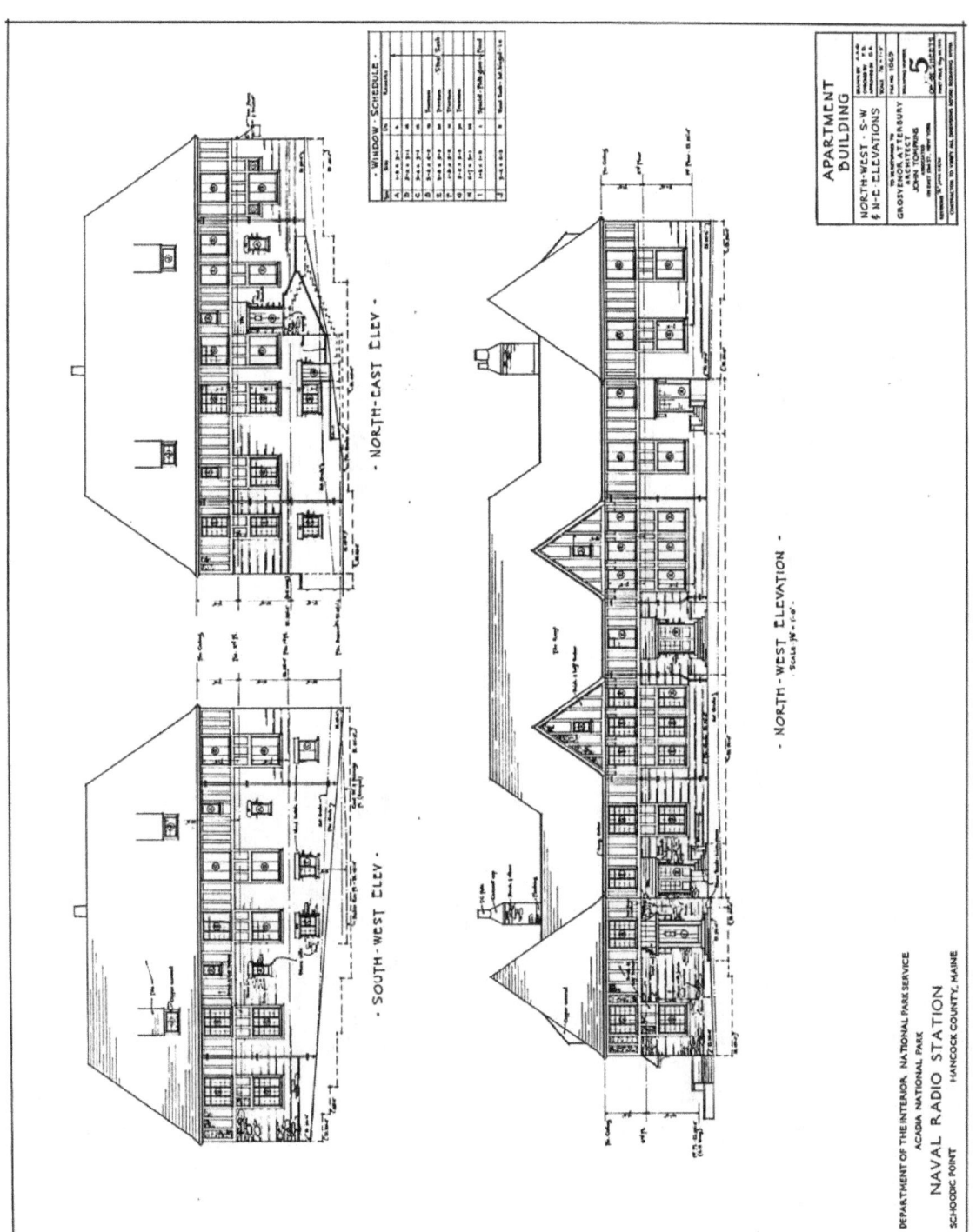

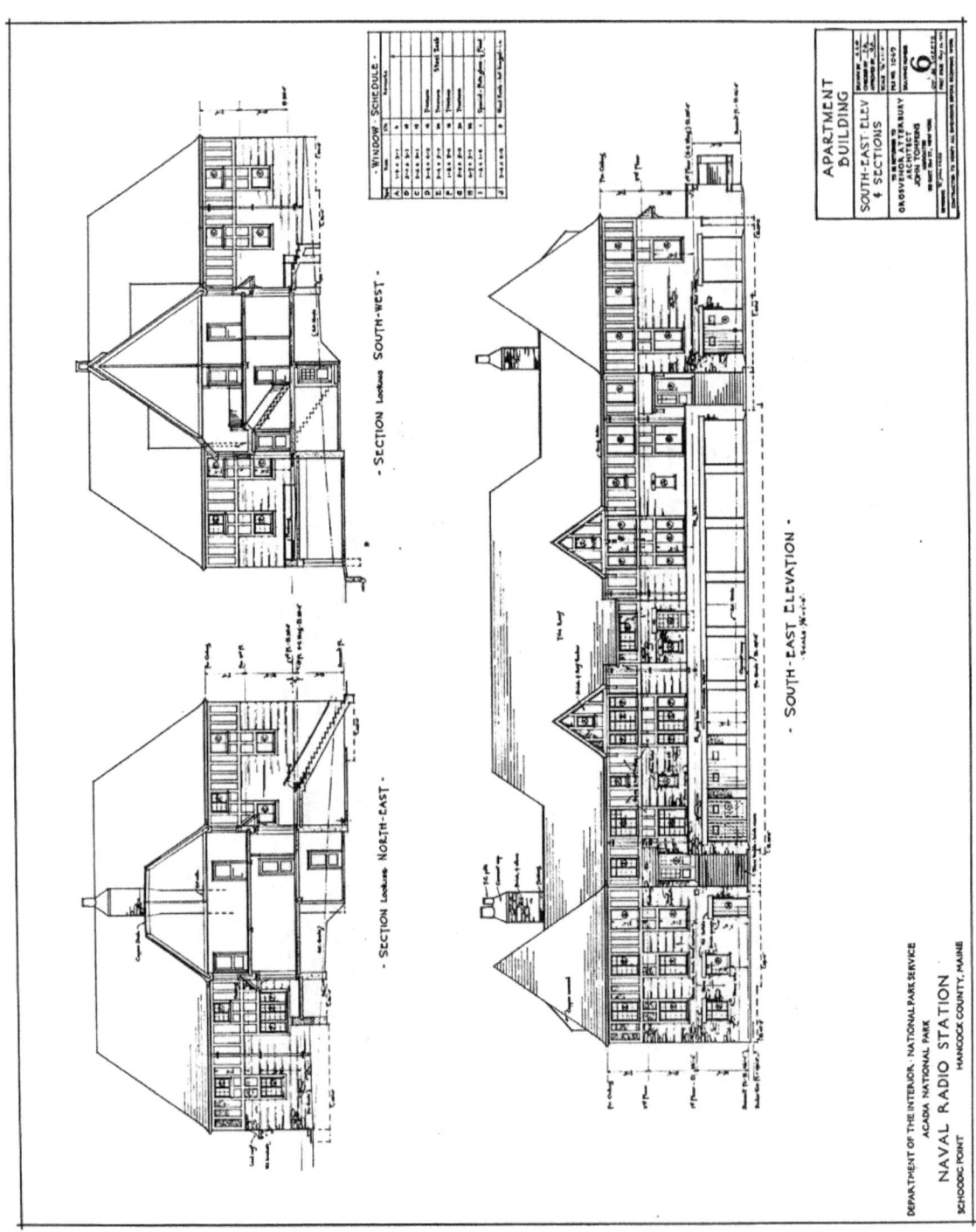

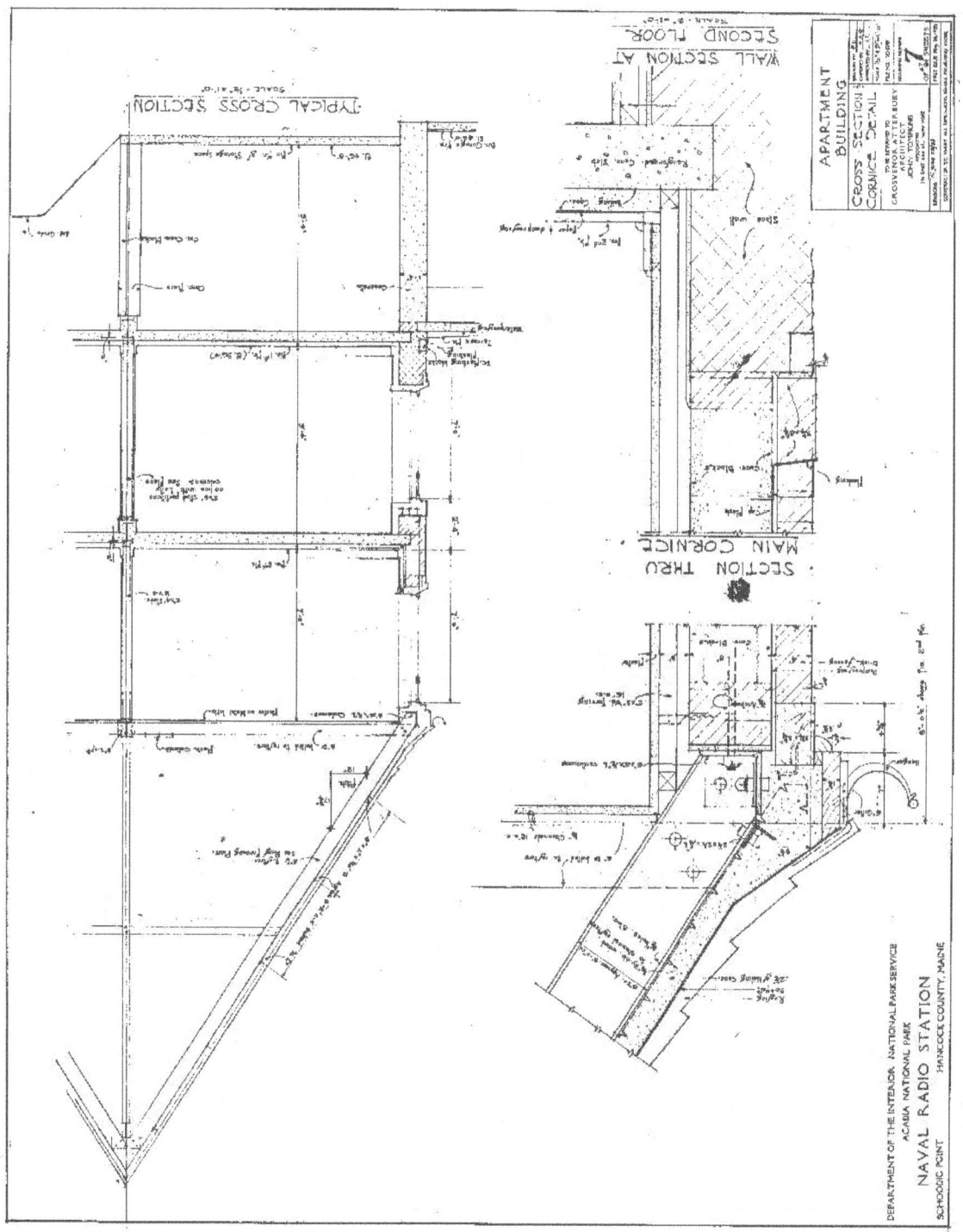

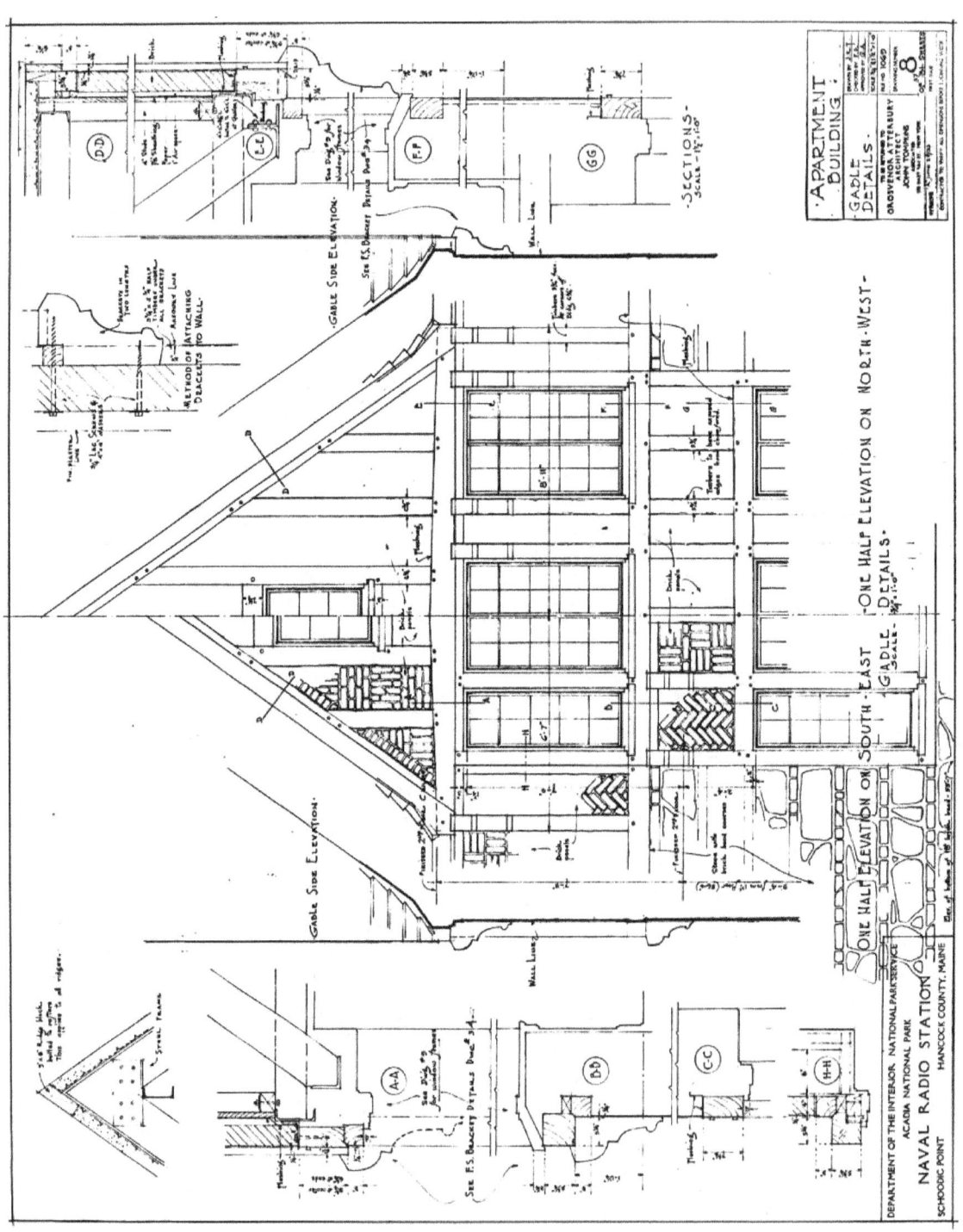

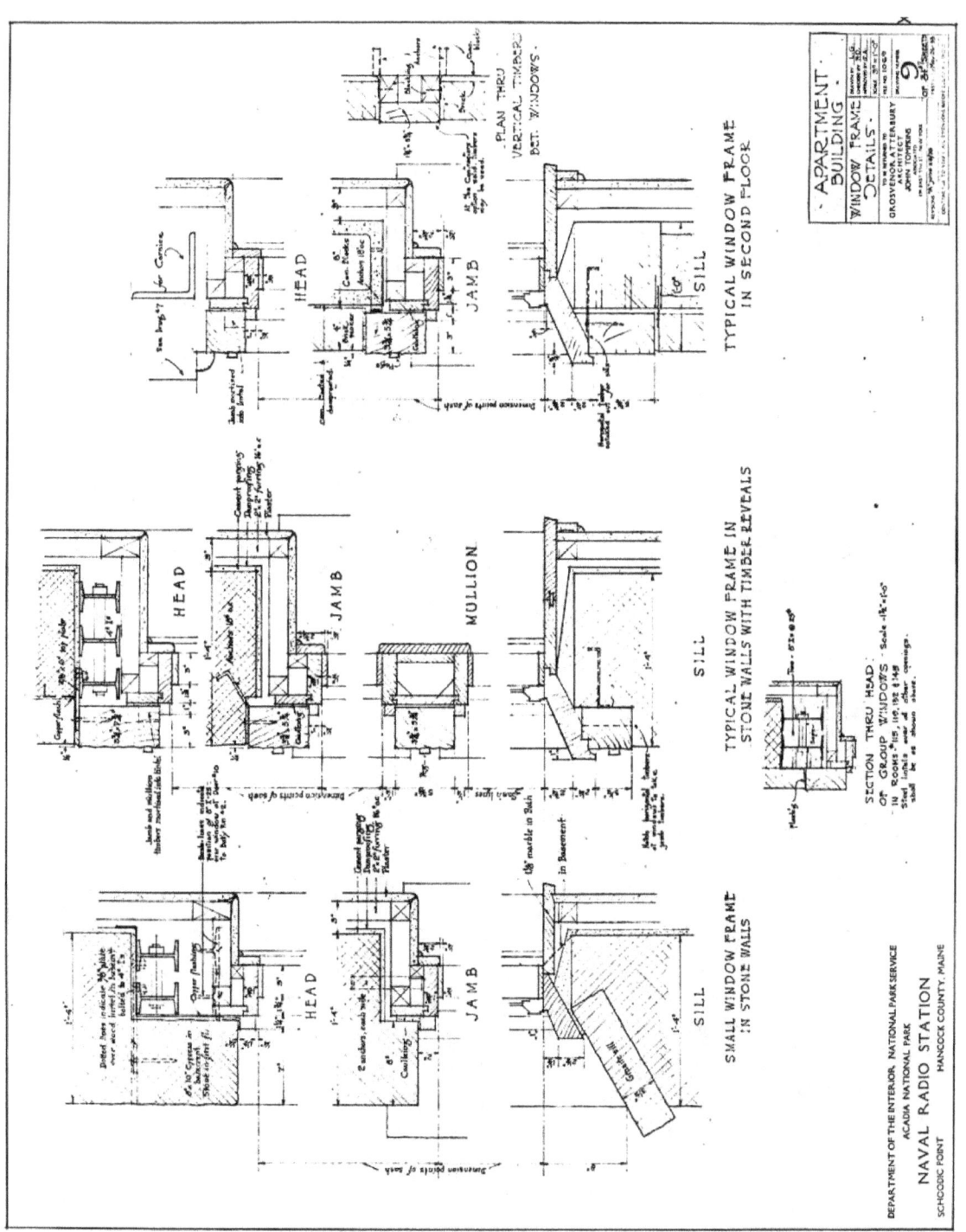

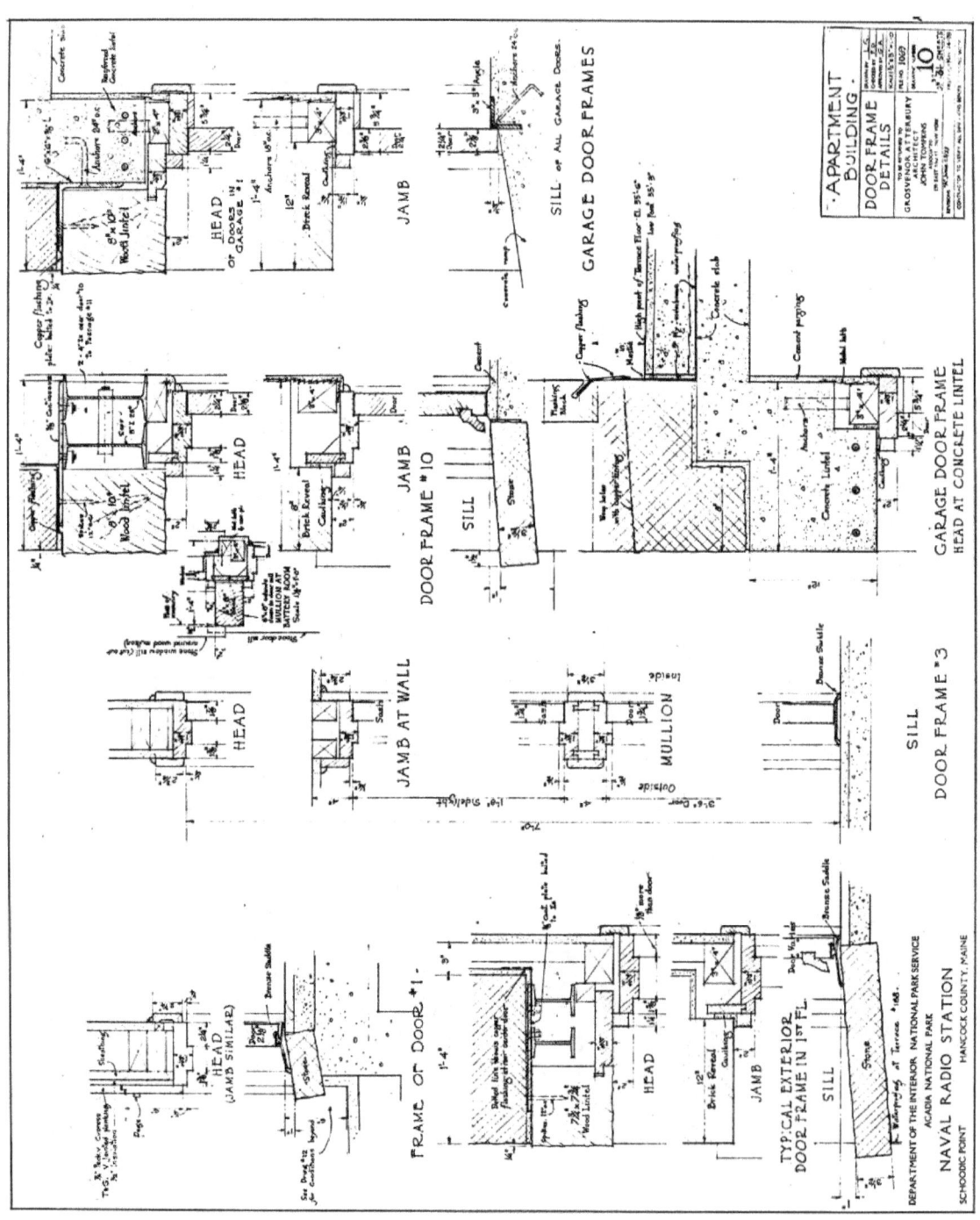

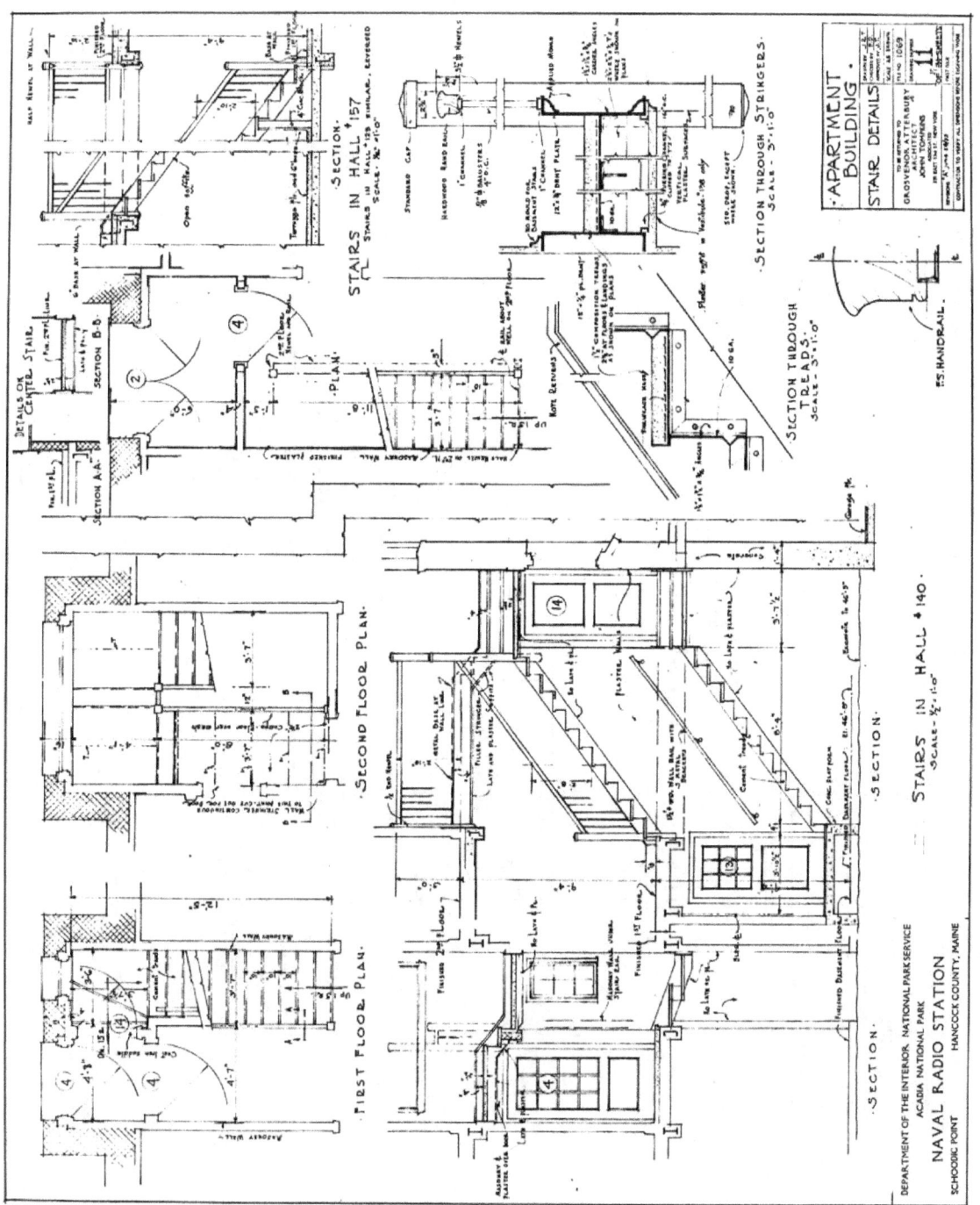

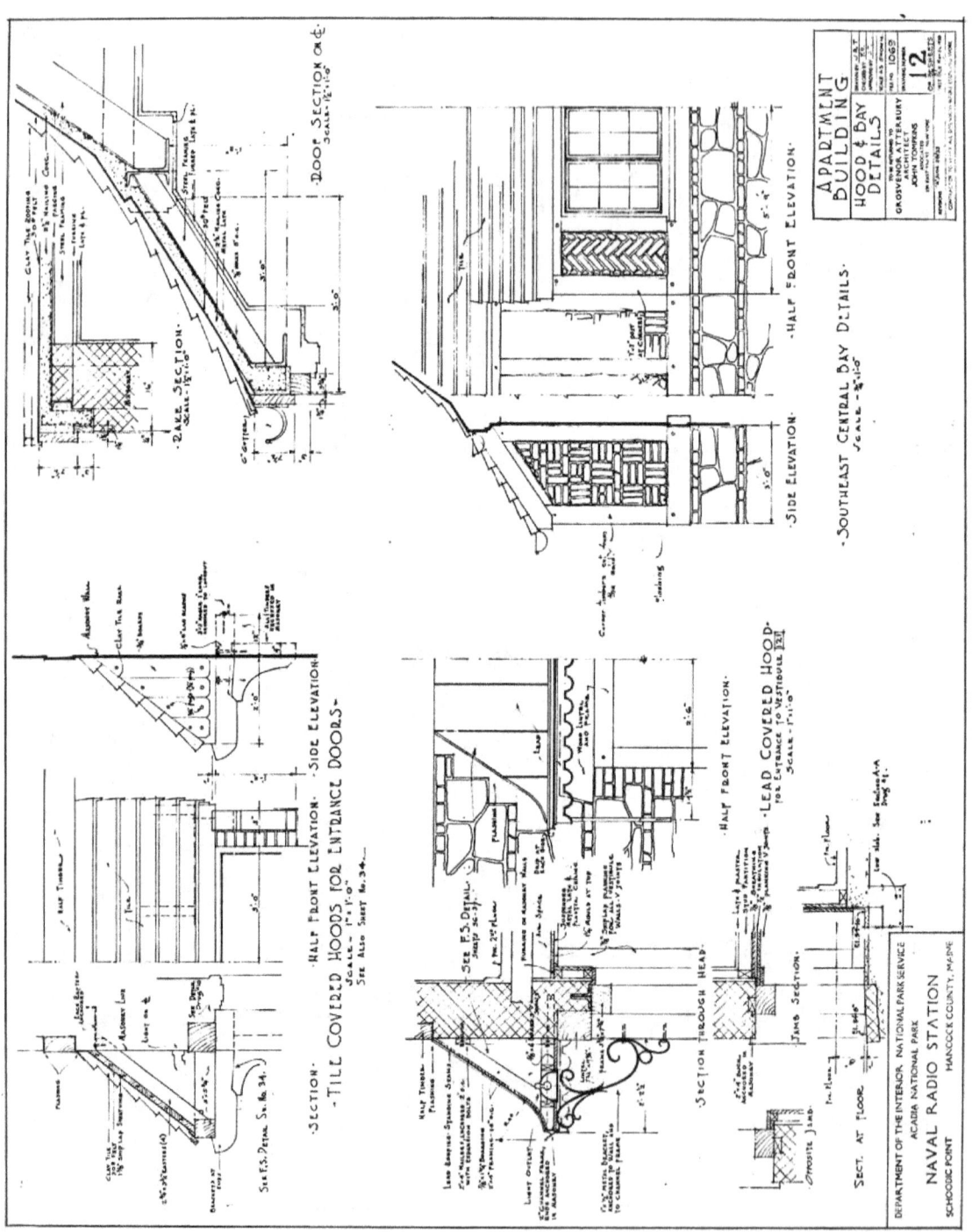

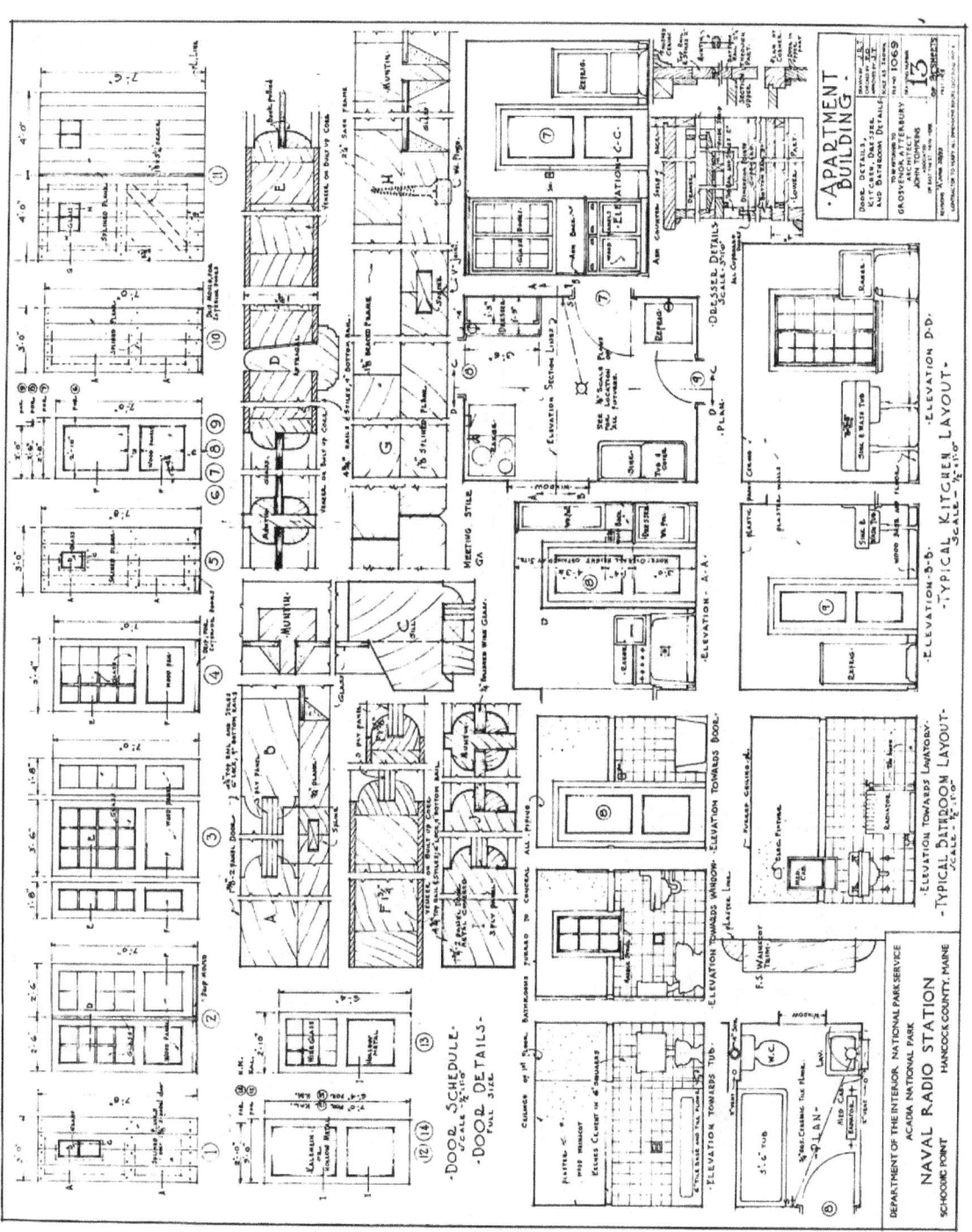

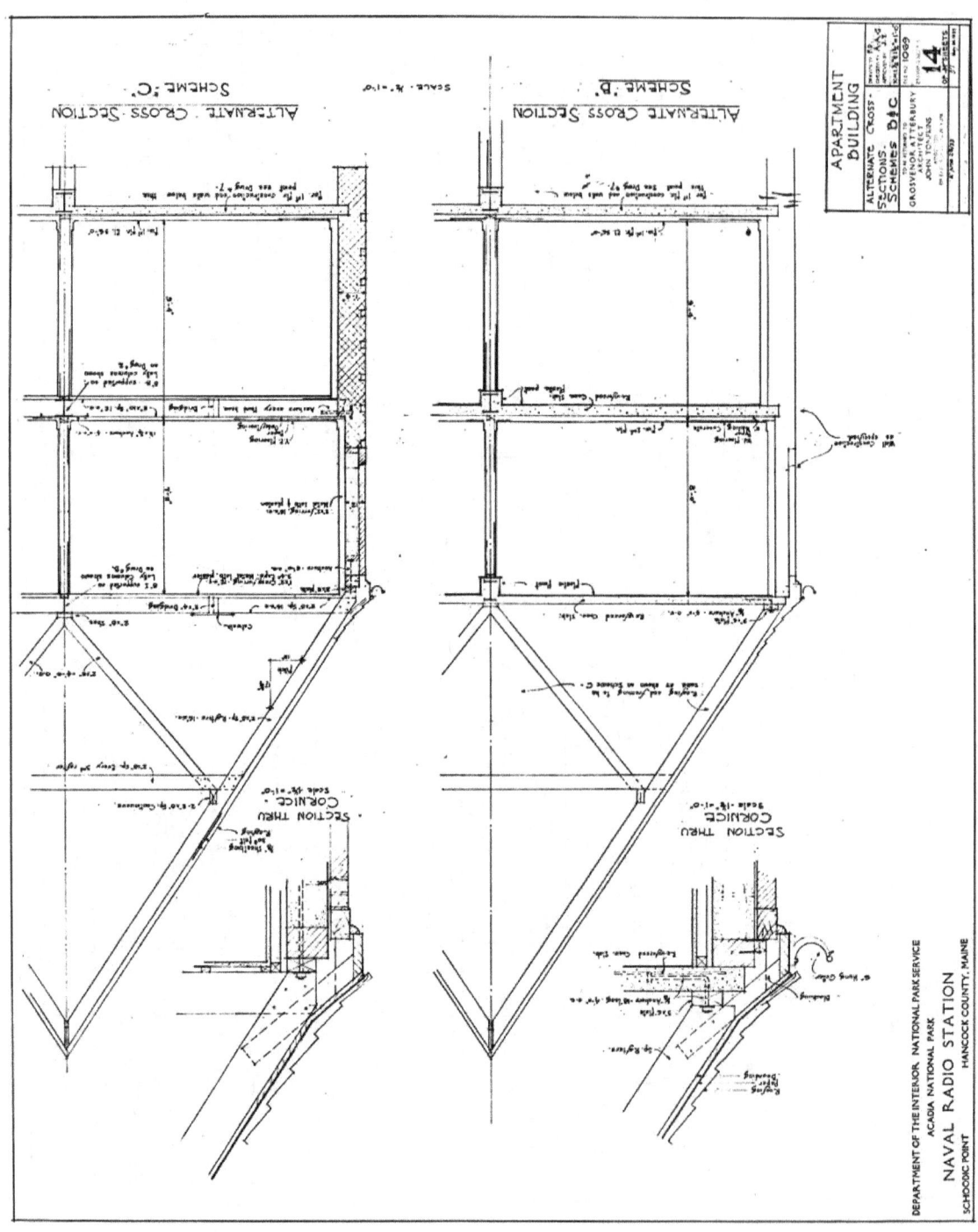

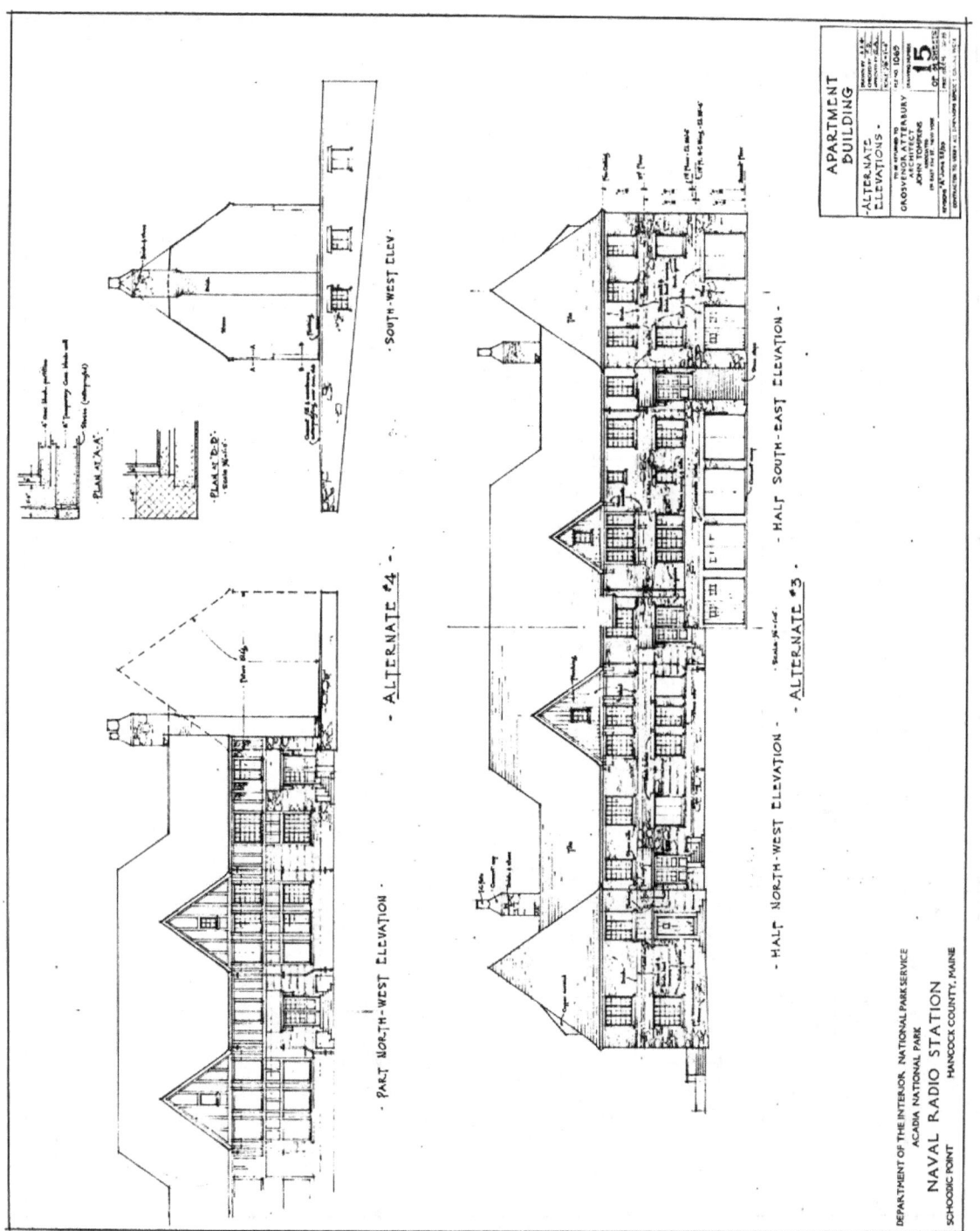

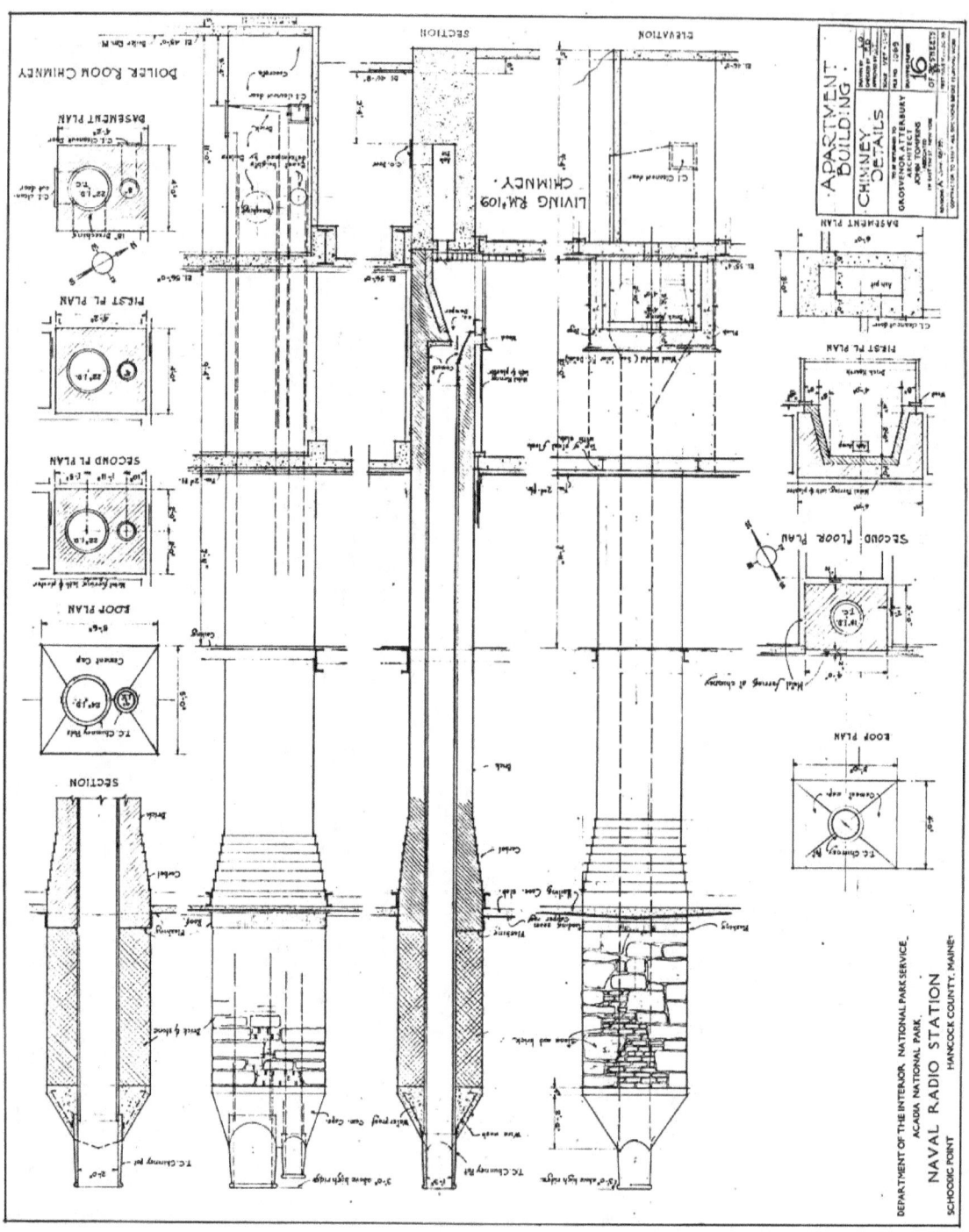

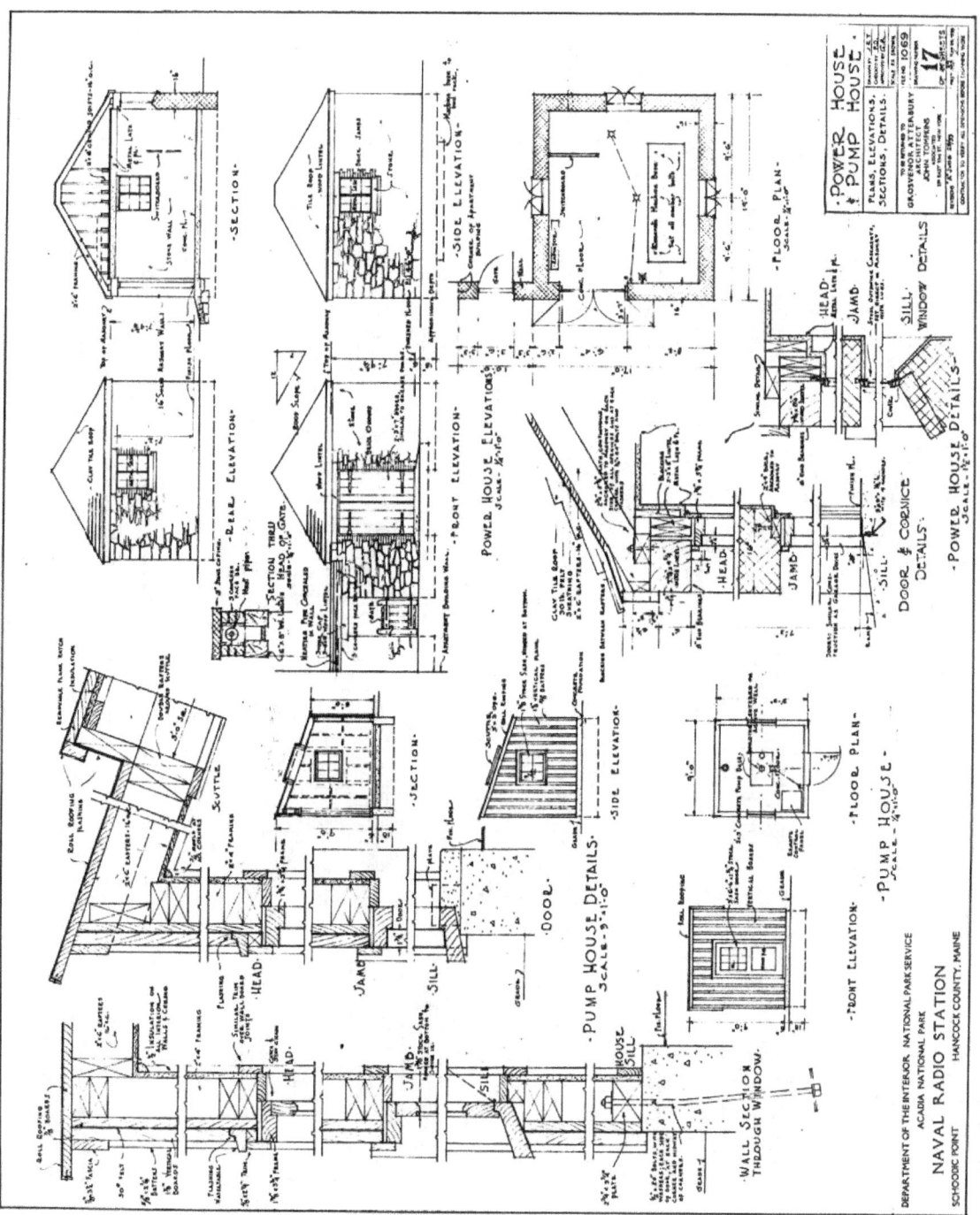

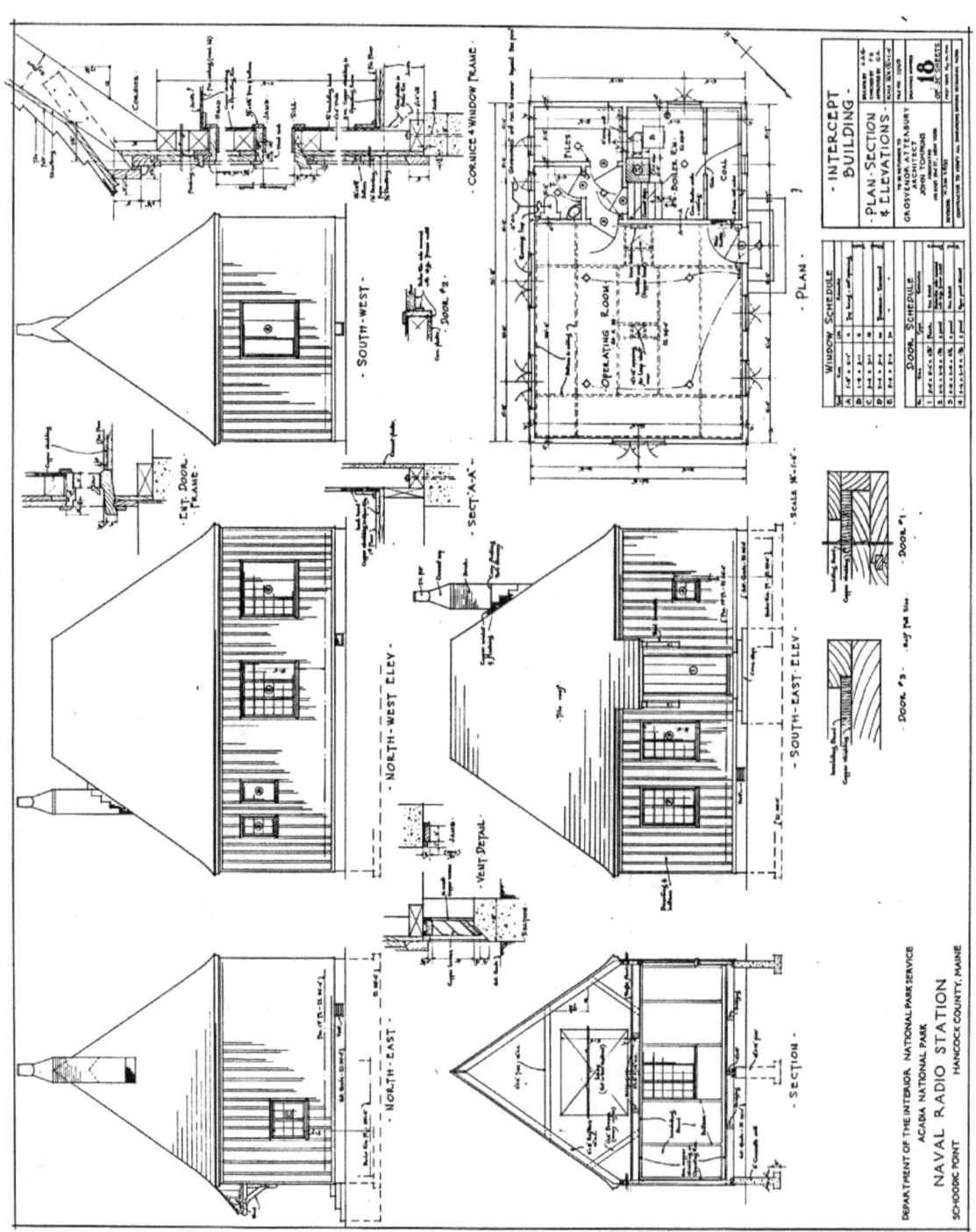

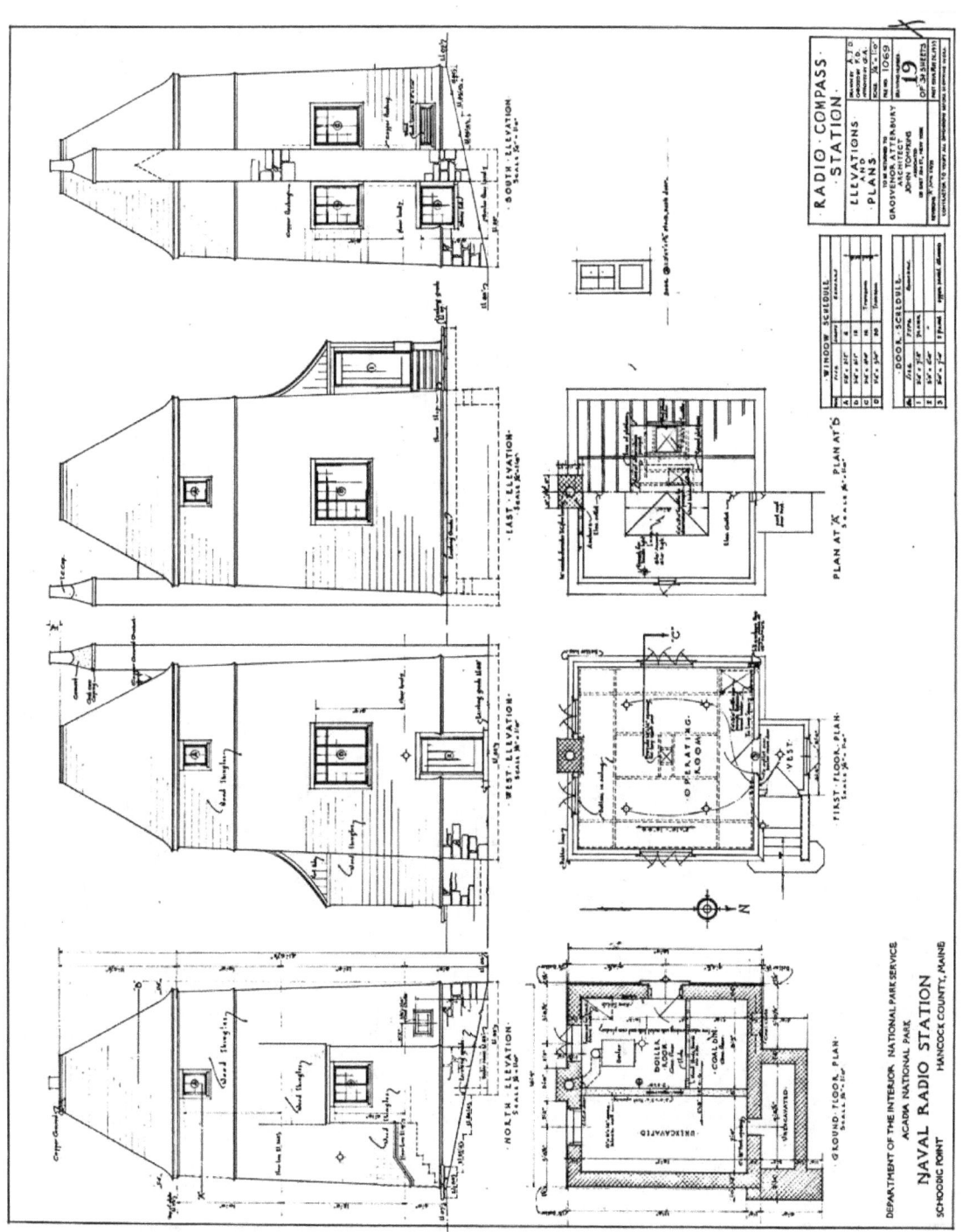

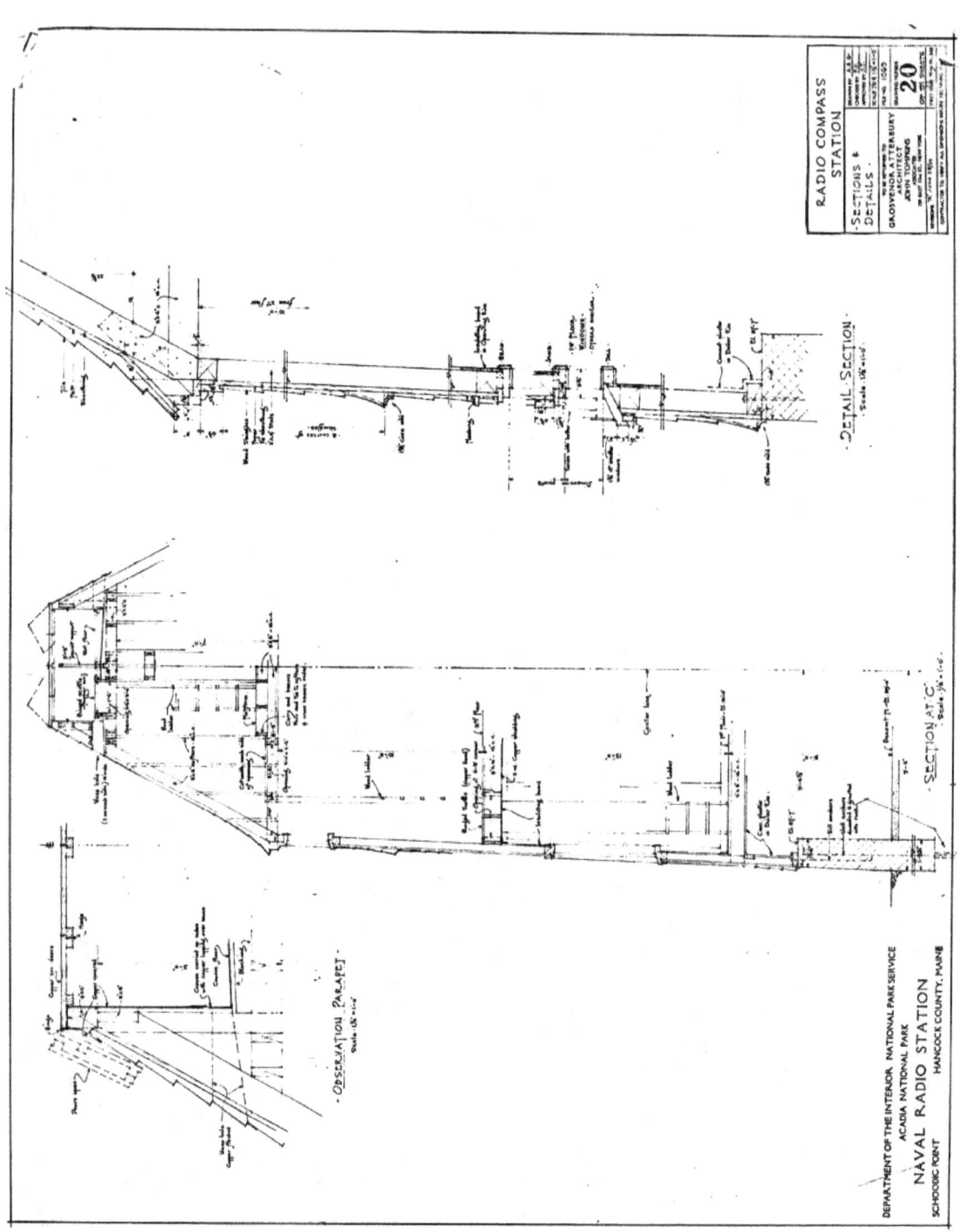

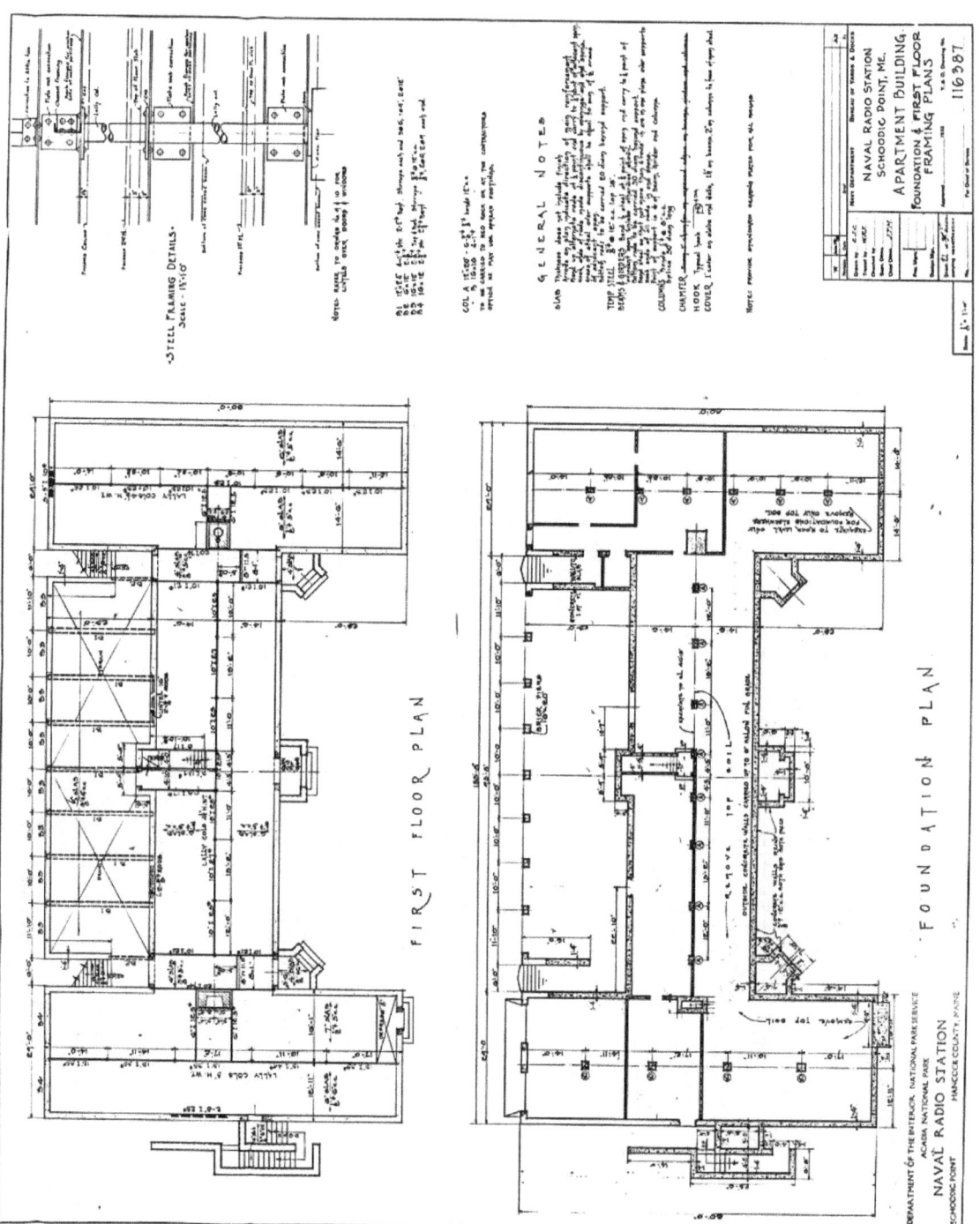

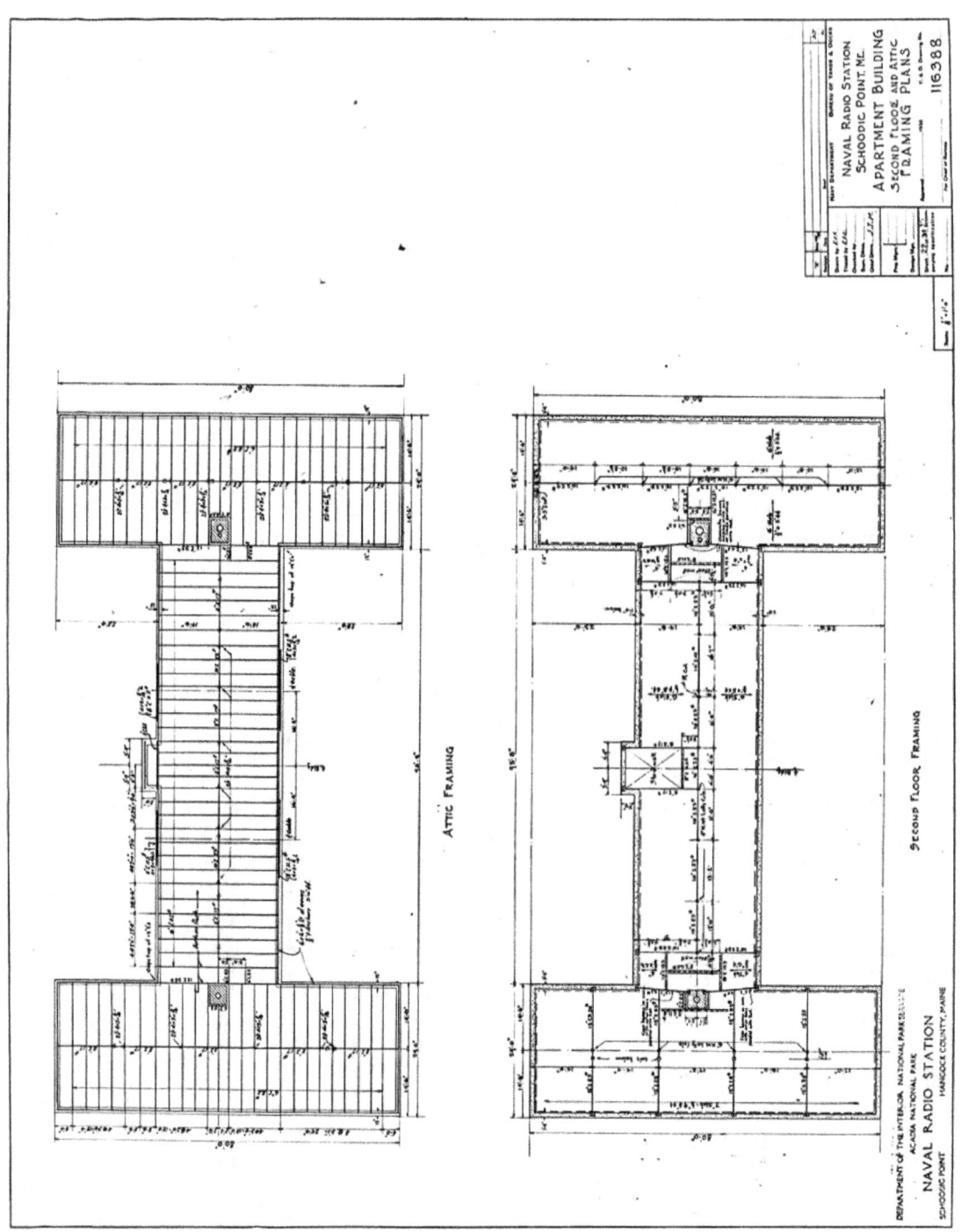

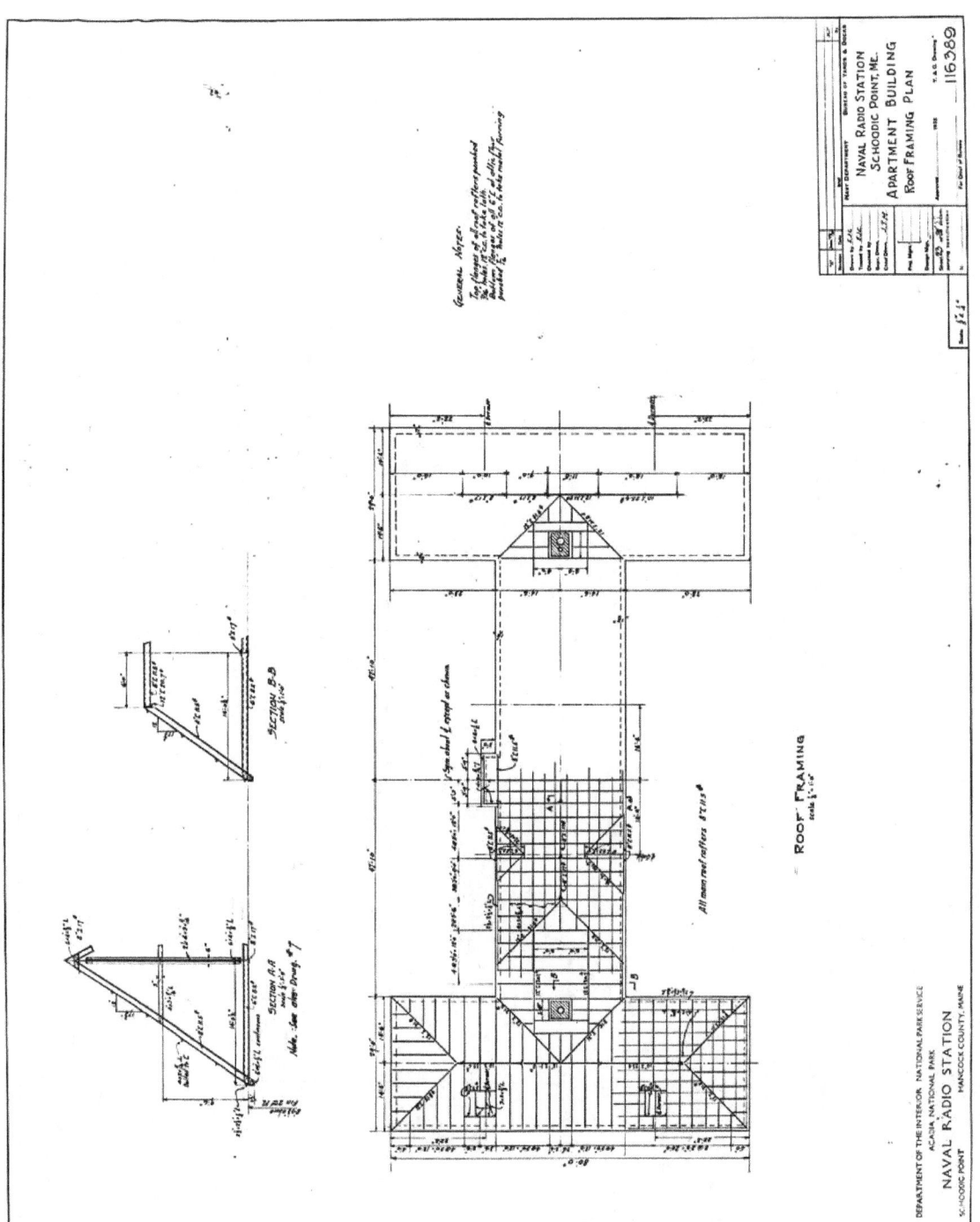

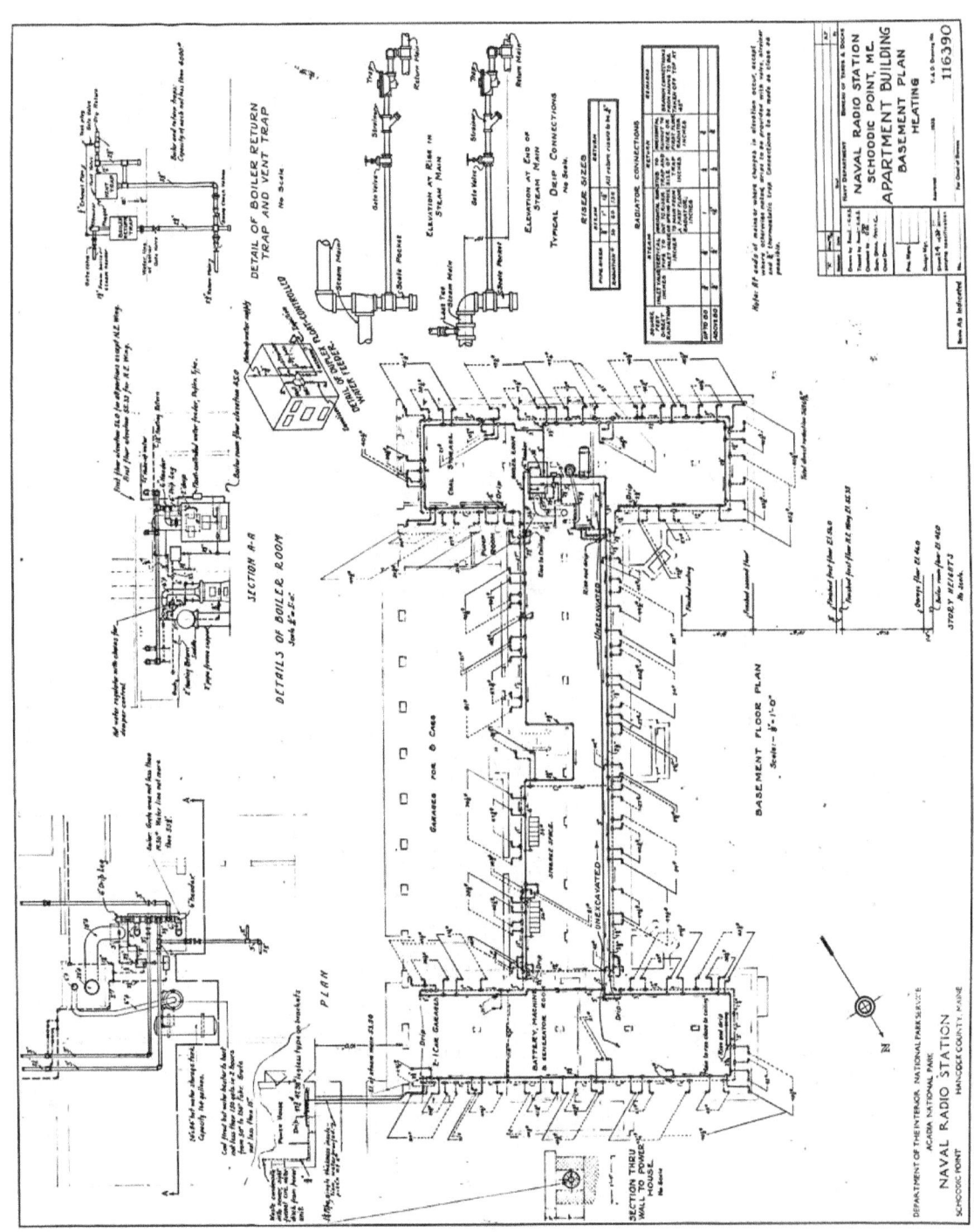

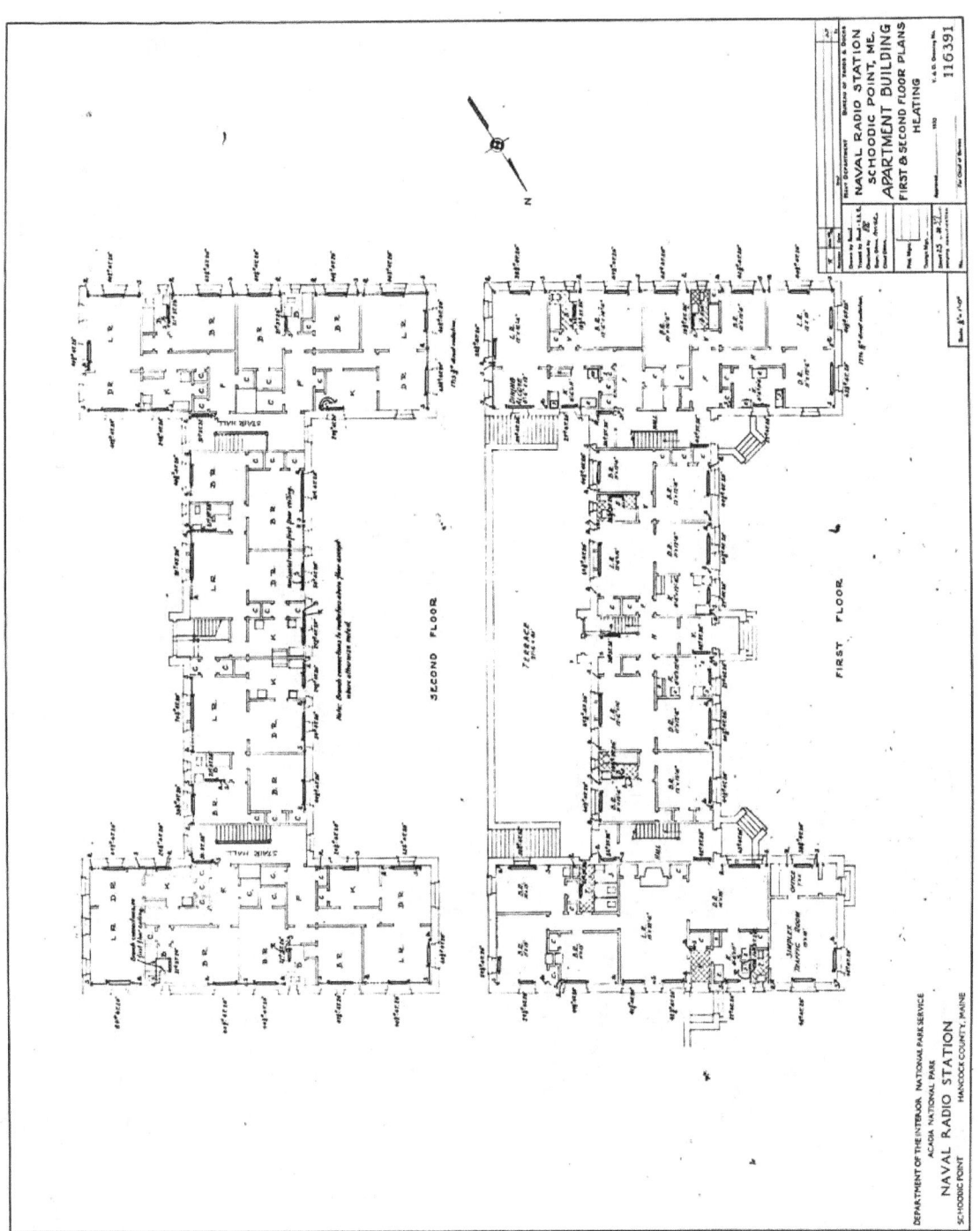

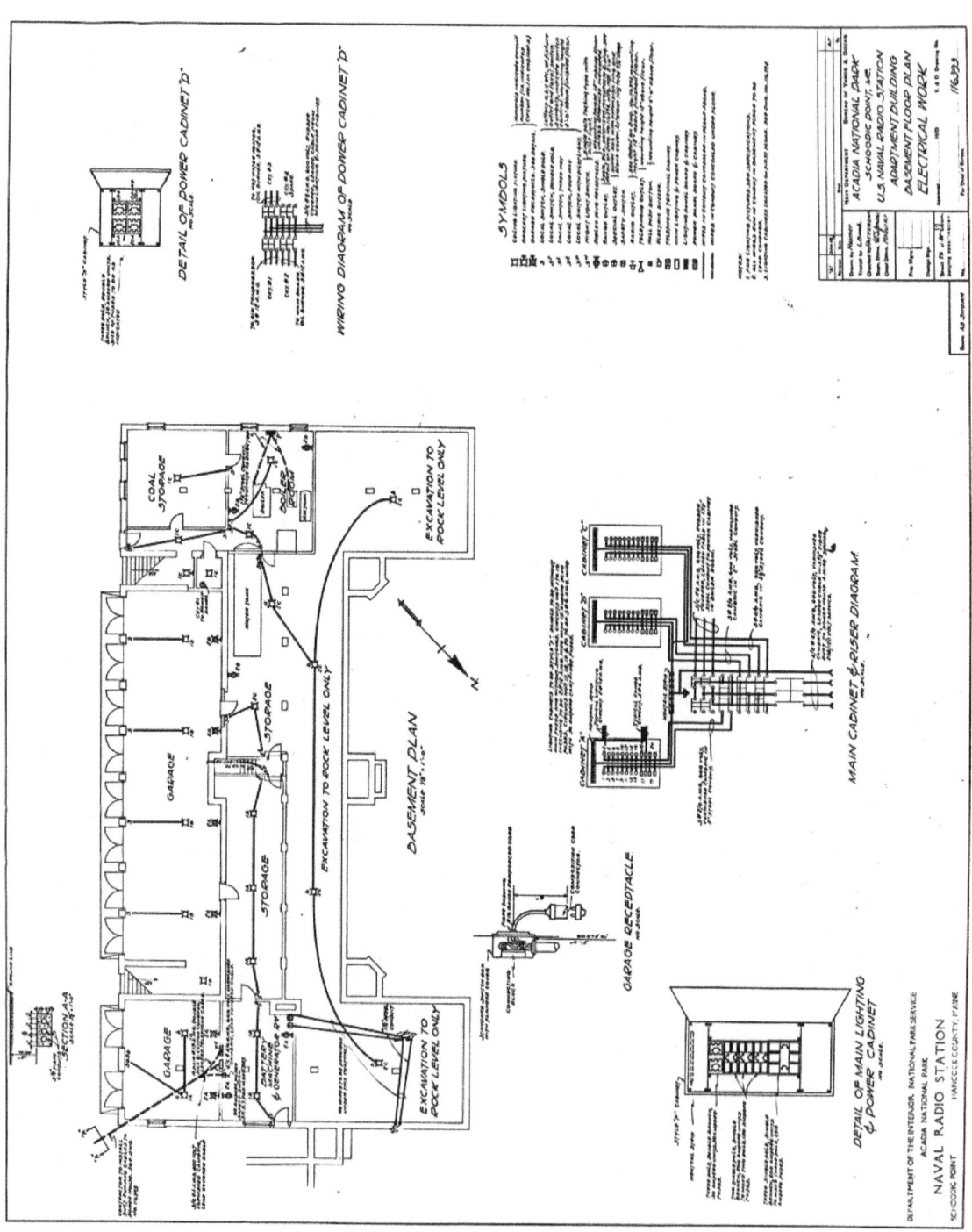

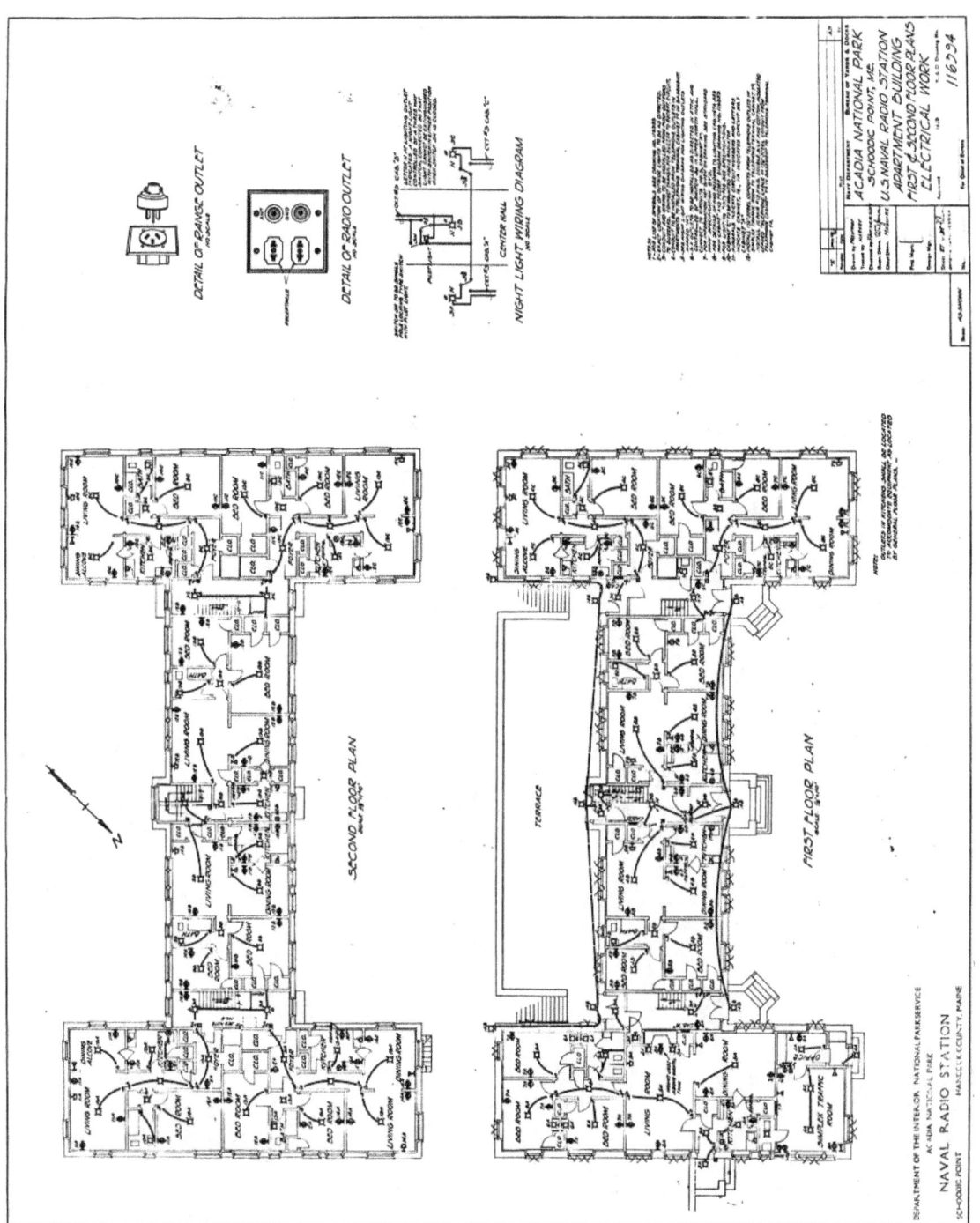

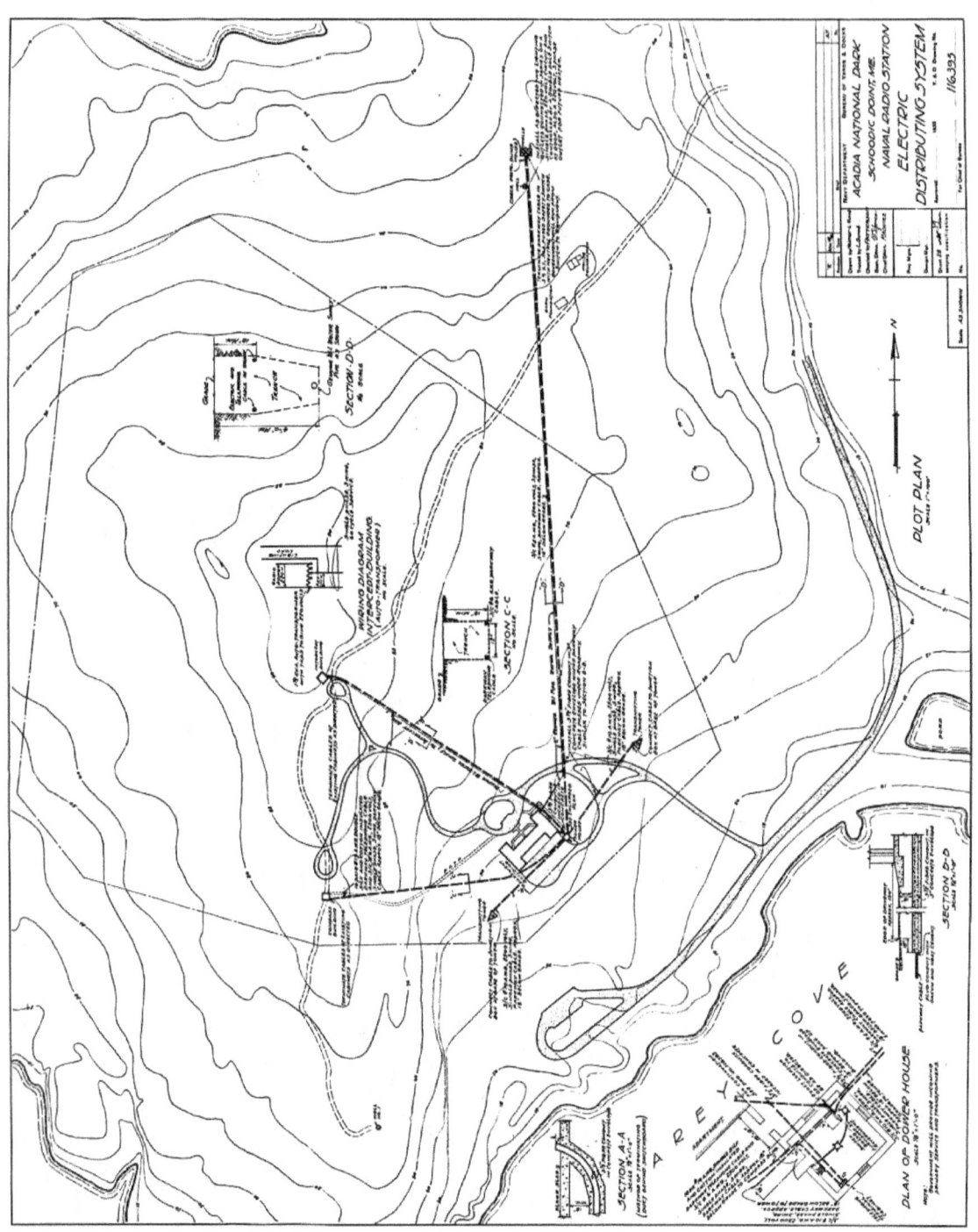

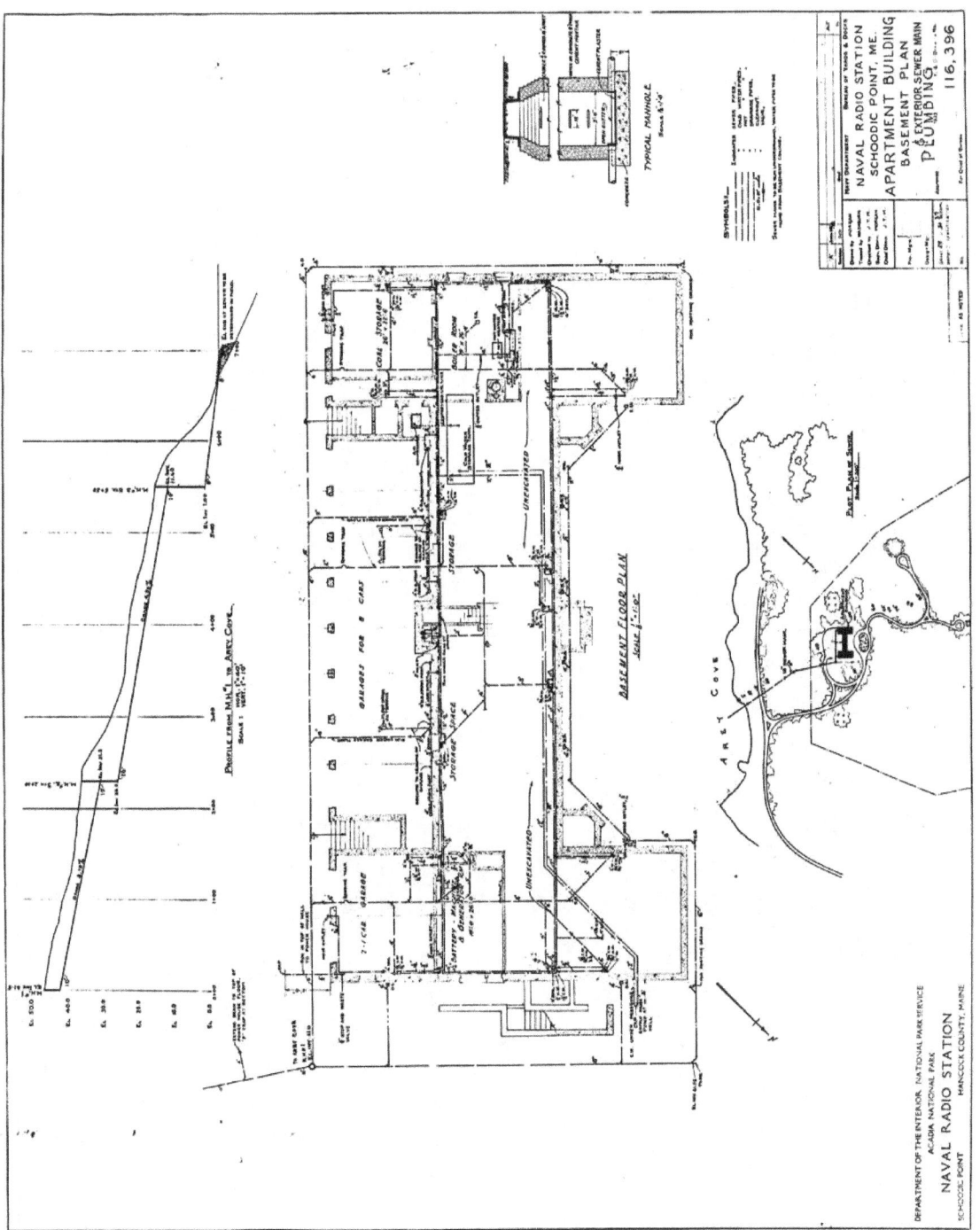

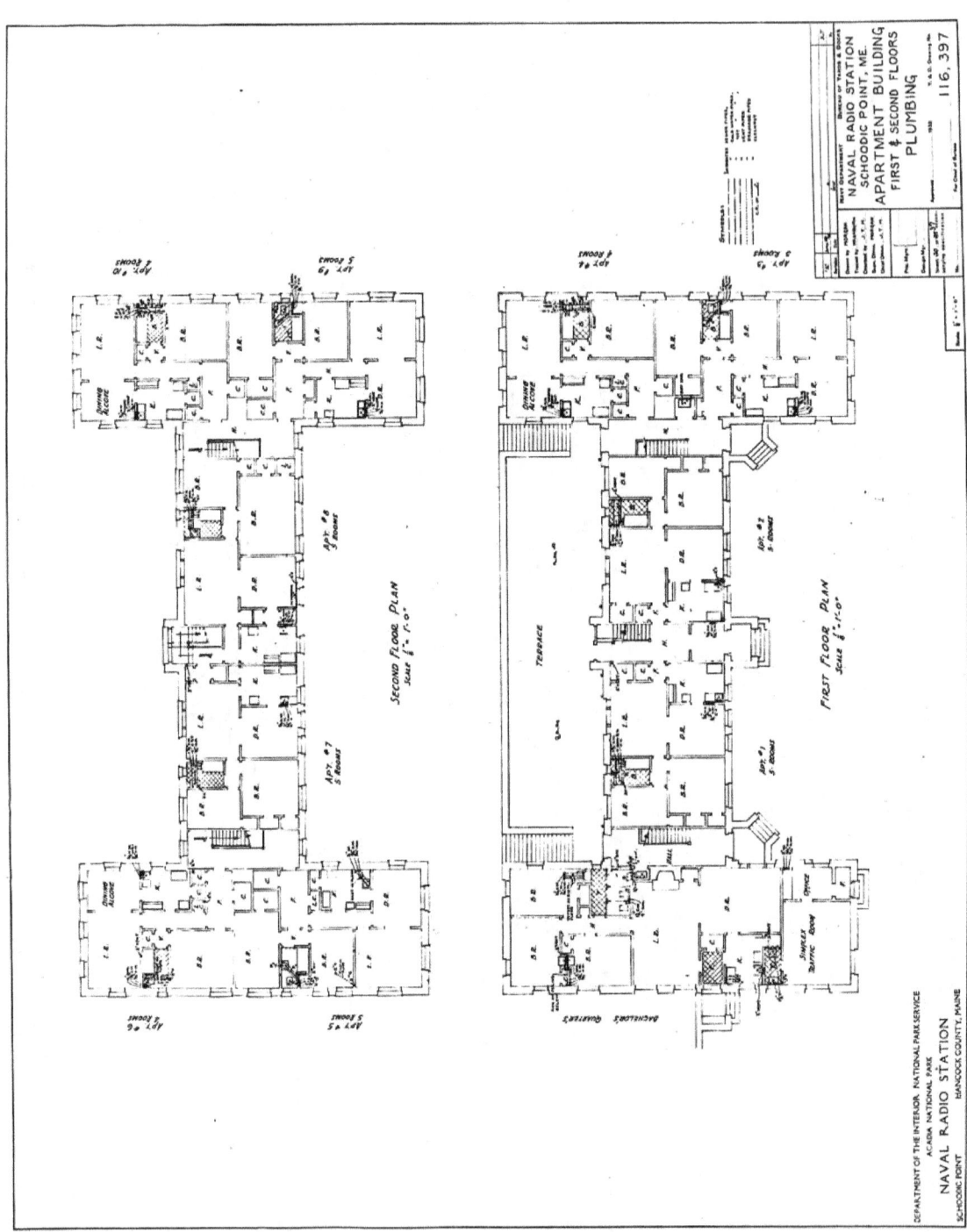

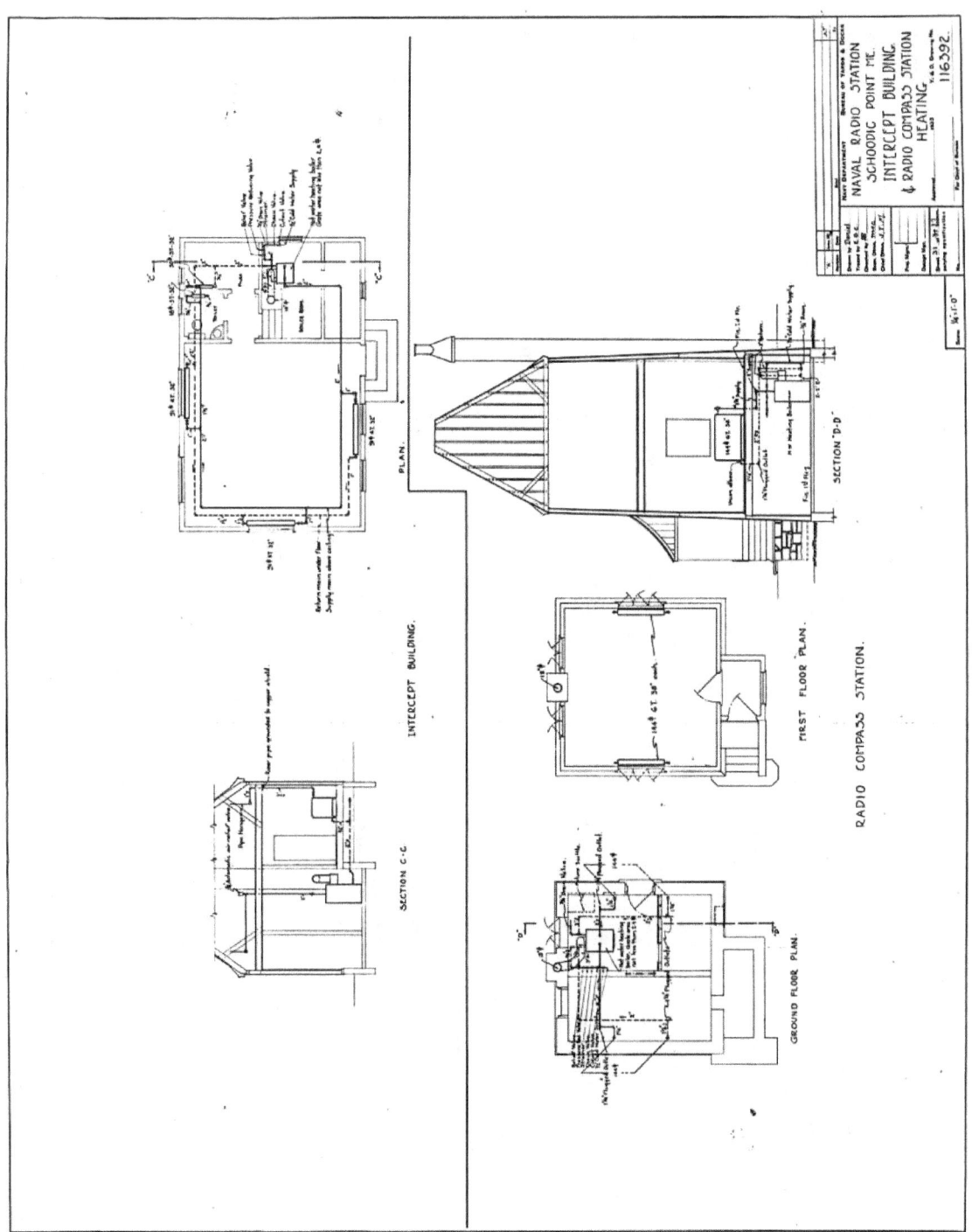

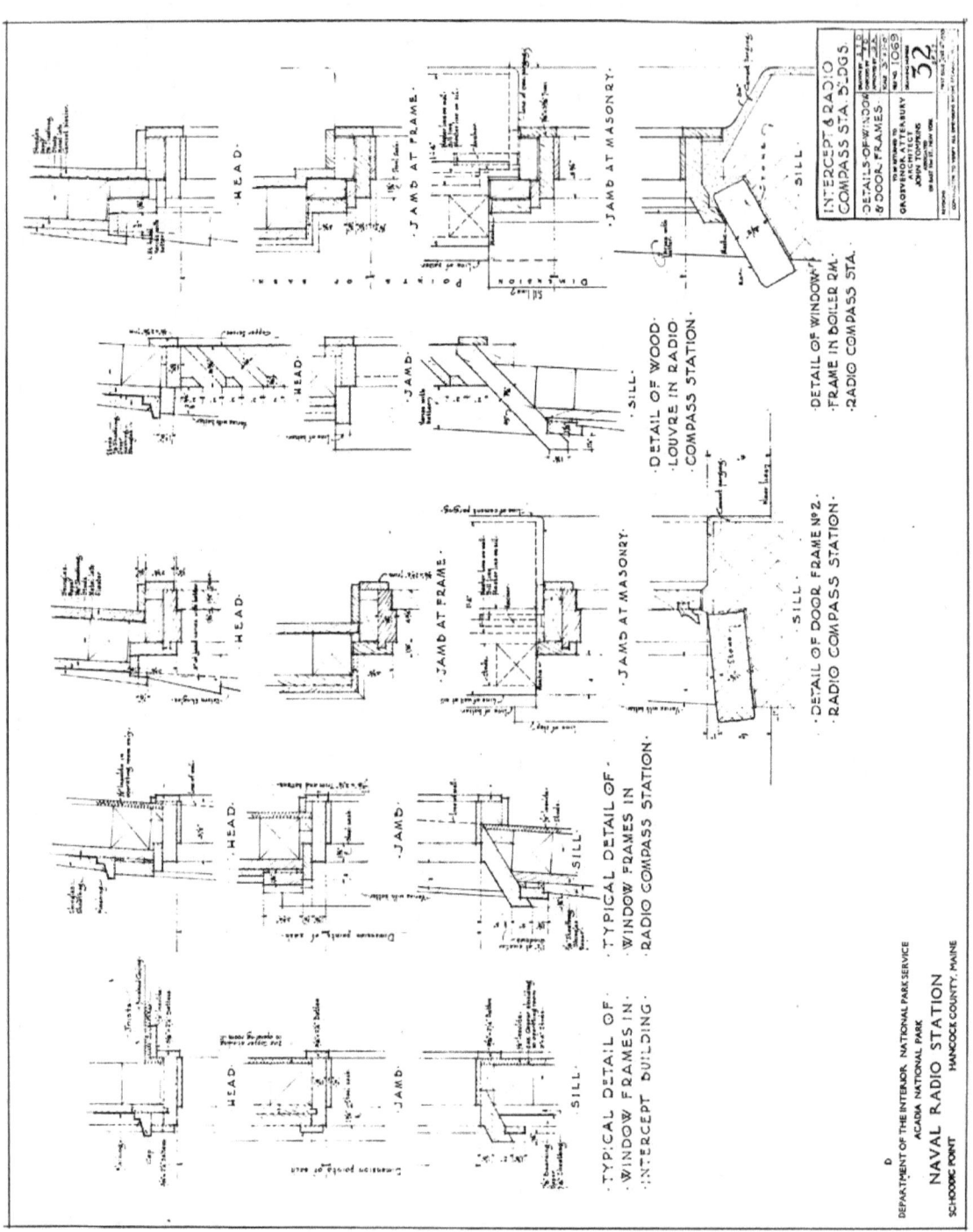

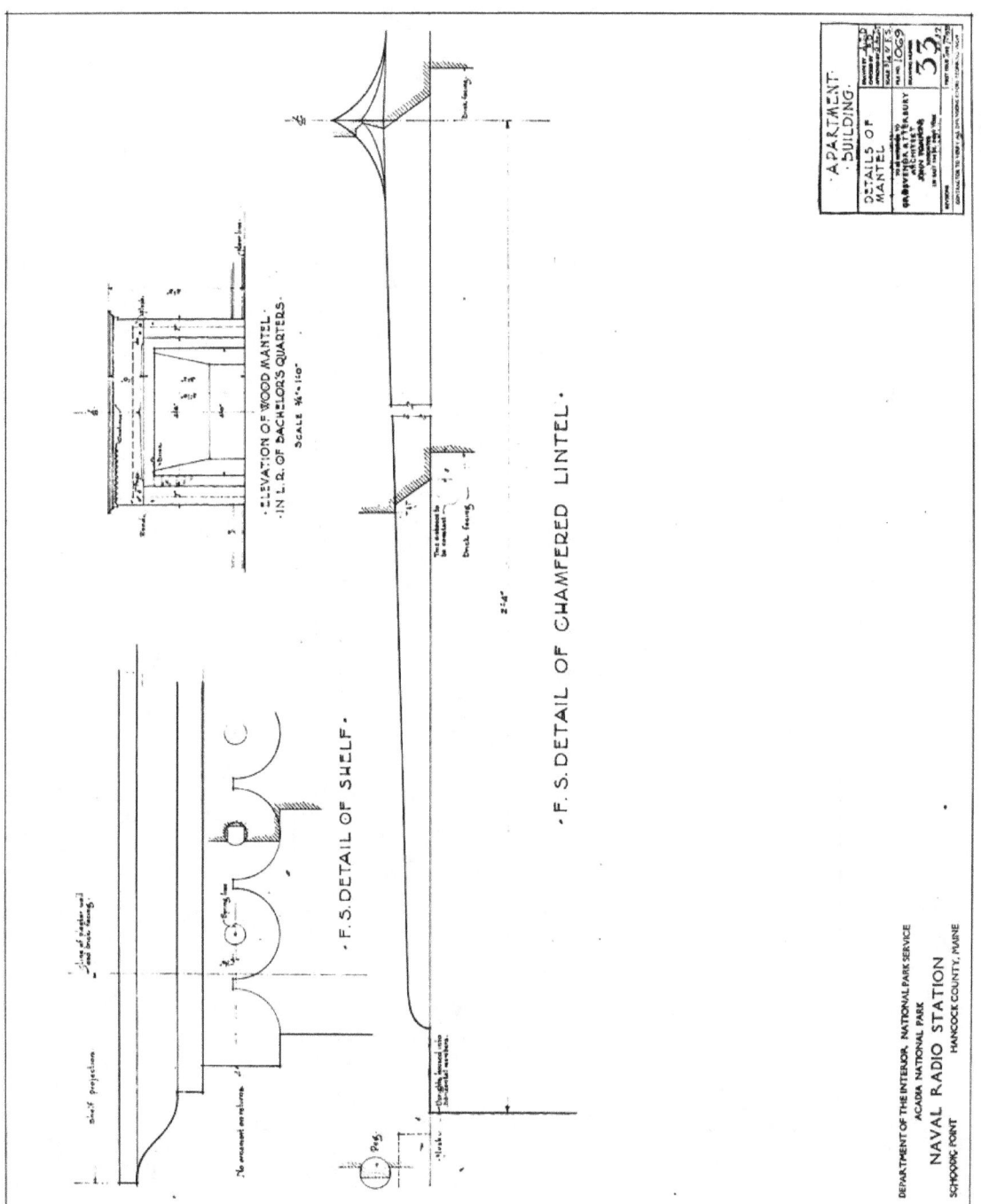

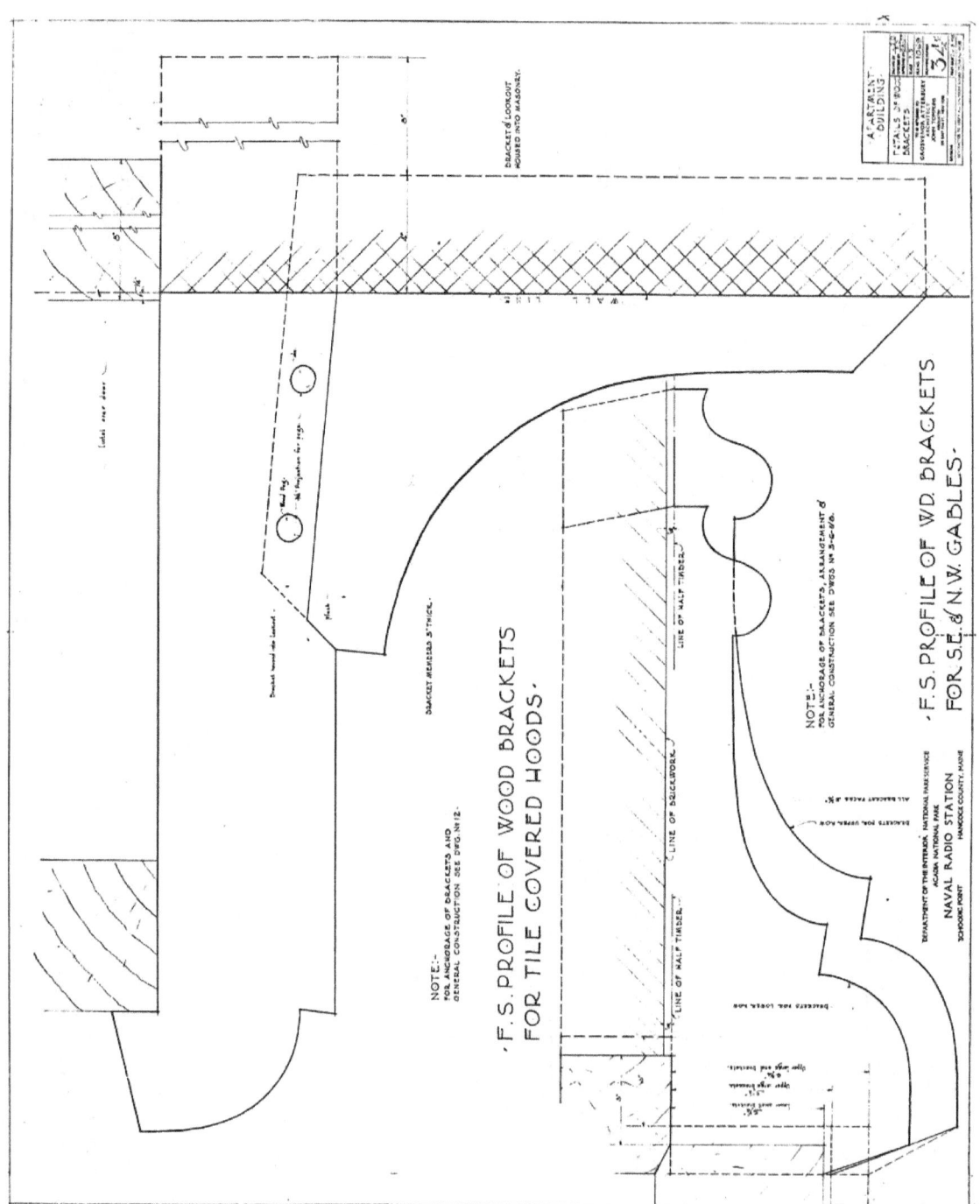

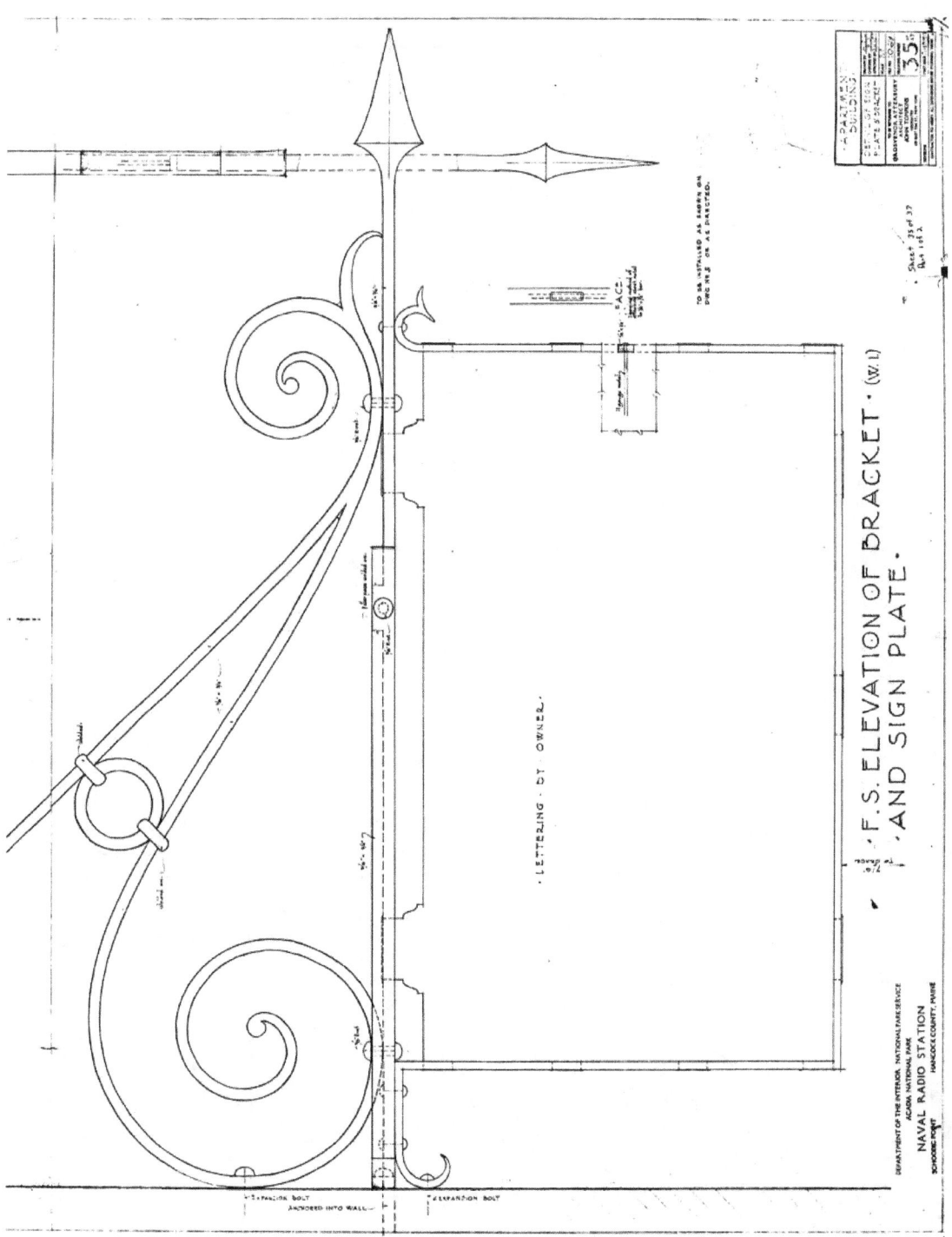

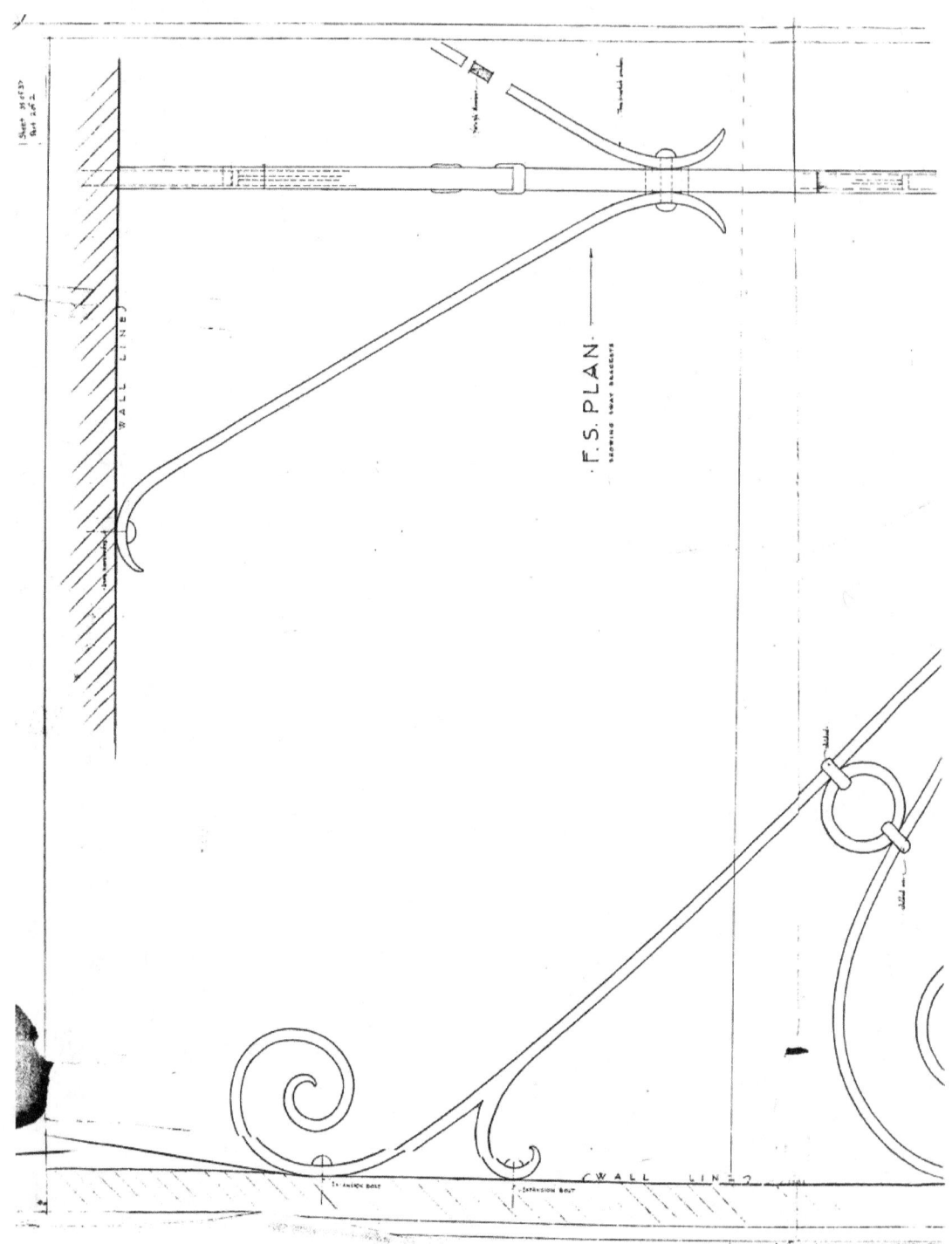

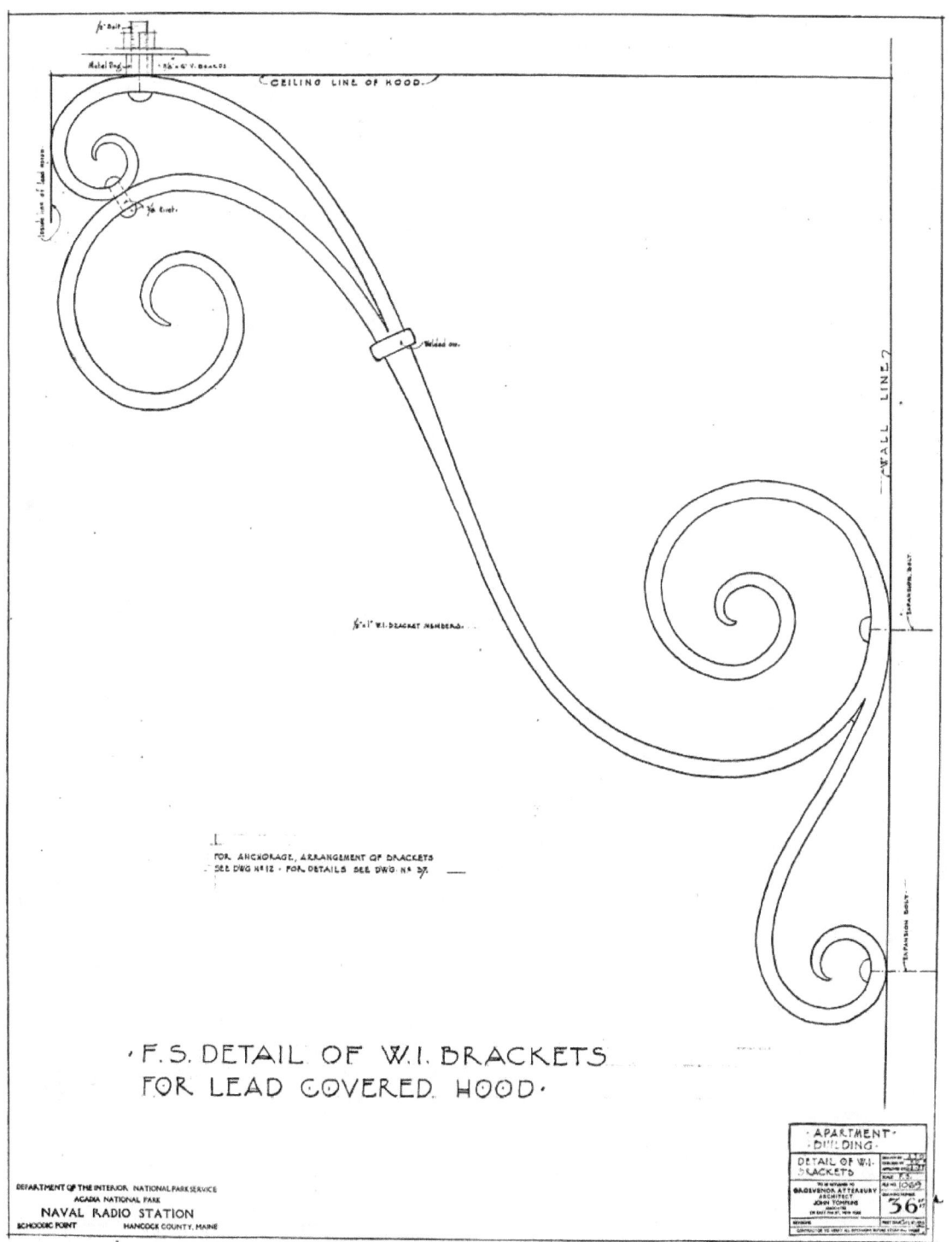

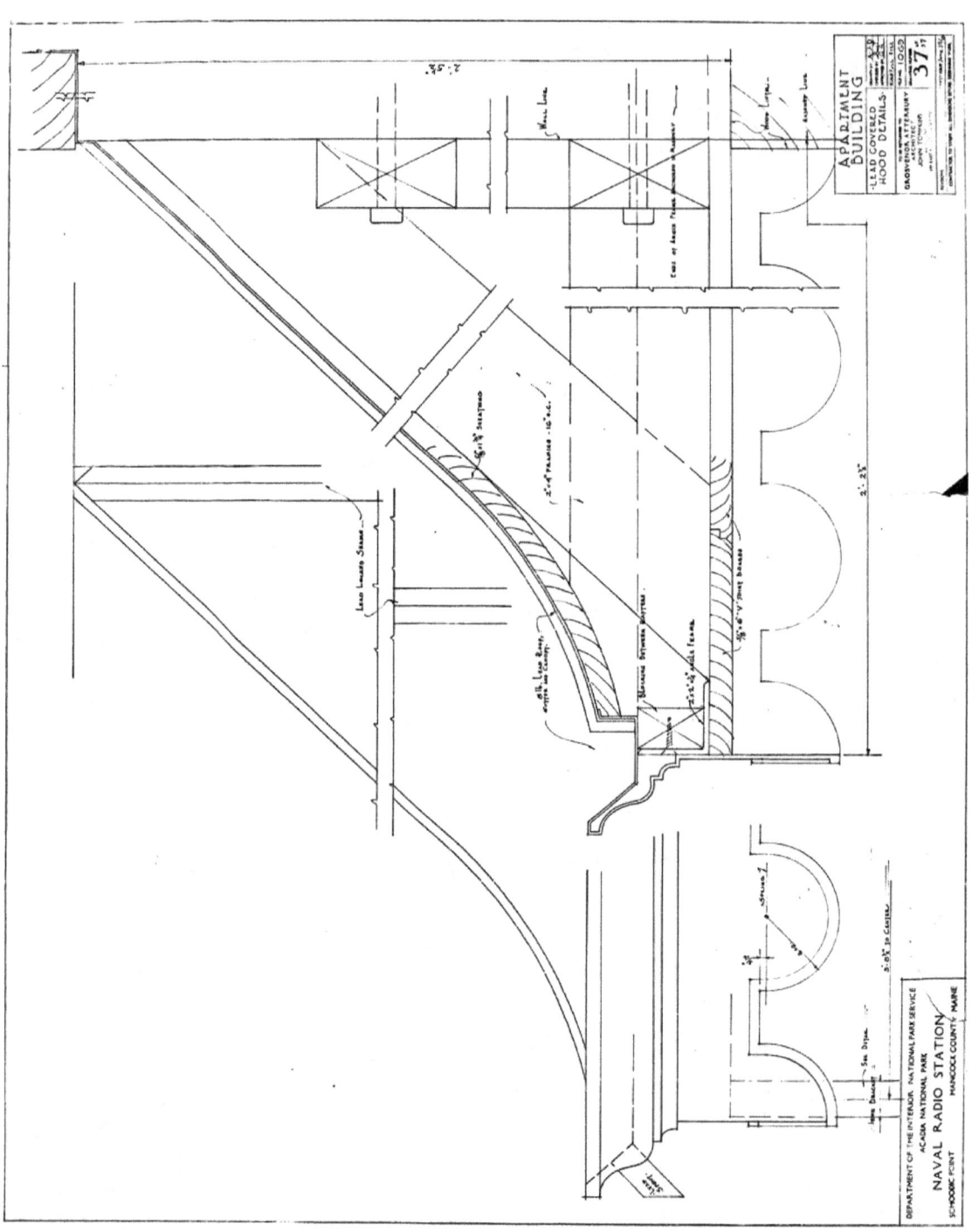

APPENDIX B

Apartment Building
Progress Reports Photographs, 1933 through 1935[185]

---

[185] "Naval Radio Station, Schoodic Point, Me., Progress Photos" 1933 – 1935; NPS Technical Information System, Denver Services Center, Denver, CO. (copies at ACAD Archives, Bar Harbor, ME).

-NAVAL RADIO STATION-
Schoodic Point, Me.
-PROGRESS PHOTOS-
Mar. 8, 1934.

Intercept Bldg.
From North

Apartment Bldg.
From S.W. Radio
Tower

P67 1 of 73

Int. View of Nailcrete
Roof slabs - Ap't Bldg.

P67 2 of 73

MAR 28 1934

-NAVAL RADIO STATION-
Schoodic Point, Me.

Nailcrete Roof Slab Construction
Nearing Completion

Apr. 14/34.

S. E. Side

Gable
S. E. Side

NAVAL RADIO STATION,
Schoodic Point, Me.

Progress Photos
April 28, 1934.

Intercept Bldg.
From S. E.

ACADIA NATIONAL PARK   123/P-67
NAVAL RADIO STATION   1933-35

Apartment Bldg.
Gable-S.E. side

P67 7 of 73

Apartment Bldg.
Gable-N.W. side

P67 8 of 73

Radio Compass Bldg.
From N. W.

Radio Compass Bldg.
From N. E.

NAVAL RADIO STATION
Schoodic Point, Me

PROGRESS PHOTOS
May 10, 1934.

Apartment Bldg.
S. E. side

P67 11 of 73

N. W. side

P67 12 of 73

S. W. side

P67 13 of 73

-NAVAL RADIO STATION-
Schoodic Point, Me.

-PROGRESS PHOTOS-
May 16, 1934

Apartment Bldg.
S.W. Side

P67 14 of 73

S. E. side

P67 15 of 73

S. E. side

P67 16 of 73

ACADIA NATIONAL PARK 123/P-67

NAVAL RADIO STATION 1933-35

Intercept Bldg
S. E. side

P67 17 of 73

R. C. Bldg
S. side

P67 18 of 73

- NAVAL RADIO STATION -
Schoodic Point, Me

PROGRESS PHOTOS
June 2, 1934

Apartment Bldg.
From South Tower

Apartment Bldg.
S. E. side

Intercept Bldg.
From S. E.

Pump House
From South

P67 22 of 73

Radio Compass Bldg.
From S. W.

P67 23 of 73

ACADIA NATIONAL PARK   123/P-67

NAVAL RADIO STATION   1933-35

-NAVAL RADIO STATION-
Schoodic Point, Me.

PROGRESS PHOTOS
June 30, 1934

Apartment Bldg.
N.E. side

S.E. side

S.W. side

Apartment Bldg
N.E. side

P67 27 of 73

Radio Compass Bldg
North side

ACADIA NATIONAL PARK	123/P-67
NAVAL RADIO STATION	1933-35

P67 28 of 73

Radio Compass Bldg
East side

P67 29 of 73

-NAVAL RADIO STATION-
Schoodic Point, Me.

-PROGRESS PHOTOS-
Sept. 15, 1934

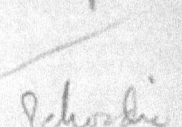

Schoodic

Radio Compass Bldg
from S. W.

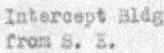

Intercept Bldg
from S. E.

-NAVAL RADIO STATION-
Schoodic Point, Me.

-PROGRESS PHOTOS-
Sept. 15, 1934

p67

-APARTMENT BUILDING-

S. E. side showing
Power House

S. E. side

S. W. side

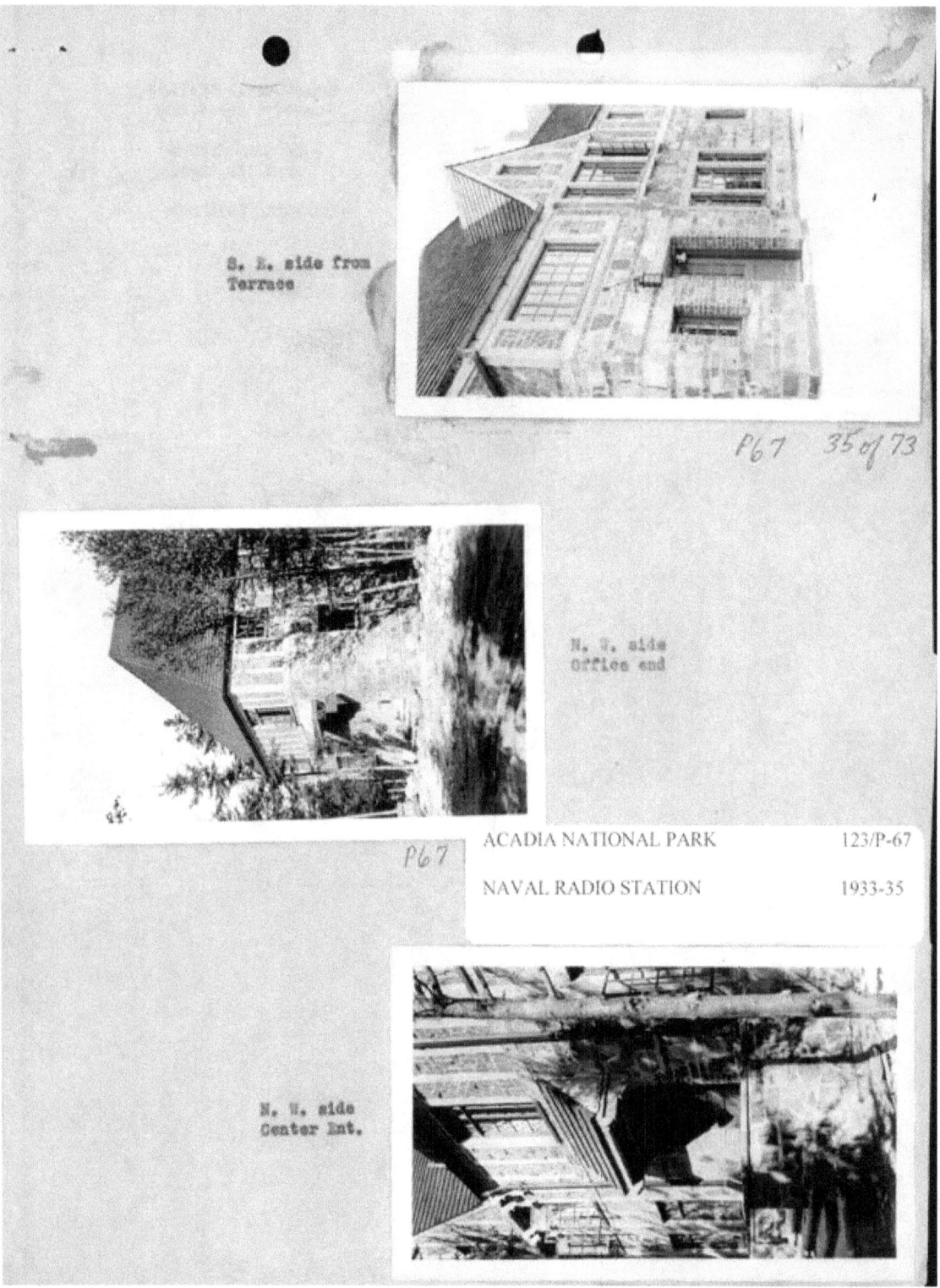

S. E. side from Terrace

N. W. side Office end

N. W. side Center Ent.

ACADIA NATIONAL PARK 123/P-67

NAVAL RADIO STATION 1933-35

NAVAL RADIO STATION
Schoodic Point, Hancock County, Maine.

Construction Photographs.

Apartment Building:
Nov. 13, 1933.

View from the East;
Garages under N.E. wing.

Apartment Building:
Nov. 16, 1933.

View from Terrace;
Brick panel detail under
Southerly Gable

Apartment Building:
Nov. 16, 1933.

View from the West;
Brick panel detail above
first floor window on
S.W. wing.

NAVAL RADIO STATION
Schoodic Point, Hancock County, Maine.

Construction Photographs.

Apartment Building:
Nov. 22, 1933.

View from South Radio Tower;
S.W. wing of Apartment with steel roof framing in progress.
All of roof framing supported on shores, the masonry walls being
built under afterwards. This allowed all steel to be bolted without
stresses in anchor bolts or masonry.

Apartment Building:
Nov. 23, 1933.

View of Second floor of N.E. wing, soon after Second floor
slab was poured. Under the thick bed of straw a waterproof
tarpaulin was laid. Salamanders were used beneath this floor,
the openings below being boarded up. These precautions were
taken for below freezing temperatures.

P67 43 of 73

The Radio Apartment Building from the service court entrance,
June, 1935. Surfacing of drive and court, finish grading,
seeding and some planting and cleanup work has still to be done.

The Radio Room Wing, in October, 1934. Grading has been partially completed.

The same view in June, 1935, showing the results of fall planting. Pruning and cultivation of these shrubs and trees is badly needed. It is hoped to complete the landscape work by means of a sub camp from Ellsworth this summer.

Panorama showing the Radio Apartment Building as it was in November, 1934, after planting had been partially completed. Subgrade of driveways and paths is in place. loam has been placed in planting beds and areas to be seeded.

Another view of the building from the service court in October, 1934. (See location on attached plan)

The same view in June, 1935, showing the curb in place on the service court, with landscape work still to be done.

Three views of the entrance court.

No. 1 shows the court in October, 1934, before selective cutting was done.

No. 2 shows the effect of selective cutting, and grading as partially completed in November, 1934.

No. 3 shows the court in June, 1935, after fall planting was completed, but with road and path surfacing and seeding still to be done.

The service court after drainage and sub-grade had been completed in November, 1934.

The same view in June, 1935, after the curb had been installed and planting partially completed at the end of the court. Planting must still be done around the court, and cleanup has not been begun.

A corner of the Radio Apartment Building from the entrance court, as photographed at the completion of the construction contract. October, 1934

The same corner, June, 1935. Planting is nearly complete, but the driveways and paths are still to be surfaced. Seeding is to be done in front of the planting along the drive.

The Radio Office entrance wing in November, 1934, before grading and topsoiling were begun.

The same corner with shrub planting completed, but surfacing of drives and paths, seeding, and cleanup work still to be done.

A rear view of the building, from a corner of the drying yard, October, 1934.

The same view from a point inside the trees shown above. Spruce has been planted in the drying yard screen; curb is in place in the service court. All other work is still to be done.

P67 58 of 73

P67 59 of 73

NAVAL RADIO STATION
ACADIA NATIONAL PARK

Apartment. S.E. Side from Terrace.
September 15, 1934.
P67 62of73

Apartment. S.E. Side Showing Power House.
September 15, 1934.
P67 60of73

Apartment. S.W. Side from Radio Tower.
September 15, 1934.
P67 61of73

255

NAVAL RADIO STATION
ACADIA NATIONAL PARK

Radio Compass Station
S. W. Bldg.
September 15, 1934.

P67 73/73

Emergency Building, E.& Side.
September 22, 1934.

P67 71/73

Pump Eqpt. Bldg., South Side.
June 2, 1934.

P67 72/73

www.ingramcontent.com/pod-product-compliance
Lightning Source LLC
Chambersburg PA
CBHW082032300426
44117CB00015B/2459